The Cost Management Toolbox

The Cost Management Toolbox

A Manager's Guide to Controlling Costs and Boosting Profits

Lianabel Oliver

AMACOM
American Management Association
New York • Atlanta • Boston • Chicago • Kansas City • San Francisco • Washington, D. C.
Brussels • Mexico City • Tokyo • Toronto

This publication is designed to provide accurate and authoritative information in regard to the subject matter covered. It is sold with the understanding that the publisher is not engaged in rendering legal, accounting, or other professional service. If legal advice or other expert assistance is required, the services of a competent professional person should be sought.

Library of Congress Cataloging-in-Publication Data

Oliver, Lianabel.
      The cost management toolbox : a manager's guide to controlling costs and boosting profits / Lianabel Oliver.
          p.   cm.
      Includes bibliographical references and index.
      ISBN 0-8144-7053-X
      1. Cost accounting.   2. Managerial accounting.   3. Activity-based costing.   I. Amacom.   II. Title.
      HF5686.C80453   1999
      658.15'52—dc21   99-36915
                                                                         CIP

Printing number

10   9   8   7   6   5   4   3

To my husband
Without your constant encouragement and
support this book would have never been
written.

Contents

Preface   ix

Acknowledgments   xiii

Part I   The Basics

  1 How Good Is Your Accounting Information?   3
  2 Different Costs for Different Purposes   13

Part II   Planning and Budgeting

  3 The Planning Cycle   33
  4 The Budgeting Process   49
  5 Budget Preparation Procedures   70
  6 How to Prepare Your Departmental Budget   91
  7 Capital Investment Analysis   100
  8 Performance Measurement and Reporting   125

Part III   Costing Principles and Systems

  9 The Costing Process   149
 10 How to Cost a Product   161
 11 How to Cost a Service   179
 12 Cost Allocations   200
 13 Standard Cost and Variance Analysis   216

14 Activity-Based Costing   235
15 Cost Analysis for Management Decision Making   262

Part IV Conclusion

16 How to Apply Cost Management Tools to Your
    Organization   287

Appendix A: The Basic Financial Statements   291
Appendix B: Mission Statement Example, Los Cidrines   298
Appendix C: How to Calculate Total Available Labor
                Hours   300
Appendix D: The Austin Division: A Budgeting Example   303
Appendix E: A Capital Budget Justification Example   310
Appendix F: Performance Summary Example   313
Appendix G: How to Trace Labor Costs to Activities   314

Glossary   317

Bibliography   337

Index   343

Preface

"Our real problem is these damn charts."

Many business professionals rely on their accounting experts to present and interpret financial information for management decision-making purposes. Moreover, they expect this information to be an accurate representation of the current state of their business. Unfortunately, the preparation of financial information is not an exact science. This information, whether historical or projected, is based on assumptions, estimates, and preparation methods that affect the results and ultimately the interpretation of the numbers. Users should understand how financial information is prepared and reported so that they can evaluate their organization's performance more effectively. The following example illustrates the importance of understanding the assumptions underlying financial information.

I once reviewed the financial statements of a proposed business venture for a clinical laboratory. The preparer of the financial statements used a simple average method to calculate the projected revenue per laboratory test based on selected industry data. Since a clinical laboratory performs many tests, each with a different price, I recalculated the average revenue per test using a weighted average method. This method takes into account not only the price of each test but also the frequency of its administration during a given time period. Therefore, it is a more accurate representation of the average revenue per test. The revised number, based on available price and volume data from similar labs in the area, was significantly lower than the revenue estimate included in the original proposal. This change in the revenue assumption caused the projected net income to drop from a healthy profit to a significant loss in the first year alone! The business proposal went from profitable venture to a losing operation by changing a single assumption.

This book focuses on the preparation and interpretation of financial information for internal use. This is the information that managers and employees use to evaluate how well their business is performing, diagnose any existing financial or operational problems, evaluate new business propositions, and forecast trends. It encompasses activities such as budgeting, forecasting, cost analysis, cost projections, and standard costs. This book will not teach you the fundamentals of accounting, debits or credits, or how to read a financial statement. There are many good books on the market that can teach you those skills. My goal is to explain the basic financial concepts and show how you can apply these to manage your business more effectively. I mesh theory with practice, drawing on my experience as an accounting manager, a controller, and a business consultant. I also incorporate material from other disciplines, such as finance, organizational behavior, and operations management, because effective cost management requires a multidisciplinary approach.

The book is organized by major topics, which build on each other. For example, you must understand basic cost terminology before you read about standard costs. I encourage you to read the book in sequence. However, individuals with some financial training may wish to focus on those chapters that cover their particular areas of interest.

The book is divided into four major parts. Part I, The Basics, introduces cost terminology and defines the user responsibilities in ensuring the accuracy of financial information. It discusses basic cost concepts and definitions that you will encounter throughout the book.

Part II, Planning and Budgeting, explains the planning and budgeting cycle. It discusses the strategic planning process and its integration into the annual budgeting cycle. It describes the annual budgeting process and explains how to prepare an operating budget and a departmental budget. This part also discusses the nature of capital investment analysis and how it fits into the overall planning process, performance reporting, and the importance of relating financial information to the key business indicators.

Part III, Costing Principles and Systems, covers basic costing principles, the different types of cost systems used in organizations today, and cost analysis techniques for management decision making. It provides a systematic framework for approaching any costing exercise and explains in detail how to develop the costs of a product or service. I have devoted a chapter to cost allocations because of their impact on total costs and the controversies that cost allocation methods may generate in an organization. Standard cost and activity-based accounting systems are also discussed in this part.

Part IV, Conclusion, summarizes the key themes of the book and provides some general guidelines on how to apply cost management tools in your organization.

This book provides a set of tools that you can use to understand and use financial information more effectively. I present the cost concepts, practices, and calculations in simple, nontechnical terms and include detailed explanations for most of the financial calculations in this book to satisfy the curiosity of readers who want to work through the computation of the numbers. Understanding the detailed mechanics of a cost calculation, however, is not the essence of this book.

Financial information does not have to be boring or complex. Even in its simplest form, it can help you manage the business more effectively if you know how to interpret and use the information available. However, improved financial information only highlights opportunities for action. You must act on this information by identifying and implementing actions that will control costs and boost your company's profits. Moreover, you will have to tailor this information to your needs and to reflect the business environment in which you operate. One size does not fit all.

I hope you find this book useful as well as entertaining. I am confident that as you expand your depth of financial understanding, you will discover a whole new perspective on your business.

Acknowledgments

I give special thanks to Professors Ricardo González Méndez, of the University of Puerto Rico School of Medicine, and Alicia Rodríguez Castro, of the University of Puerto Rico, Rio Piedras Campus, for reviewing and commenting on the contents of this book. They provided valuable feedback to make this book more understandable to the nonaccounting professional.

I am also grateful to my clients for their willingness to adopt new ideas and their faith and trust in my ability to lead the way.

Finally, I thank the participants of my public training seminars who continually urged me to put my ideas down on paper.

Part I

The Basics

Chapter 1

How Good Is Your Accounting Information?

F inancial statements are the primary mechanisms for communicating information on an organization's financial performance. There are four major financial statements: the **balance sheet**, the **income statement**, the **statement of stockholders' equity** (or **statement of capital**), and the **statement of cash flows**. The income statement is a familiar document for many business professionals. Most companies use it as a measure of managerial performance and emphasize revenue growth, expense control, and profits. The balance sheet, the statement of cash flows, and the statement of stockholders' equity are less well-known among nonfinance professionals. They are prepared primarily for external users, such as banks, stockholders, or government agencies, and are typically not used for internal performance measurement. The explanation of these financial statements is beyond the scope of this book. Appendix A, however, provides an overview of these statements and explains their purpose and contents.

A company may produce other financial reports on a regular basis besides the formal financial statements. The monthly departmental-spending reports, for example, compare the actual to the budgeted costs for a particular department, process, project, or program. Cost reports provide a breakdown of how much it costs to build a product or to service a customer. Standard cost variance analysis shows the differences between the actual and standard costs by major cost category (labor, material, and overhead) and by the type of variance (price, quantity, or volume). The type of reporting and its frequency of preparation varies with the size of the company and its managers' informational needs.

Managers often need more detailed financial information than the standard financial reports provide. For example, you may want to identify the optimal mix of products or services to maximize revenue, determine the cost of excess capacity in your manufacturing facilities, figure out how much it costs to service a customer, or calculate the value of a repeat client. This type of financial information does not reside in your company's accounting system. It is prepared on demand and requires the use of both historical and projected data, such as sales price per unit, cost per unit, industry data, usage estimates, vendor quotes, operational data, and market trends. The validity of the underlying data and assumptions will determine the accuracy and reliability of information generated.

Accounting as an Information System

Figure 1-1 shows a diagram of the typical accounting cycle in an organization. The cycle begins with a business transaction, which results in an exchange of goods or services. This transaction typically generates a document, such as an invoice, a shipping document, or a receiving report, that provides physical evidence of the exchange.

Figure 1-1. *The Accounting Cycle.*

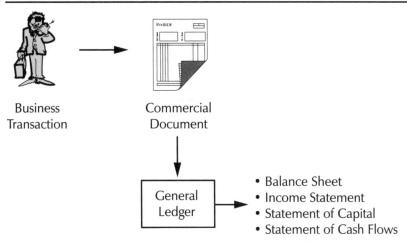

Business
Transaction

Commercial
Document

General
Ledger

• Balance Sheet
• Income Statement
• Statement of Capital
• Statement of Cash Flows

Transactions are recorded, summarized, and reported by major categories that satisfy legal requirements and are meaningful to the company's management. These categories are known as **accounts**. The **chart of accounts** is a listing of all the categories within an organization that may be used to classify financial information.

In some organizations, managers and employees assign the account number when placing a purchase order requisition or authorizing the payment of an invoice. If they make an error, they generate inaccurate financial information. For example, suppose you purchase office supplies but code the invoice into the account number for maintenance supplies. Your financial reports will not accurately reflect the amount of maintenance or office supplies that you have consumed during that period. If you rely on this data to prepare a budget or project future costs, you could seriously distort your cost estimates. Proper usage of a company's account structure is critical to ensure the accuracy, reliability, and comparability of financial data.

All business transactions are coded according to the company's chart of accounts and recorded in the **general ledger**, the file, book, or database that contains all the company's accounts. The general ledger is summarized into the four major financial statements that are used to measure overall performance (see Figure 1-1). The general ledger is also the basis for other financial reports, such as departmental spending and cost analysis, that are used for management decision making, performance evaluation, and cost control.

Ensuring the Integrity of Your Accounting Data

Managers rely on accounting to produce accurate financial reports. However, as we have seen, users of financial information can play a significant role in this process. Here are several suggestions for improving the accuracy of your financial reporting:

■ *Make sure you understand the chart of accounts for the department or area.* The chart of accounts determines how business transactions are recorded in the accounting system. You should understand what accounts are commonly used to record transactions for your area. This understanding will ensure that they are entered in a consistent manner, increasing the reliability and accuracy of your financial information. You should also determine the level of detail that you require in your financial reports. The level of detail will dictate the complexity of the chart of accounts. For example, maintenance costs can be recorded in one account, maintenance, or in various accounts such as facilities, equipment, preventive, or corrective maintenance. Whether you use one or more accounts will depend on the level of detail desired in your financial reports. Accountants should strive to keep their chart of accounts as simple as possible given the informational requirements of the business. Simplicity decreases the chances of coding errors, thereby increasing the accuracy of the financial reports.

■ *Ensure that transactions are coded correctly.* Accounting professionals should train the employees who code and process purchase requisitions or invoices on the proper use of the chart of accounts. Coding errors should be brought to the attention of the initiator. This type of training will increase the accuracy of the financial reports and minimize the amount of rework associated with improperly coded transactions.

■ *Ensure that your systems (whether manual or computerized) have the proper internal controls.* Groups or departments that are responsible for a particular task or process, such as inventory management, sales order processing, or shop floor control, generate transactions that are expressed in monetary terms and recorded in the general ledger. These systems should have the proper controls so that all transactions are entered, reviewed, and reconciled on a regular basis. A lack of procedural or system controls in your key processes could distort financial and operational data. Since operational data is often used in the preparation of financial analyses, any error could affect the reliability of the information produced. Suppose you want to calculate the cost per purchase order (PO) issued. As you review the data in the purchasing system, you discover that noninventory POs are not processed through the system. If you had used the statistics generated by the system, you would have overstated the cost per PO. Your finance support can review the adequacy of the internal controls in your area and help you to develop or implement control procedures accordingly.

- *Review weekly or monthly financial reports.* This review will allow you to detect and correct errors in a timely manner. In addition, it will give you a better understanding of costs. Be particularly attentive to what accountants call **accruals**, which record expenses that have been incurred but not yet paid or revenues that have been earned but not yet received. This accounting method is known as **accrual accounting**. Most medium-size to large organizations use accrual accounting to comply with **generally accepted accounting principles (GAAP)**. GAAP are the standard accounting concepts, rules, and procedures that govern accepted accounting practices at a particular time. They arise from a broad agreement of accounting practitioners in academia, government, and industry and evolve with changes in business conditions.

Cash basis accounting recognizes revenues and expenses on the basis of cash received or cash paid. Its popularity with small businesses and individual proprietorships stems from its simplicity and ease of use. Because cash basis accounting does not comply with GAAP, many small organizations have adopted a **modified accrual approach**. Under this method, the organization maintains its books on a cash basis throughout the year. At year-end, the appropriate accounting entries are made to convert the financial records from cash to accrual accounting.

The following example illustrates the difference between cash-based and accrual accounting. Suppose you hire a consultant to perform a business valuation of your company. Under cash basis accounting, your accountants record this cost when the invoice is received and paid. Under accrual accounting, they record the estimated cost of the consultant's services on completion of the valuation project. This estimate is an accrual. The receipt or payment of the actual invoice from the consultant does not determine when the expense is recognized on the books. Once the service has been received and there is an obligation to pay, accrual accounting requires that you record the expense on the books. Users of financial information often have difficulty understanding the fundamentals of accrual accounting. They do not always notify their accountants when services are rendered, goods are shipped, or inventory is received. Consequently, revenue, expense, and inventory transactions are not always recorded in the proper accounting period. This situation distorts the company's financial performance when comparing actual results to the budget or to prior periods. It can seriously affect a manager's performance if a purchase or service that was budgeted and rendered in the prior fiscal year is recorded against the current year's budget.

■ *Question financial information.* If you have any questions or doubts about your financial reports, ask your accountants—particularly if the information is inconsistent with your knowledge of the business. They should be able to shed light on the situation and correct any errors. Do not wait until quarter- or year-end to investigate an unusual item. If you are not satisfied with your accountant's explanation, keep asking questions.

A couple of years ago, I was called in by a client to mediate a dispute between the manufacturing and the accounting personnel. The manufacturing group argued that there was something very wrong with their financial statements. They were particularly concerned about an accounting adjustment at year-end that turned their profits into losses. The accountants counterargued that their financial statements were accurate and that the manufacturing managers simply did not understand the accounting procedures of the company. When I was hired to unravel the mystery of the missing profits, I found that both groups were right: The accountants learned that their financial information was not accurate, and the manufacturing managers learned that they did not know how the operational controls and procedures affected their financial results. The project improved communications significantly between both areas and increased the accuracy and reliability of their financial reporting.

Is Your Accounting System Obsolete?

Accounting is an information system that measures, processes, and communicates financial information about an organization or its subdivisions. **Financial accounting** is designed primarily to meet the needs of external decision makers, such as banks, stockholders, or regulatory agencies, and is governed by GAAP. **Management accounting** provides financial information for internal use and is not governed by GAAP. Accounting systems have traditionally focused on the external users. Financial information for internal use is often a by-product of the financial accounting system.

Recent changes in management philosophies have highlighted the deficiencies of traditional accounting practices and placed greater demands on accounting organizations to provide more timely and detailed financial information. Financial information should accurately reflect how an organization consumes its resources and highlight areas for improvement or areas of opportunity. Managers have also stressed the need to tie the operational data to the financial results in one coherent package. Few accounting systems, manual or automated, currently perform this function.

Accounting systems do not become obsolete overnight and are often the result of dramatic changes in the business processes and practices of the organization. The symptoms show themselves slowly and are often hard to detect. Some common symptoms of an obsolete accounting system are as follows:[1]

- *Managers complain that the financial results do not accurately reflect the business or are just plain wrong.* This situation typically occurs when financial results do not meet management expectations in terms of revenue, cost reductions, or profitability. Accountants should follow up on management concerns to ensure that accounting transactions are being properly recorded and that the system design reflects management needs for information.

- *Managers gather cost data and develop their own cost models for management presentations.* I once managed the worldwide costing function for a major Fortune 500 company. One day the product cost manager stormed into my office fuming over a recent discussion with a product development engineer. He had met with the engineer to discuss his cost estimates for a particular product. The engineer disagreed with the calculated cost, ran his own cost model, and showed the manager his version of the same numbers. This anecdote demonstrates a fundamental point: If nonfinancial managers do not agree with the established company methodology to estimate costs, they will develop and use their own models.

- *Managers ignore requests for information from the accounting staff.* I have had several clients who publish monthly performance reports for major departments or cost centers that compare actual versus budgeted performance for the area. Some accounting departments require explanations for any cost overage or underage in excess of 10 percent of the budgeted amount. Managers often see this as a worthless exercise because the variances resulted from changes in the business (e.g., a change in volume or product mix) that everybody knows about and understands. They either ignore the request or provide cursory explanations to get the accountants off their backs.

■ *Managers do not use financial reports generated by the accounting system to monitor their operating results.* During one rushed month at one of my former employers, my staff and I decided not to publish two standard reports, the monthly operating results and the worldwide inventory report, since both required a substantial amount of preparation time and effort. During the weeks that followed, I got calls from individuals all over the company asking me for a copy of the worldwide inventory report. We availed ourselves of the opportunity to ask the users how they used the report and how we could improve it. We even discovered users who were not on the official distribution list. In contrast to the flurry over this report, not a soul inquired about the monthly operating results. This simple exercise led us to reevaluate the internal management reporting for our division.

■ *Department or business unit managers have their own accounting systems that run parallel to the official accounting system.* I have visited subsidiaries of major Fortune 500 corporations where department managers are suspicious of the numbers generated by the organization's accounting systems and set up a parallel accounting system to track and monitor the expenses in their departments. Parallel accounting processes consume a significant amount of resources that could be used more effectively in other areas of the organization.

■ *The accounting department spends an excessive amount of time on special analyses and projects.* When simple requests for information consistently turn into special projects, you should evaluate the ability of your financial system to meet the needs of the business. You should pinpoint whether the problem is related to people (you do not have the right skill mix), systems, or procedures, or a combination of these factors.

■ *The operating data shown in the management performance reports is inconsistent with the operating data used to record finan-*

cial information. Many financial transactions are based on operational data, such as the number of units sold per product or the number of hours spent servicing an account. This operating data may also be included in management reports that summarize the financial and operational performance for the period. If the data reported in the management reports does not tie to the data recorded in the general ledger, a potential problem may be hiding in your accounting system.

If your accounting system is showing any of these symptoms, you should ask yourself the following questions:

- Does the current accounting system reflect the reality of my business?
- Does it provide me with accurate and timely information?
- Is it flexible?
- Does it meet my current and future business needs?

Financial information is a critical element of many business decisions. Obsolete accounting systems can lead managers astray by providing an inaccurate representation of the company's financial position.

Chapter Summary

The accounting system is not an island within the organization. It depends on other management information systems, such as purchasing, customer order processing, production control, and inventory management, to record and cost business transactions. If these management systems (manual or automated) cannot collect and report reliable data, the accounting system will be unable to produce any meaningful financial information. Managers and employees can greatly contribute to increase the accuracy of their financial information by:

- Understanding the company's account structure
- Ensuring that all transactions are properly coded when the purchase order is placed or when the vendor invoice is sent for management approval

- Investigating immediately any unusual items on their financial reports

As the organization grows and evolves, management must update its accounting system to reflect the current business practices and management philosophies. An obsolete accounting system can become a source of waste and result in poor management decision making.

Notes

1. In "You Need a New Cost System When . . . ," *Harvard Business Review* (January–February 1989), Robin Cooper describes the symptoms of an obsolete cost accounting system. I have found that the symptoms that Cooper describes in this article also apply to outdated accounting and control systems. Cost accounting systems are highly integrated to the financial accounting structure and the operational control systems of the organization. When the cost accounting system is obsolete, there are usually other aspects of the accounting and control systems that must be overhauled as well, such as month-end close procedures and internal control procedures. I have focused on those symptoms that manifest themselves internally in an organization and have added observations from my own experience. Cooper discusses other symptoms that are external manifestations of a potentially outdated cost system.

Chapter 2

Different Costs for Different Purposes

The driver of a pickup truck rapped at the door of the farmhouse and asked the farmer, "How much is that old bull out there on the road worth to you?"

The farmer replied with a question of his own. "It depends,"
he replied. "Are you the tax assessor, do you want to buy him, or did you run him down with your truck?"

Copyright © 1991 Sylvia Simmons.[1]

Costs do not come in a one-size-fits-all category. There are different costs for different purposes depending on the question that is being asked.[2] Moreover, cost information that is prepared for one purpose may be totally inappropriate for another.

Suppose you want to calculate the monthly cost of driving to work. You could start by identifying the costs of owning a car, such as loan payments, insurance premiums, licensing fees, maintenance costs, and gas. These are the costs directly associated with owning a car. Some costs are fixed, such as the monthly loan payment, but others, like maintenance and gas, vary with the number of miles you drive during the month. Since you use the car for multiple purposes, you can include only a portion of these costs in your calculations. Therefore, you must find a reasonable way to assign these costs to the specific use of driving to work—for example, the total number of miles driven or the number of days of the week. In addition to the costs of owning the car, you must add other incidental costs, such as parking fees and highway tolls, to obtain the total cost of driving to work. Finally, you must decide how to present the information you have collected in a meaningful manner. In this example, you could report cost per mile, cost per day, or total costs per month. Your needs as the user of financial information will determine the most appropriate reporting method.

Let us further suppose that you are using this information to decide whether to drive to work or take public transportation. Since you already own the car, some costs would not be relevant to this decision process. The loan payment is fixed no matter how you use the car. Other costs, such as insurance, gas, and maintenance, may vary with the number of miles you drive or the particular use of the car. For these costs, you would consider only the incremental amounts that you must pay for these items as a result of driving to work. If you use the total costs of owning and operating a car in your analysis, you would overstate the cost of driving to work as compared to the cost of public transportation. The total cost figures include items such as the loan payment and insurance premiums that you must pay anyway, regardless of how you use the car.

What Are Costs?

Costs are an estimated measure of the resources consumed to provide a product or service. I emphasize the word *estimated* because accountants sometimes portray an erroneous notion that costs can be calculated to the nearest penny. Suppose you purchase $100 of office supplies for your department. Was the actual cost to the company of purchasing these supplies $100—or something else? Theoretically, the company consumes other resources for the purpose of purchasing the office supplies—for example, the time and materials required by the buyers to prepare and process the order and the time and materials used by warehouse employees to receive and store the merchandise. The actual cost of the office supplies is not just the invoice price but the cost of *all* resources the company consumed in ordering, receiving, and storing these items. Since it is not economically feasible to include all the costs associated with a particular product, program, or service, costs represent our best estimate of the resources that the organization uses to achieve a specific objective.

Unit Costs, Total Costs, and Averages

Organizations compute costs on a total or on a per unit basis. **Total costs** represent the aggregate resources consumed by the organization or a part of the organization, such as a department, a work area, a product, or a service. For example, an income statement summarizes the total costs incurred to generate the reported revenue for a period. Total costs are generally summarized by major cost categories (e.g., labor, material, and facility costs) or by functional areas (e.g., accounting, manufacturing, legal, and sales).

A **unit cost** is the cost of one unit of measure (UM) of a good or service. The UM should identify the output of the goods or services of the organization in a meaningful manner—for example, labor hours, machine hours, units of products, hours of service, number of patients attended, number of passenger miles flown, and number of permits issued, among others.

Unit costs can be calculated by using an **average cost**, which establishes a relationship between the costs and the activity level or volume. It is calculated by dividing some total cost (the numerator) by some total measure of activity (the denominator). The activity level is expressed in a unit of measure that is meaningful to the users. Suppose a school incurs annual operating costs of $765,000 and has an enrollment of 340 students per year. The average cost per student would be $2,250 per year ($765,000 ÷ 340). Average costs are also used in manufacturing. Suppose a beverage company incurs total manufacturing costs of $1,744,000 and produces 1,000,000 gallons per month. The average production cost would be $1.744 per gallon.

Average costs are useful to measure productivity or detect significant cost trends. However, for decision-making purposes, they should be interpreted with caution. Average costs include both fixed and variable cost components. Variable costs are affected by changes in activity levels, but fixed costs are not.

The Importance of Cost Classifications

Managers in organizations use costs in many different situations. They seek to answer questions such as what products should be sold, what services should be subcontracted, or what is the profitability of a special customer order. The nature of the question determines the appropriate cost to use in each situation.

Accountants classify costs according to the purpose for which they will be used. Different costs have different purposes. Costs that are classified and recorded for one purpose may not be appropriate for another. Suppose you are evaluating the profitability of a special customer order. The full manufacturing costs, which are calculated for inventory valuation purposes, may not be appropriate for this type of analysis. You may wish to prepare the analysis based on the costs that can be directly traced to this customer order.

Figure 2-1 shows the common cost classifications that accountants use to record and report costs. An understanding of these classifications and how they are used in different situations is a fundamental building block for analyzing and interpreting financial information. The rest of the chapter explains the nature and purpose of each type of cost classification in detail.

Cost Behavior Pattern

In classifying costs by cost behavior pattern, we establish a relationship between the cost of an item (the cost object) and how it reacts to changes in volume or usage levels. The **cost object** is the item being measured; **activity levels** are measures of volume or usage that vary according to the cost object. Costs are classified as fixed or variable with respect to the cost object and how it behaves with changes in volume or usage. **Fixed costs** do not change in total with changes in volume or activity levels. **Variable costs**, on the other hand, change proportionately with increases or decreases in activity levels.

Costs are considered fixed only in the **short run**, a brief period of time in which the quantities of the available resources cannot be varied. In practice, it is usually defined as less than one or two years. In the long run, all costs are variable: plants can be shut down, branch offices closed, employees laid off, and equipment sold. It is only in the short run that costs are considered fixed for decision-making purposes.

Let us return to the example of driving to work to illustrate the

Figure 2-1. *Common Cost Classifications.*

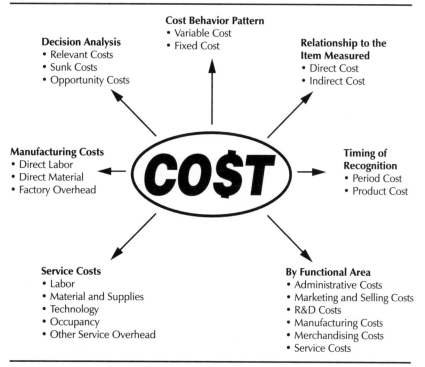

concept of fixed and variable costs. Our cost object is the drive to work. Let us reexamine these costs in light of the cost behavior pattern of each item. Suppose your car payment is $500 per month. Whether you drive 500 miles or 1,000 miles, your car payment will remain the same; it is fixed. However, as you drive more miles, the unit cost per mile will decrease, from $1.00 ($500 ÷ 500 miles) to $.50 ($500 ÷ 1,000 miles).

Fixed costs per unit must be interpreted with extreme caution. Fixed costs are not sensitive to changes in volume. In this example, your $500 car payment will remain unchanged whether you increase or decrease the number of miles you drive during the month. However, these costs are fixed only in the short term. In the future, you may decide to sell the car or transfer ownership and thereby eliminate this fixed payment.

Variable costs vary directly with changes in sales or production volume or some other measure of activity. Gas is considered a variable cost because it will increase or decrease in proportion to the number of miles you drive each month. If the number of miles doubles, the amount of gas consumed will increase proportionately. Total variable costs change as the activity level changes; however, on a per unit basis, they remain constant. Suppose you estimate your monthly gas cost at $.06 per mile. If you drive 500 miles, your estimated cost of driving to work would be $30 ($.06 × 500 miles); if you drive 1,000 miles, it would be $60 ($.06 × 1,000 miles). Although your total costs increase as you drive more miles, on a per unit basis they have remained constant at $.06 per mile.

Some costs are **semivariable**; they have a fixed and a variable component. Car maintenance is an example of a semivariable cost. Although some maintenance costs are fixed (e.g., a three-month or 3,000-mile oil change), a higher usage will probably result in higher maintenance costs. Individuals can easily identify semivariable costs; however, the quantification of the semivariable portion is difficult and often arbitrary. Some companies use mathematical models to identify the fixed and variable components of a cost item. I recommend a simple approach: Classify all costs as either fixed or variable. This approach will avoid endless discussions on the methods used to identify the variable portion and will keep reports simple and understandable.

Fixed and variable costs are valid only for a range of activity. Outside this range of activity, called the **relevant range**, the cost-volume relationship will change. Suppose you work in a fast-food restaurant that can serve 100–200 customers per hour. The owner has identified her fixed and variable costs for this level of activity. Beyond 200 customers, the owner will require more space and more staff to provide consistently good service. Below 100 customers, she would be forced to lay off employees and trim amenities. Therefore, any activity level outside the range of 100–200 customers is beyond the restaurant's short-run capacity and changes the established cost-volume relationship.

The high end of the relevant range is a measure of the organization's **short-run capacity**: the maximum output that can be attained without making an additional investment in the plant or equipment or straining the company resources. In the restaurant example, 200 customers is the restaurant's short-run capacity.

Some costs, such as travel and training, are difficult to categorize as either fixed or variable. They are not fixed because managers determine the level of spending required in these areas; they are not variable because they bear no relationship to volume or activity levels. Travel and training are examples of **discretionary costs**: costs that are incurred at the option of a manager. Although these costs are neither fixed nor variable, they are classified as fixed costs for management-reporting purposes because they do not change directly and proportionately with changes in the activity level of the organization.

Relationship to the Item Measured

Costs are also classified as a function of their relationship to the cost object or the item being measured. **Direct costs** can be directly traced to the cost object. Parking fees and highway tolls are direct costs of driving to work. Indirect costs are common to one or more cost objects. The indirect costs of driving to work include the car payment, the insurance premiums, the maintenance expenses, and the fuel costs. A cost may be direct with respect to one cost object and indirect with respect to another. For example, the monthly car payment is an indirect cost of driving to work and a direct cost of owning and operating a car.

Because indirect costs cannot be traced specifically to a cost object, they must be assigned in some reasonable manner to obtain the total or **full cost** of the item being measured. This method should bear some causal relationship between the incurrence of the cost and the basis used for cost assignment. Suppose you calculate the monthly costs associated with driving to work as follows:

Direct costs

Parking	$3.00/day	@ 20 days	$ 60.00
Tolls	$1.00/day	@ 20 days	20.00
Subtotal direct costs			**$ 80.00**

Monthly ownership and usage costs

Car payment	$500.00
Insurance premium	70.00
Estimated maintenance costs	100.00
Licensing fees	12.00
Fuel	50.00
Total indirect costs	**$732.00**

The monthly ownership and usage costs represent the total costs of owning and operating a car. Since you use the car for multiple purposes, you must assign a fair share of these monthly expenses as commuting related. How would you know what is a fair share? Here is where your judgment comes into play. The assignment basis should have a causal relationship between the cost object and the cost incurred.

One possible basis would be the actual number of miles you drive to and from work during the month. This procedure could be quite time-consuming, however, because you would have to log your mileage each time you drive the car to work. Another option would be to estimate the number of miles driven in a given month and determine the percentage that is work related—for example:

Estimated number of miles driven per month (based on historical data from prior year)	1,000
Estimated commuting mileage per month (5 miles round-trip × 20 workdays/month)	100
Percentage of work-related miles	10%

Therefore, your total cost of driving to work during a month would be $153:

Direct costs	$ 80
Indirect costs (10% × $732)*	$ 73
Total costs of driving to work	**$153**

*rounded to the nearest dollar

Suppose you use the number of workdays in the month as the basis of your cost assignment. Then the costs would increase dramatically, as follows:

Direct costs	$ 80
Indirect costs	
(20 workdays ÷ 30 workdays/month	
= 67% × $732)*	$490
Total costs of commuting to work	**$570**

*rounded to the nearest dollar

The use of workdays is an inappropriate basis for assigning indirect costs because the cost of owning and operating a car is not a function of the number of workdays in a month. The use of an inappropriate basis can significantly distort costs and result in poor decisions.

The correct identification of direct and indirect costs affects the accuracy of cost information. Direct costs can be directly related to the cost object. Indirect costs, on the other hand, must be assigned to the cost object and are therefore less precise. Computer technology has facilitated the increased traceability of costs. The specific identification of costs provides a more accurate representation of the organization's resource consumption. It is also more costly to manage and report. Users should examine the trade-offs between information accuracy versus cost of data collection in evaluating the direct and indirect cost classification for their organization.

Costs by Functional Area

Costs are classified according to the functional area in which they are incurred. You are probably most familiar with this classification since it is used for both internal and external reports. **Administrative costs** are the support costs of running the organization and include areas such as human resources, accounting, tax, treasury, information systems, legal, and corporate. **Marketing and selling costs** are those used to market and sell a product or service. These costs may include new business development, product marketing, sales, service, and support. **Research and development costs** (R&D) refer to the costs incurred for research and development of new products, processes, or technology. A manufacturing facility may perform R&D functions if it is involved in the development or testing of a new process or product. Sometimes R&D carried out in manufacturing facilities is erroneously classified as a manufacturing cost. This misclassification distorts actual product costs since it includes the cost of items that are unrelated to the current products being manufactured.

Manufacturing costs are the costs required to produce a product for resale: the sum of labor, material, and overhead. **Service costs** are the costs incurred to provide or deliver a service. Service costs also have labor, material, and overhead elements, although it may be more difficult to identify these components with a particular service. Manufacturing and service costs are explained in more detail in the next section. **Merchandising costs** are the costs of acquiring merchandise for resale. This category includes not only the purchase price of the item but also freight, tax, insurance, and any other costs required to prepare the merchandise for sale. These costs are found in retail or wholesale outlets. Pure service organizations typically do not have manufacturing or merchandising costs.

Cost classification by functional area seems fairly straightforward, but in practice, many judgment calls are required. Suppose you are the controller for a manufacturing facility. How would you classify the cost of the support services such as accounting, human resources, and information systems? These are administrative costs for running the plant, but they could also be considered indirect manufacturing costs of the product. What about the manufacturing manager's salary: Is it an administrative or manufacturing cost? It could be classified either way depending on how the company wants to report its costs. I have seen both approaches used in practice. Although the costs of support services are collected in a separate cost center, these are later redistributed to the product as indirect costs (overhead).

Often organizational politics determine how the classification by functional area is to be made. I worked in an organization where the product marketing function reported to the vice president of R&D. These costs were reported as R&D on the financial statements, although they arguably were a sales and marketing expense. Cost classifications by functional area are not always black and white; judgment calls are required.

Manufacturing Costs

The manufacturing cost includes all costs incurred to complete and place the product in a sellable condition. Generally accepted accounting principles require that these costs remain as inventory until the goods are sold. When inventory items are sold, they are reported as cost of sales or cost of goods sold. Manufacturing costs are composed of three major elements (see Figure 2-2): labor, material, and overhead. The sum of direct material and direct labor is called **prime costs**.[2] The sum of direct labor and overhead costs is also called **conversion costs**.

Direct materials cost includes the costs of all raw materials that are used to manufacture the finished product. This cost is the sum of all expenditures and charges, direct and indirect, that were incurred in bringing the materials to their existing condition or location. It typically includes the purchase price of the goods plus other costs, such as freight, insurance, royalty payments, sales tax, broker-

Figure 2-2. *Elements of Manufacturing Cost.*

Prime Costs < +Direct Materials
+Direct Labor > Conversion Costs
+Overhead

= FULL MANUFACTURING COST

age fees, and duties. Any cash or trade discounts should reduce material costs. Materials-related costs such as purchasing and receiving should be allocated to the direct materials cost if it can be done in a reasonable and economical manner (e.g., materials dollars purchased). In my experience, most companies include these materials-related costs as part of overhead.

Direct labor costs are composed of all labor costs related to the time spent manufacturing a product. This category typically includes the wages of direct labor personnel, plus fringe benefits, payroll taxes, bonuses, and any other type of special compensation.

Each company has its own definition of what it considers direct labor costs. Some companies include only the wages paid to the direct labor employees and charge fringe benefits and payroll taxes as an overhead cost. Others include the sum of all labor-related costs. It is important to understand the particular definition in your company and know the components of labor costs that are included or excluded in this definition.

A frequently asked question is whether to treat overtime as a direct labor cost or factory overhead cost. If the overtime was incurred due to the heavy workload in the plant, then it should be included as overhead and assigned to all products. It would be wrong to penalize a particular product or group of products with higher costs because they were produced with overtime hours. However, if the overtime can be specifically attributed to a problem with a particular product or production line, then it should be charged to the product or group of products to which it specifically relates.

In the past, direct labor costs included only the cost of individuals working directly on the production floor. With advances in manufacturing technology and the formation of a service economy, the definition of what constitutes direct labor needs to be changed. Engineers have focused on reducing labor costs on the factory floor through automation and the redesign of manufacturing processes. Line operators are now performing many jobs that were once considered indirect labor, such as maintenance, data gathering, reporting, and quality control. Many high-technology companies have eliminated labor tracking because direct labor is no longer a significant component of product cost. In these companies direct labor is just another component of factory overhead.

Factory overhead consists of all other manufacturing costs that are not included as direct labor or direct material. For example:

- *Indirect labor*—the total labor costs of maintenance, supervisory, and support personnel on the manufacturing floor and those individuals who work in manufacturing but are not directly involved in the production process.

- *Indirect materials*—the cost of miscellaneous production supplies such as glue, screws, minor tools, and tape.

- *Depreciation*—the cost of machinery and equipment that is assigned to each accounting period in some consistent and uniform manner. Most companies have established uniform depreciation policies by type of equipment, which are used to calculate the depreciation expense that will be charged each accounting period.

- *Utilities*—electricity, water, gas, fuel, and telephone.

- *Rent*—the cost of leasing or renting the production facility or warehouse.

- *Maintenance*—parts and labor used to maintain or repair production equipment or facilities. In highly automated factories, these costs can be significant.

- *Allocated costs*—a fair share of the costs of support departments such as purchasing, receiving, material handling, quality control, and quality assurance that are assigned to production departments. General and administrative costs such as accounting, human resources, and information systems may or may not be allocated to production departments depending on company policy.

Overhead costs are usually incurred in a production department or a business unit and are related to more than one product or product family. Therefore, accountants must assign these overhead costs in some meaningful and systematic way to individual products. This process is called overhead allocation. Overhead allocations are discussed in Chapter 10.

Service Costs

Service costs are the costs of providing a service to the customer. This category is the service equivalent of manufacturing costs. Service organizations have a lot in common with their manufacturing counterparts. They have labor, which is the time spent performing the service. They have materials, which are the food ingredients or supplies used in dispensing the service. They have overhead costs, which are all the other support costs incurred to deliver the service. They have capacity requirements and limitations determined by facilities, equipment, or manpower or a combination of these factors. Therefore, we can analyze service costs by applying the basic cost concepts used in manufacturing organizations. The following example will illustrate this point.

Suppose you own a company that provides janitorial services to small- and medium-size organizations. You have several services available, each with its own pricing structure. In order to determine which services are most profitable for the company, you need to understand how much it costs you to provide each type of service. Each service has three major cost elements:

■ *Direct labor*—time your maintenance personnel spend in delivering each service.

■ *Direct materials*—the particular cleaning tools and supplies used in each type of service.

■ *Overhead*—other resources in the organization that provide support to field personnel. Overhead costs could include transportation, scheduling, and administration. Because these costs relate to more than one type of service, they must be assigned in some reasonable manner to each service provided. This cost assignment is the same overhead allocation process mentioned in the discussion of manufacturing costs.

As you can see, the cost concepts for service organizations are similar to those used in manufacturing. However, managers may find it difficult to apply manufacturing cost concepts to a service environment. Service costs are not carried as inventory on the balance sheet or typically reported as cost of sales on the income statement. Costs such as raw materials, which are significant in manufacturing, may be insignificant or nonexistent in service industries. Therefore, managers in service organizations may wish to define the cost composition of their services in different terms from those traditionally used in manufacturing. Below is a suggested approach for classifying and reporting service costs.

Service costs can be divided into five major cost components: service labor, materials and supplies, technology costs, occupancy costs, and other.

- **Service labor** is the cost of those employees who provide services to the customer. It can also be defined as the total labor costs related to the time spent providing a service. Service labor costs include wages and salaries, fringe benefits, payroll taxes, bonuses, and any other special type of compensation.

Service labor can be further divided into frontline labor and support labor. **Frontline labor** refers to employees who are directly involved in providing service to a customer—for example, a bank teller, an insurance agent, or a customer service representative. **Support labor** includes maintenance, supervisory, and administrative personnel who do not have direct customer contact but provide essential support services to the frontline employee. Management may choose to report frontline and support labor as separate cost elements or summarize them as one cost category, called service labor costs.

- **Materials and supplies** are the cost of consumable items used in providing the service—for example, fuel, paper, cleaning compounds, hospital supplies, packaging materials, or promotional literature. In the food service industry, the ingredients used in food preparation and the packaged goods offered for resale (e.g., beverages or bakery products) are also considered materials costs. Some food service organizations report these items as a cost of sale. Materials costs can be included as part of other overhead if they are not a significant cost component.

- **Technology costs** consist of all costs relating to the acquisition and use of equipment and information technology—for example, depreciation, maintenance contracts, repair parts and labor, support personnel, and miscellaneous equipment purchases (e.g., a $200 printer).

■ **Occupancy costs** are all costs incurred to maintain the facilities and the surrounding areas—for example, building depreciation, rent, building repair and maintenance, janitorial services, landscaping, security, utilities, insurance, and property taxes. These costs generally represent a significant percentage of total costs.

■ **Other service overhead costs** consist of all other service costs that are not included as service labor, materials and supplies, technology costs, or occupancy costs. Other costs may include the following items:

—Employee-related expenses: Expenses incurred for the benefit of employees that are not payroll related (e.g., training, recruitment, employee relations, and travel)

—Royalties, franchising, and licensing fees: Compensation paid to another person or corporation for the use of property, technology, or brand name

—Outside services: Support services such as security or cleaning that are subcontracted to outside contractors and professional service fees for consultants, accountants, and lawyers

—Allocated costs: A fair share of the costs of support departments such as the cafeteria, information systems, human resources, and accounting

If any one item in the category of other service overhead costs represents a significant portion of total service costs, it should be reported as a separate cost category.

Because there is such a wide variety of service organizations, managers must decide which cost categories are meaningful for their business and how these should be reported. Let us suppose that labor and occupancy costs represent 80 percent of your company's total costs. Your company may choose to report only three cost categories instead of five: service labor, occupancy costs, and other service overhead costs. Service costs can also be reported in total or on a per unit basis. If service costs are reported on a per unit basis, you should determine the appropriate unit of measure (e.g., per order, per customer, per patient, per mile).

Because cost accounting practices were developed in the factory to meet the information needs of manufacturing management, service costing is a relatively new area for cost accountants. Even advanced cost management practices such as activity-based costing originated in a manufacturing setting. As the business environment becomes more competitive, service organizations will require a greater refinement of cost information to manage their resources effectively. (Service costing procedures are discussed in Chapter 11.)

Timing of Recognition

Costs are also classified according to when they are recognized as expenses on the financial statements. **Product costs** or manufacturing costs are all costs that are assigned to the items produced. These costs are reported as inventory until sold, as required by generally accepted accounting principles. **Period costs** are recognized in the period in which they are incurred. Some examples are sales and marketing expenses, research and development costs, and general and administrative costs. These costs cannot be inventoried. There are, however, some gray areas with period costs. The section on manufacturing costs discussed how the general and administrative costs of a manufacturing facility could be allocated as factory overhead and included as a product cost. The classification of costs as product or period costs is primarily used for financial statement preparation and reporting. Service costs are generally considered period costs and are reported on the income statement by major functional area (e.g., sales and marketing, R&D, general and administrative).

Decision Analysis

Many business decisions are based on or are influenced by cost information. Depending on the situation, costs can be relevant or irrelevant to the decision-making process. The following cost classifications provide guidance on how to classify costs for decision-making purposes.

Incremental costs (also known as **relevant** or **differential costs**) are expected future costs that differ with each alternative. Suppose you are considering purchasing a new copier for your office. You have received quotations from Suppliers A and B, as follows:

	Supplier A	Supplier B
Purchase price	$1,500	$1,500
Copier supplies per month	$30	$20
Maintenance contract per year	$250	$450

Since the purchase price of the new copier is the same under either alternative, it is not considered relevant to this decision. The financial analysis would be as follows:

	Supplier A	Supplier B
Copier supplies per year[3]	$360	$240
Maintenance contract per year	$250	$450
Total annual costs	$610	$690

If you base your decision on costs alone, Supplier A is clearly a better alternative than Supplier B. However, nonfinancial considerations may sometimes override any cost advantage of one alternative over another. For example, you may want to look at the average downtime of the machine, the service response time for the suppliers, and what types of customers the suppliers support. The importance of machine reliability and service response time depends on the type of business in which the machine will be used. A high-volume copy shop has very different needs than does a home-based consulting business. Therefore, in this example, your needs will determine whether nonfinancial considerations can justify the cost differential between the two alternatives.

To continue the example, let us say that the new copier will replace an existing machine. The existing machine had an original cost of $2,500 and has a net book value (NBV) of $1,000.[4] The original cost of the asset and the net book value are **sunk costs**. These costs have already been incurred. They are the result of past decisions that cannot be changed, and therefore are not relevant to the decision-making process. Classic examples of sunk costs are inventory and equipment.

In the example, your company spent $2,500 in cash on a copier years ago. Nothing can change this fact. Not true, you protest: "I can sell the machine for scrap or trade it in for a discounted price on a new model." You are absolutely right! You may make decisions regarding the old machine that will result in incremental costs or revenues that must be included in the financial analysis. However, the fact that you purchased a $2,500 copier in the past will not change. Moreover, the value on the books may or may not reflect its current value on the market.

Now let us say that you decide to evaluate alternative uses for the $1,500 you plan to invest in the new copy machine. The best available option is to invest in a certificate of deposit earning a 5 percent annual interest rate. The interest earned on this investment becomes the **opportunity cost** of buying a new copier: the profit forgone from the best available alternative as a result of choosing a particular course of action. This cost is not reflected in the accounting books and is often implicit in the decision-making process. It answers the question: Can I invest this money in a more profitable manner? The opportunity cost is relevant only if resources are limited and you must choose between competing alternatives.

Chapter Summary

As we have seen in this chapter, different costs are used for different purposes. As a nonfinancial manager, you should understand the basic cost concepts since they are the building blocks of a good financial information system and are used extensively in planning, reporting, and analysis. Their use (or misuse) can affect the accuracy of the financial information generated and, ultimately, the quality of management decisions that rely on this information.

Notes

1. Reprinted from *How to Be the Life of the Podium* by Sylvia Simmons. Reprinted by permission of AMACOM, a division of American Management Association International, New York, NY. All rights reserved. http://amanet.org.
2. Different costs for different purposes are a recurring theme in many cost-accounting textbooks. See Charles T. Horngren, George Foster, and Srikant M. Datar, *Cost Accounting: A Managerial Emphasis,* 9th ed. (Upper Saddle River, N.J.: Prentice Hall, 1997), Chap. 2, and Harold Bierman, Jr., Thomas R. Dyckman, and Ronald W. Hilton, *Cost Accounting: Concepts and Managerial Applications* (Boston: PWS-Kent Publishing Company, 1990), Chap. 2.
3. Supplier A = \$30/month $\times$ 12 months; Supplier B = \$20/month $\times$ 12 months.
4. The net book value is the original purchase price of the equipment less the amount that has been systematically recognized as an expense during its useful life. Accountants call this amount the accumulated depreciation. In nonfinancial terms, this is known as "the value on the books." The NBV does not bear a relation to the market value of the equipment.

Part II

Planning and Budgeting

Chapter 3

The Planning Cycle

LONG-RANGE PLANNING

ILL EAT, I'LL CHASE MY SHADOW, AND I'LL LOOK AT THE CHAIR LEG FOR A WHILE THEN, MAYBE, I'LL TAKE A SNOOZE

© 1994 SIDNEY HARRIS

The annual planning cycle instills fear in the hearts of many managers. They face deadlines, paperwork, meetings, meetings, and more meetings. Strategies are debated back and forth. Numbers are done, redone, and then may be done again. If the process is not managed properly, it can generate a high level of stress and frustration among managers and employees.

Planning, however, does not have to be a painful process. Managers should view planning as a continuous cycle rather than as something that happens once a quarter or once a year. It is not something that can be done by your accountants in a vacuum. Good planning requires constant revision and a high involvement from operational managers.

This chapter provides an overview of the planning process and its purposes within an organization. It defines the nature of strategic planning and positions this process as a necessary first step in the development of long-range strategies and short-term plans. Finally, it discusses the integration of the strategic-planning process into the annual budgeting cycle of the company.

What Is Planning?

Planning is the identification of long-range goals and the strategies and action plans required to achieve them. These plans are eventually translated into budgets, which are used to track and monitor performance. The **budget** is a financial document that quantifies in monetary terms the action plans of the company over a short period of time, typically a year. During the budgeting process, managers strive to maximize the utilization of resources in line with the company's long-term objectives. The budget is a means to an end, not an end in itself. Sometimes during the budget preparation process, we get so absorbed in presenting the "right" numbers that we forget the strategies and actions that are driving these numbers.

Why Plan?

Planning and budgeting requires a large investment of time and resources. We invest such a significant amount of resources in this effort because a well-orchestrated plan serves several important functions within the organization. For example:

■ *Resource allocation.* The planning process forces managers and their associates to think beyond the day-to-day effort and plan the distribution of limited resources to support the organization's stated goals and objectives. An anecdote from one of my former employers illustrates this point. One year at the start of the annual planning cycle, the chief executive officer published the major strategies of the organization for the upcoming year. One of the major strategies was the training and development of its human resources. My division management, however, had allocated less than 1 percent of the budget for training, development, and employee relations. When this inconsistency surfaced during the budget review process, the strategies and resources were realigned to support the company's long-term goals.

- *Control.* The planning and budgeting process plays a major role in the management control system of an organization. Through the budgeting process, management authorizes an amount of money to achieve specific objectives. It also establishes a standard that can be used to evaluate both organizational and individual performance.

- *Coordination and communication.* The planning process should promote an understanding of the interdependencies among departments, business units, and related subsidiaries and encourage continuous communication among these different parts of the organization. In the current environment of continuous improvement and reengineering, it can provide a mechanism to coordinate the efforts of various parts of the organization and minimize duplicating functions and resources. Once while I was reading the strategies for the sales division of a former employer, I noticed its plans to penetrate the federal government market. I know that the federal government has strict requirements in terms of product configuration, availability, and delivery and called the controller of the appropriate manufacturing facility to ensure that it had the necessary resources to support this strategy. The plant controller had no knowledge of this strategy and confirmed that there were no resources in the budget to support it. Fortunately, by meeting with their counterparts in sales and marketing, they were able to clarify and correct the situation before the budget was finalized.

- *Feedback.* The planning process results in a measurable plan that can be used to monitor and evaluate performance. It also provides a systematic mechanism to update the plan at least once a year based on changing business conditions. It can also establish the key financial and nonfinancial indicators, such as units sold, customer complaints, percentage of on-time shipments, and unit cost, that can be used to measure performance against the plan.

- *External demands.* Outsiders, such as Wall Street analysts, investors, and banks, may require that you provide them with information on your company's future direction. The accuracy of this information has implications for the reputation of the organization in the financial community and can ultimately affect the stock price. In 1994 Pfizer learned this lesson the hard way, as the following report illustrates:

> If Pfizer did manage its earnings, though, it made a critical misstep: failing to warn Wall Street. Analysts had expected a 24% rise in earnings from continuing operations for 1993, and investors reacted badly to the reported 15% gain on Jan. 19. Pfizer's share price dropped $5, to just under $63. Since then, it has recovered only to 64 or so.[1]

■ *Simulations.* The planning process allows you to perform what-ifs and understand their financial implications without actually playing them out. Thus, you may foresee difficult situations and develop contingency plans before a crisis occurs.

The planning process can serve multiple purposes in an organization. By increasing your understanding of the usefulness of this process, you can maximize the benefits that it can provide.

The Planning Cycle

Figure 3-1 shows the continuous nature of the planning cycle. It starts with the setting of long-range objectives and the formulation of strategies to achieve these objectives. These strategies are translated into short-term action plans that form the basis of the annual or biannual budget. As the year progresses, the action plans are implemented and evaluated against the desired results. This evaluation may result in either a change of strategy (long term) or a change in action plans (short term), creating the need for the planning cycle to begin anew.

What Is Strategic Planning?

The planning cycle begins with the strategic planning process. **Strategic planning** is the process of determining the goals of the organization and the strategies required to achieve these goals. These plans, set at a high level, define the general direction in which the organization is headed. There are three important aspects of strategic planning:

Figure 3-1. *The Planning Cycle.*

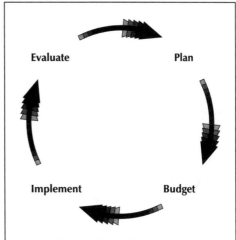

1. *Setting objectives.* This is the first and most critical stage of the process. In this step, the organization defines its identity and determines its long-term goals. The organization finds answers to the following questions:

- Who are we?
- Where are we going?
- How are we going to get there?

2. *Resource allocation.* This aspect, done at the macrolevel, involves making decisions as to the best way to allocate the organization's resources to achieve the stated objectives. For example, a multinational corporation might want to develop a specific line of business, or a nonprofit may want to focus on a particular client group. The resource allocation should support the direction in which the organization is headed.

3. *Establishment of policies.* Policies are general guidelines that provide a framework for decision making and actions in an organization. During the strategic-planning process, management should ensure that the company policies support the organization's objectives.

Strategic planning envisions a desired future and identifies ways to make it happen. It links company goals to intermediate-range plans to short-term action plans in a systematic manner. It allows management to examine the organization as a whole and provides a mechanism for moving different parts of the organization in the desired corporate direction. Strategic planning enables managers to make better current decisions by aligning alternative courses of actions with the company's objectives. Moreover, it allows them to understand the risks and payoffs of each possible alternative in light of a changing business environment.

The Strategic-Planning Process

Strategic planning begins with the determination of the corporate mission. The **corporate mission statement** identifies the essence of the company and provides a framework to establish its long-term direction. It seeks to answer these questions:

- Who are we?
- What do we do?
- What values are important to us?

The corporate mission should pass the test of time and circumstances. If it is well-defined up front, it should remain relatively unchanged over time.

The **vision** or **long-term direction statement** defines the long-range goals of the organization—typically 10 years or more into the future—and must support the corporate mission. It answers these questions:

- Where are we going?
- Where do we want to be?

The definition of the long-term direction also involves identifying the **critical success factors** for the business: the key dimensions of performance that determine the long-term success of the organization. For example, safety is a critical success factor for an aircraft manufacturer. Critical success factors are discussed in more detail in Chapter 8.

Strategies are long-term objectives that are defined for a specific period of time. They must support the long-term direction of the organization and the corporate mission. Companies often define strategies for three to five years. Management seeks to answer this question:

- What do we do to get there?

As part of the strategy formulation, managers should identify the key performance indicators that will be used to measure progress toward these objectives. Key performance indicators, discussed in Chapter 8, are quantifiable measures that the organization uses to evaluate and communicate performance against expected results.

Action plans are short term in nature (one to three years) and should support the strategic objectives. They describe the specific actions that the organization will take to attain its long-range objectives. They answer the question:

- What specific actions are we going to take to achieve our long-term strategies?

Key performance indicators provide a critical feedback mechanism to evaluate the effectiveness of short-term plans.

Figure 3-2 summarizes the strategic-planning process. Appendix B contains the mission statement and corporate values of a local manufacturer in Puerto Rico, Los Cidrines, to demonstrate that even small to medium-size businesses can reap significant benefits from this process.

Strategic planning is the responsibility of everyone in the organization. At each level of the organization, managers make short- and long-term plans. Although the scope and impact of their decisions may vary, each level must take into account the corporate goals

Figure 3-2. *The Strategic-Planning Process.*

and the internal and external environment in determining the direction of the organizational unit.

Figure 3-3 shows a hypothetical structure of a multinational corporation with offshore operations. Each organizational level has a different set of strategic decisions. At the plant level, these may involve issues of capacity, employee skill set, or the introduction of new manufacturing technology. At the manufacturing operations level, the decisions may center on product transfers, tax benefits, and overall production capacity. The division level may focus on customer needs, market share, competitor strategies, and new product development. The corporate level may be concerned with mergers, acquisitions, earnings per share, and financing options.

Finally, strategic planning is a continuous process. Although many companies set aside a specific period of time for planning purposes, the constantly changing business environment requires that plans be continually revised and updated. Long-term strategies, however, should not change dramatically from month to month or year to year. Strategies should exist until changes in the internal or external environment prompt a need for revision.

Strategic Analysis

Once the corporate goals have been established in the mission and long-term direction statement, managers should perform a strategic

Figure 3-3. *Structure of a Multinational Company With Offshore Operations.*

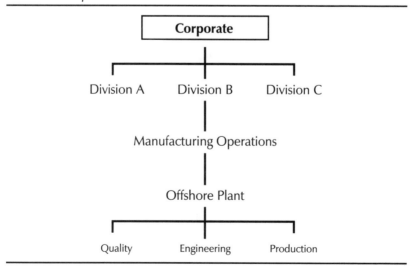

analysis. **Strategic analysis**, shown in Figure 3-4, is a thorough examination of the external and internal factors affecting the organization for the purpose of developing strategic plans.

An analysis of the external environment and the company's strengths and weaknesses will allow you to assess your current position—where you are today. The desired position—where you want to be—is determined by analyzing your corporate objectives in light of the external forces that affect your organization. The difference between your current position and your desired position is the **strategic gap**.[2] Strategic plans should be designed to close this gap and bring the organization closer to its desired position over a reasonable period of time. There is a strategic analysis, implicit or explicit, behind every company plan.

Company plans culminate with the preparation of financial statements, which quantify the monetary impact of the proposed actions. These plans should reflect the results of the strategic analysis and be consistent with the long-term direction of the organization. Long-range plans are sometimes, but not always, quantified at a very macrolevel (e.g., on a business segment or geographical region) in what is known as an intermediate-range plan (IRP). Short-term plans are reflected in the annual budget and are updated monthly or quarterly through financial forecasts. Figure 3-5 shows the different types of plans that are prepared during a planning cycle.

Figure 3-4. *Strategic Analysis.*

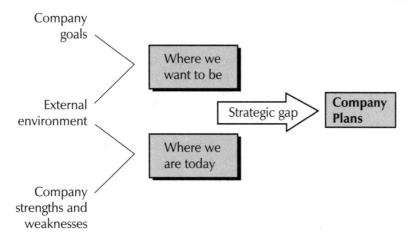

Source: Adapted and reprinted from *Business Horizons 15,* © 1992 by Indiana Kelley School of Business. Used with permission.

Figure 3-5. *Types of Company Plans.*

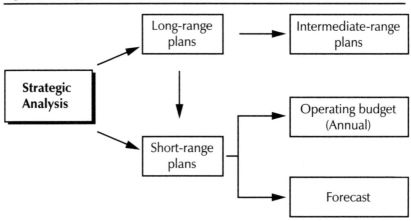

The External Environment

Strategic analysis requires an assessment of the external environment in which the company operates: the market, the industry structure, technological changes, the government, demographics, and the economy. Management should consider the impact of these forces when developing the company's strategies and action plans.

The Market

An analysis of the market focuses on the customer. Who is the customer? What are the customer's current and future needs? What tendencies can we identify that may affect the organization? In analyzing the market, the management team should look at the following aspects:

- The size of the market and its projected growth rate
- The current market share and what needs to be done to grow at, above, or below the market growth rate
- How the product will be sold—whether directly to the end customer or through intermediaries
- The actions of major competitors and where the organization is positioned in relation to the competition

The Industry Structure

Some industries are more competitive than others by the nature of their product. An understanding of the industry structure is key in developing the basis of the organization's competitive advantage. This structure should be analyzed in terms of the collective strength of the five competitive forces:[3]

■ *Barriers to entry* describe the difficulty in entering the industry—for example, technology, capital requirements, economies of scale, retaliation from existing companies, or government regulations.

■ The *bargaining power of customers* focuses on the influence of the buyers. Some factors to examine are the number of buyers, their ability to integrate backward, buyers' costs of switching to another product or company, and the impact of the business on buyers' operations and costs.

■ The *bargaining power of suppliers* focuses on the influence of the vendors, such as the number of suppliers, the availability of substitute products, their ability to integrate forward, and the importance of the company's unit volume for their business.

■ *Rivalry* examines the competitiveness of the industry in terms of growth, product differentiation, number and diversity of competitors, industry capacity, and exit barriers.

■ *Threat of substitutes* looks at relative price to performance, the buyers' cost of switching, and the buyers' tendency to substitute.

The strength of these five forces determines the level of competitiveness of the industry in which you operate. The pharmaceutical industry is a good example of an industry that has seen radical changes over the past 10 years. This industry was traditionally one in which the five competitive forces were weak: there were high barriers to entry, the buyers were not organized, and the threat of substitutes was virtually nonexistent. With the high cost of health care, the pharmaceutical industry has come under attack from Congress and insurance companies to reduce costs. Buyers have become more organized and more demanding in terms of price versus perceived benefits. The rise of generic and over-the-counter (OTC) drugs has prompted major pharmaceutical organizations to enter these markets. Some companies manufacture the generic and OTC version of their own prescription drugs.

Technological Changes

Technological innovations can have far-reaching implications for an organization. New technology can create new markets or destroy old ones (the typewriter comes readily to mind). It can dramatically alter the workplace by providing new and better tools to get the job done. A company must stay abreast of the technological changes in its industry: What changes in technology are foreseen for the next 5 to 10 years? What new technologies that are under development may be commercialized in the future? What technological changes will affect the way we live and work?

The Government

In a global economy, managers should analyze the potential impact of government policy and regulations of any country in which they do business. They should stay abreast of legislative changes or international treaties that could affect how, when, and where they do business. Tax legislation is particularly important for corporations with offshore operations that are operating with tax incentives. Legislation such as the Clean Air Act, the Clean Water Act, the Americans With Disabilities Act, and the increase in the minimum wage have had a significant financial and operational impact on companies doing business in the United States. International treaties such as Maastricht in Europe and the North American Free Trade Act (NAFTA) have also affected companies doing business in these regions.

Demographics

Changing demographics can have a large impact on markets. Managers should consider the following questions:

- How will the population change in age and sex in those countries where I plan to do business?
- What impact will this change have on our product?
- Can we foresee new trends that may open new markets?
- What tendencies do we observe at the local, national, or international level?

The Economy

In a global economy where the fate of nations is deeply intertwined, it is critical to have an understanding of the economic trends that may affect your business. What is the economic outlook on a global basis? Regional basis? National level? Locally? What are the key economic indicators (growth in gross national product, the inflation rate, interest rates) that affect the business? Where are interdependencies? During the Gulf War, the United States experienced firsthand the nature of a global economy. Kuwait and Iran, thousands of miles away, are key suppliers of oil to the Western world. Oil and gas prices skyrocketed and fear of shortages was widespread.

The Internal Environment

A strategic analysis also involves an understanding of the internal environment of the organization. What are the strengths and weaknesses of your organization? Are you prepared to cope with the changes brought on by external forces? Five major areas should be examined: people, facilities, information systems, procedures, and the financial condition of the company.

People

This area examines the issues relating to the organization's human resources. Some possible areas to review are training, recruitment, employee retention, and succession plans. For example, how will changes in technology affect the organizational model? How about changes in management philosophy? Do the workers have the right skill sets? Are the workers adequately trained? Is there a morale problem? Is there an established succession plan for each key manager?

Facilities

Facilities relate to the physical conditions of the general workplace, including the building and the equipment. Are the facilities adequate for the current and future level of operations? What is the current capacity level? Where are the bottlenecks? Is it necessary to shut down or relocate facilities? Do the facilities comply with government regulations? What areas are in noncompliance?

Information Systems

An analysis of information systems looks at the state of the company's information technology. It analyzes whether the current system platform will support the future direction of the business. It looks at new technology that could improve the accessibility of information or provide a competitive advantage with the customer. For example, many banks have capitalized on new technology to create a competitive advantage by offering financial services through the Internet.

Procedures

All organizations have policies and procedures. These can be implicit in the organizational culture or clearly defined in a manual or some other type of company material. Company policies and procedures should support the mission and values of the organization. As part of the internal analysis process, a manager should evaluate the current policies and procedures. What procedures hinder the business processes? How can the current procedures be simplified? Does the organization have the proper internal controls to safeguard assets? What procedures are obsolete? What new policies or procedures will be required in the near future to support changes in the business?

Financial Condition

A good strategic plan requires a commitment of resources. A review of the financial condition of the company will allow you to determine whether it has the economic capability to meet future resource requirements. Is the business operating at a profit? Are there cash flow problems? What are the overall trends in terms of revenue and expense growth? How do the key financial ratios compare to those of major competitors?

A detailed financial analysis may be required that looks at sales or cost trends by customers, channels of distribution, products, or services. Other important factors may affect a company's financial position that are not necessarily reflected in the financial statements: the company's legal and tax structure, the strength of its banking relationships, its bill payment and collection practices, and its ability to raise capital through additional debt, public offerings, or venture capital.

*   *   *

An analysis of the internal environment will provide you with a better understanding of your current competitive position and identify areas of opportunity to close the strategic gap. The strategic plan should capitalize on the organization's strengths and address any areas of weakness that hinder a company's ability to compete effectively.

The Planning of the Budgeting Process

The budget is an integral part of a company's planning cycle. The budget process starts with the identification or reevaluation of short-term strategies to achieve long-term goals. The budget is not just a bunch of numbers thrown together by management. Behind these numbers are projects, programs, and action plans that move the organization closer to its long-term goals. You cannot arbitrarily cut a well-thought-out budget without affecting the future plans or operations of the business.

The budgeting process can flow more efficiently if the management team discusses, agrees on, and communicates its strategic direction at the start of the budget cycle. The prioritization and communication of strategies can facilitate the budget process and minimize rework. A couple of years ago, a client asked me to prepare a seminar that explained the company's budgeting process to the managers and supervisors. As I examined the process, I noticed a curious detail: Managers were asked to prepare the budget in the summer for corporate approval in the fall. In November, the general manager of the facility would assemble his management team to discuss and agree on the strategies for the upcoming fiscal year—the same fiscal year for which the budget had already been finalized! This inconsistency in the budgeting process typically led to a lot of frustration and rework because the November strategy session usually resulted in changes that had not been budgeted for. When I pointed out this inconsistency to top management, the process was changed so that the strategy session with key managers occurred before, not after, the start of the budgeting cycle.

Chapter Summary

Planning involves the setting of long-term goals and the development of strategies and actions to move the organization in the desired direction. Planning accomplishes several important functions within an organization, including resource allocation, management control, coordination, and communication.

The planning process begins with the determination of the company mission that defines the company identity and provides a framework for setting its long-term direction. This vision or long-term direction establishes the long-range goals of the organization and requires the development of detailed strategies to achieve these objectives.

Strategy formulation requires a careful assessment of the external environment and a thorough understanding of a company's strengths and weaknesses. Strategies give rise to short-term action plans, which form the basis of the budget. The budget summarizes the short-term plans in monetary terms and is used to measure and evaluate the performance of the organization.

Notes

1. Joseph Weber, "Did Pfizer Doctor Its Numbers," *Business Week,* February 14, 1994, p. 34.
2. See Louis V. Gerstner, Jr., "Can Strategic Planning Pay Off?" *Business Horizons* 15 (December 1972). Gap analysis is also discussed in George A. Steiner, *Strategic Planning: What Every Manager Must Know* (New York: Free Press, 1979), pp. 23–26.
3. See Michael Porter, *Competitive Advantage* (New York: Free Press, 1985), pp. 4–11.

Chapter 4

The Budgeting Process

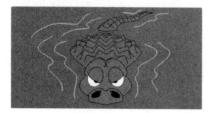

When you're up to your ass in alligators, it's difficult to remember that your initial objective was to drain the swamp.

Copyright © 1991 Sylvia Simmons.[1]

This quotation is particularly appropriate to describe the budgeting process. Often managers get so wrapped up in the mechanics and the politics of the budgeting process that they forget its true purpose. The goal becomes to finish, get approval, and move on with what is regarded as the "real business" of managing the organization. The budget process, however, is critical to the organization's long-term success. During this process, management defines the short-term actions that are required to support the strategic direction of the business. Unless the short-term plans are consistent with the long-term direction, the organization will have difficulty achieving its long-range goals.

This chapter provides an overview of the budgeting process. It describes the budgeting cycle, discusses the major contents of the annual business plan, and explains the review process. It also discusses some undesirable consequences of the budgeting process and its impact on human behavior. Finally, it explains the various budget

preparation methods and presents some specific recommendations
to facilitate the budgeting process in your organization.

The Budgeting Process

Figure 4-1 is a flowchart of the annual budget cycle in a typical organization. The cycle begins with a review of the company direction
and strategies. In this **strategy review**, management develops short-
term plans that support the company's long-term objectives and establishes the company priorities. This consensus on plans and priorities will facilitate the allocation of resources later in the process.

The next step is to determine the new products, services, or

Figure 4-1. *The Budgeting Process.*

```
┌──────────────┐
│   Strategy   │
│    Review    │
└──────┬───────┘
       │
       ▼
┌──────────────┐      ┌──────────────┐
│ New Products,│      │   Sales or   │
│ Services, or │ ───▶ │   Revenue    │ ─────────────┐
│  Processes   │      │ Projections  │              │
└──────────────┘      └──────┬───────┘              │
                             ┆                       │
                             ▼                       ▼
                      ┌──────────────┐  ┌─────────────────────────┐
                      │  Production  │  │  Resource allocation    │
                      │     Plan     │──▶ • Production cost        │
                      │              │  │ • Service cost           │
                      └──────────────┘  │ • Departmental expenses  │
                                        │ • Operating expenses     │
                                        └───────────┬─────────────┘
                                                    │
                                                    ▼
                                        ┌─────────────────────────┐
                                        │      Operating          │
                                        │       Budget            │
                                        └─────────────────────────┘
```

processes that may affect sales. "Products" refer to both manufactured items and services. New products may open market niches or affect the sales of existing products. New processes can give the company a competitive advantage that could translate into increased sales. This information, plus historical sales data and market research, is used to prepare the **sales budget** for the new fiscal year. After possibly many rounds of negotiation with top management, the sales budget is finalized. The sales budget drives the resource allocation for the rest of the organization. It sets an upper limit on the monetary resources that are available to cover operating expenses and still produce the desired level of profitability.

Next, each major area or department estimates the level of resources required to obtain the planned level of sales. This **resource allocation** process occurs throughout the organization. Manufacturing entities, however, must translate the sales budget into a **production plan** before they can estimate their resource requirements for the upcoming year. The production plan considers not only the budgeted sales volumes but also the desired inventory levels for the year.

The production plan details the quantities of each major product that will be manufactured during the year and is expressed in physical terms (e.g., units, pounds, gallons). Managers use the production plan to estimate the resources required in the manufacturing operations to achieve the planned volume levels. These resources are usually budgeted by department or work area and are reported as manufacturing costs.

Service organizations generally do not prepare a production plan for their frontline operations. They instead estimate their resource requirements based on the planned sales volume. However, some service organizations that provide a combination of goods and services may prepare a detailed production plan. For example, a company that provides food services must plan the number and types of meals that will be required during the year by major customers. Since meals cannot be inventoried, the expected sales would equal the planned production volume for the year. Similar to manufacturing organizations, managers estimate the resources required for their frontline operations by department or work area.

Service and manufacturing organizations also budget for operating expenses in addition to their manufacturing or frontline operations. Operating expenses may include research and development, sales and marketing, and general and administrative support. The investment in these areas is often dependent on the level of sales.

The budgeted sales, the production or service costs, and the operating expenses become the operating budget for the next fiscal year. The **operating budget** consists of an income statement and all supporting budgets. Nonfinancial managers are actively involved in the preparation and use of an operating budget. They have limited participation in the preparation of other budgets, such as the cash budget, the capital budget, and the budgeted balance sheet.

The Annual Business Plan

The budget process culminates with the preparation of an annual business plan. This document provides the company management with detailed information on the upcoming year. It should include a management narrative, financial schedules, and operational schedules that provide supplemental information to support the proposed plans. Figure 4-2 summarizes the suggested contents of an annual business plan.

The Management Narrative

The management narrative discusses the company's direction, the environmental factors affecting the organization, and the strategic objectives for the next fiscal year. The management narrative should contain the following information:

1. *Summary of the major strategies and objectives.* This section details the organization's short-term strategies and objectives for the year. It should explain any major programs or projects and how these support the company's strategic direction.

2. *Analysis of the internal and external environment.* This section describes the general environment in which the company will operate. It should analyze the company's current strengths and weaknesses and how it is positioned for the future.

3. *Key assumptions.* This section highlights any key assumptions that underlie the preparation of the budget. Key assumptions usually center on new product introductions or transfers, facility expansions, government legislation, taxation, price increases, interest rates, and foreign exchange rates. For example, if the government is expected to increase the minimum wage and this increase is included in the calculation of salaries and fringe benefits, it should be explicitly mentioned in this section.

Figure 4-2. *Suggested Business Plan Contents.*

Management Narrative
- Strategic objectives
- Environmental assessment
- Key assumptions
- Risks and opportunities

Financial Schedules
- Financial statements
  - ⇛ Income statement
  - ⇛ Balance sheet
  - ⇛ Statement of cash flows
- Capital budget
- Cash budget
- Sales revenue
- Product cost
- Departmental budgets
- Other financial analysis

Operational Information
- Key performance goals
  - ⇛ On-time delivery
  - ⇛ Manufacturing yields
  - ⇛ Inventory accuracy
  - ⇛ Customer satisfaction
  - ⇛ New product introductions
- Market share by segment
- Unit growth from new products
- New customer acquisitions
- Customer turnover
- Head-count plan

4. *Risks and opportunities.* Any business plan has risks. Some risks are financial (e.g., the interest rates will go up), and others are operational (the product will be unavailable). There are also opportunities; for example, a supplier may lower prices, or interest rates are projected to go down. Risks and opportunities are identified but are not included in the financial plan. However, the financial implications should be quantified and taken to the bottom line, if possible. This assessment will provide management with a tangible measure of the degree of risk involved with the plan.

The management narrative is followed by detailed financial and operational schedules that quantify the expected performance for the next fiscal year. The level of detail required depends on the size and complexity of the organization and management information needs.

Financial Schedules

The financial schedules should contain all the pertinent financial information for the budgeted period: usually a **pro forma income statement** that summarizes revenues and expenses by major functional category and detailed budgets for each major department or work area that tie to the budgeted income statement. The detailed departmental budgets usually include a **head-count plan** that details the staffing requirements for the upcoming year. In addition to these schedules, most companies prepare a **capital budget** that shows the expenditures required for major investments or the purchases of property, plant, and equipment by area. The capital budgeting and investment analysis process is explained in Chapter 7.

For a subsidiary of a large, multinational corporation, this description may sum up the bulk of the corporate requirements with respect to the budget. Corporate headquarters, however, may require additional information and other supporting schedules. Other financial schedules that are prepared at the end of the budgeting process are a **cash budget**, **a pro forma balance sheet**, and a **pro forma statement of cash flows**. A **cash budget** presents the expected cash receipts and cash disbursements for the budget period. It is used for the purpose of cash planning and control.

The income statement, the capital budget, and the cash budget are used to prepare the budgeted balance sheet. The pro forma balance sheet is important because it could disclose adverse financial conditions that management may want to avoid—for example, the company could be in violation of a bank loan agreement or have unfavorable financial ratios that do not conform to analysts' expectations. These situations would cause management to rework the budget. Corporate or regional headquarters usually prepare the pro forma balance sheet, the statement of cash flows, and the cash budget. Small companies may not prepare these schedules at all because they have limited utility for the day-to-day management of the business.

Management may also require supplemental schedules that provide more detailed information in certain areas, such as sales, product or service costs, and customer profitability. The format and content of these supplemental schedules are determined by the needs of the management team.

Operational Schedules

The operational schedules establish a framework for understanding the budgeted financial information. They describe the nature of the operations that underlie the budgeted figures and therefore are a necessary complement to the financial schedules. They may contain information on key performance goals, market share, and new product introductions. In contrast to the financial schedules, there are no standard operational schedules. Each company must determine the operational information that should be included as part of its annual business plan.

Financial and operational information should be linked so that management can clearly understand the financial implications of a change in operational strategy. Suppose management has set a performance goal to ship 95 percent of all orders within 24 hours. How would the budgeted resources change if this goal were set at 98 percent? Would higher on-time delivery performance result in increased sales? By linking financial and operational information, managers can understand how their business decisions affect the bottom line of the organization.

The Review Process

The most difficult part of the budget cycle is the review process. Managers spend countless hours defending their budgets in presentations and meetings, a process that can be very stressful. This section describes the typical review process and discusses some steps for managing this process more effectively.

There are two levels of review. The first level is a financial review whereby the manager reviews the budget with an accounting analyst before presenting it to the next level of management. The accounting analyst verifies that the numbers are accurate and reliable and may point out inconsistencies between the budgeted amounts and the departmental goals or objectives. I have reviewed budgets that provide for hiring new employees but do not budget desks, chairs, or computers for these individuals. The accounting analyst ensures that all costs that should be included in the budget are accounted for. Accountants should help department managers identify inconsistencies or highlight unusual trends that may be questioned by the next level of management. Why are the actual figures higher or lower than the proposed budget? Was an alternative supplier considered? Is this function duplicated in another part of the organization? The accounting analyst should verify that the budget information is complete and conforms to the expectations of the next level of management.

The management review is a negotiation process that examines the assumptions and the data that underlie the budgeted numbers. Managers will prod, probe, and question as they look for inconsistencies or duplication of functions that will result in an inefficient use of company resources. If the numbers are too high or cannot be justified to the next level of management, the presenter will be asked to rework the numbers. Figure 4-3 shows a typical management review process. As the budget moves up through the corporate hierarchy, the focus is less detailed oriented and more macro in nature. At each level of the process, however, the numbers will be subject to negotiation and scrutiny.

The review process can produce high levels of stress and frustration, particularly when budgets must be adjusted downward. Managers can make this process a lot easier on their staff by following two simple recommendations:

■ *Avoid arbitrary adjustments.* Managers sometimes receive a company directive to cut a specific dollar amount or a fixed percentage from their budget. When the budget cuts are applied equally to all areas, management may affect strategies that are a high priority for the organization. It also limits management flexibility to handle budget cuts. For example, suppose you received a management directive to cut 10 percent from the total budget of your division. You

Figure 4-3. *The Management Review Process.*

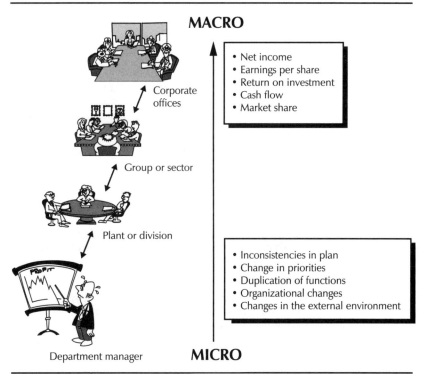

MACRO

Corporate offices

- Net income
- Earnings per share
- Return on investment
- Cash flow
- Market share

Group or sector

Plant or division

- Inconsistencies in plan
- Change in priorities
- Duplication of functions
- Organizational changes
- Changes in the external environment

Department manager   **MICRO**

may want to reduce 15 percent in one area and actually increase 5 percent in a high-priority area. Arbitrary adjustments put the organization at risk because high-priority projects may be inadequately funded. Managers should understand the impact of budget revisions on the organizational strategies and communicate possible trade-offs to the next level of management.

■ *Give key individuals input into the process.* When budget cuts are required, the manager should hold a meeting of the key individuals in the organizational unit. These individuals should agree as a team on the top priorities for the group and how the budget cuts will be spread through the organization. They should identify and communicate the impact of these cuts on the current or future level of operations and the proposed organizational strategies. Individuals often complain that the budgets are cut without their input or knowledge, yet the performance expectations remain unchanged. This process provides a forum to discuss the budget cuts as a group and understand the trade-offs for the organization as a whole. The controller is no longer the source of hard feelings since the budget reductions are reached by consensus with the management team.

The budget review process can consist of one or more iterations. Top management will continue to revise the budget until the financial results are in line with their expectations. Then a management steering committee, a board of directors, or the owner, if the company is an individual proprietorship, formally approves the budget. The approved budget is communicated to the rest of the organization and is used to measure managerial performance throughout the year.

Behavioral Considerations

The budget process can have a significant impact on human behavior in the organization. We cannot separate the mechanics of the process from the people who participate in the process. Some potentially adverse consequences of the budget process are:

- *The use of budgets as a pressure device.* Budgets are often used as a pressure device to continually raise the standard of performance. This situation can be a motivating factor as long as employees perceive that the standards are attainable. When the standards become unattainable, they will either ignore the budget or circumvent the process to achieve the targeted financial results. This situation may affect product quality or customer service levels and be detrimental to the company in the long run.

- *An emphasis on negative results.* Budget versus actual comparisons tend to focus on negative results. Although some companies require explanations for both favorable and unfavorable variances to the budget, the reality is that unfavorable variances get a lot more management attention, a situation that can be demoralizing for managers and employees. The actual-to-budget comparisons should highlight both the positive and negative results for the period.

- *The overuse of the budget as an evaluation tool.* The budget is a tool to evaluate managerial performance. Because not all aspects of managerial performance are reflected in the accounting reports, it must be used with caution. The budget is designed to alert management to potential problems. It is a feedback tool, not a mechanism to dispense reward and punishment. Moreover, the budget reflects only short-term results. A manager can sacrifice long-term objectives to improve short-term performance. Short-term actions to improve the bottom line may not be in the best long-run interests of the corporation.

■ *A lack of communication and participation.* Although lower-level supervisors and employees are often asked to provide information for the budget process, there is little exchange of information. Information tends to flow up, not down. First-line supervisors and middle managers sometimes do not understand how the information they provide fits in the larger picture and how it will affect their planned resource levels for the next year. When organizational plans are not communicated adequately, the result is a lack of commitment to attain the desired results.

■ *Budgetary slack.* This term describes what is known in management circles as fat—the cushion that protects the managers against anticipated budget cuts and provides for unexpected expenditures during the year. Managers use fat to hedge against uncertainty. Because it is so pervasive in the budgeting process, it is difficult to eliminate. We all like to hedge our bets. The following tips may help you undercover the fat in your organization's budget:

—Question the assumptions underlying the numbers. Are they reasonable? Do they seem inflated in comparison to other departments or the actual spending levels for this department? What are the historic spending patterns for this department?

—Analyze the manager's track record. Have her spending levels been consistently under budget in the past years? Does this manager have a reputation for preparing well-thought-out numbers? What kind of documentation supports the numbers?

—Tie dollars to specific business objectives. This requirement makes it more difficult to allocate a chunk of money with no identifiable purpose.

The budgeting process can be a motivating or demotivating factor in your organization. By understanding the potential pitfalls, you can structure your budgeting procedures to minimize the adverse effects.

Budget Preparation Methods

Before the start of the budgeting cycle, a company must determine which budget preparation method it will use. Each method has benefits as well as shortcomings. The choice of a particular method depends on management's information needs, the size and complexity of the organization, and its stage of maturity in terms of organizational development. A high-growth company operating in a dynamic environment has very different needs from a mature company operating in a stable environment.[2]

Static Budget

The most commonly used preparation method is the **static budget**, a detailed plan based on a single level of activity. In manufacturing operations, activity levels are defined as dollars sold, units sold, units produced, labor hours, machine hours, and others. Service industries use other activity bases, such as billable hours, passenger miles, customers serviced, orders processed, or gross sales dollars. This activity level drives the resource allocation within the organization.

The static budget remains unchanged for the duration of the budget period. Once it is approved, it cannot be altered or adjusted. The static budget is not well-suited for companies that operate in a dynamic environment or are experiencing high growth. Such companies may create other mechanisms, such as quarterly or monthly forecasts, to reflect major changes in the business environment.

Incremental Budget

The static budget can be prepared on an incremental basis. In an **incremental budget**, managers justify only expenses that go beyond a specified amount. This amount is defined as a percentage change (e.g., 3 percent), an absolute dollar increase (e.g., $5,000) or both (e.g., 3 percent and $5,000) from a base level such as the prior year's budget, the projected actuals, or some other reasonable basis.

The use of an incremental budget greatly simplifies the preparation and review process. The people who prepare the budget and the individuals who review it focus on major deviations to the established limits and do not review each budgeted item in detail. Incremental budgeting, however, has some drawbacks. It implicitly accepts that costs will increase from year to year and therefore does not support a continuous improvement philosophy. Moreover, it does not force managers to rethink their current resource allocation and tie these resources to the business strategies. In adopting an incremental budget, managers should ensure that this preparation method is consistent with the management philosophy and strategic direction of the organization.

Flexible Budget

Another type of budget preparation method is the **flexible budget**, which adjusts the budgeted costs to reflect actual activity levels. The purpose of a flexible budget is to measure performance more accurately by comparing actual costs for a given volume level with the budgeted costs for the *same* volume level. The flexible budget is dynamic. It establishes a relationship between cost and volume that can be used to develop budgets at different levels of activity. By contrast, a static budget can be developed for only one level of activity.

A flexible budget separates costs into its variable and fixed components. It adjusts the budgeted costs by changing the total variable costs according to the actual activity level attained. Fixed costs by definition remain unchanged. The flexible budget eliminates the variances between actual costs and budgeted costs created by volume increases or decreases. These volume variances are a major weakness of the static budget. The following example illustrates the difference between these two methods.

Suppose the manufacturing plant of Company X planned a volume of 10,000 units in June. Due to a change in the sales forecast, the actual units produced during the month totaled 8,000. Figure 4-4 shows the actual production costs for June (Column A) and compares these costs to the static budget (Column B) and the flexible budget (Column C). Column D shows the difference between the actual and budgeted costs using a static budget; Column E shows the same information using a flexible budget.

The company identifies materials as a variable cost, which are budgeted at $1.00 per unit. All other costs are fixed. The static budget for June is $10,000, which is the materials cost of $1.00 per unit times the planned volume of 10,000 units. Let us evaluate the actual performance of the company for June using a static budget.

If we compare the numbers in column A (the actual results) with Column B (the static budget), the difference between the actual and the budgeted materials costs is zero, as shown in Column D. One could infer that the company did a good job of controlling materials costs, because the actual costs came in at the budgeted level of $10,000. However, the company produced 2,000 units fewer than originally planned. The actual materials costs should have been *lower* than the budget of $10,000 because this item was based on a

Figure 4-4. *Comparison of a Static vs. a Flexible Budget.*

	June Actual (A)	Static Budget (B)	Flexible Budget (C)	Actual vs. Static (D)	Actual vs. Flexible (E)
Production volume (units)	8,000	10,000	8,000	2,000	———
Variable costs[a] Material	$10,000	$10,000	$ 8,000	———	$2,000
Fixed costs Labor	$ 2,750	$ 3,000	$ 3,000	($250)	($ 250)
Utilities	495	500	500	(5)	(5)
Rent	1,000	1,000	1,000		———
Other	875	1,000	1,000	(125)	(125)
Subtotal fixed	5,120	5,500	5,500	(380)	(380)
Total production costs	$15,120	$15,500	$13,500	($380)	$1,620

[a]Variable costs were budgeted at $1 per unit.
Note: Parentheses indicate a favorable budget variance.

planned production volume of 10,000 units. Because there is a significant volume difference between the actual results (8,000 units) and the static budget (10,000 units), this budget comparison presents a misleading view of the company's performance for the period.

Column C shows the flexible budget for June. The flexible budget adjusts the planned materials costs to reflect the actual production volume of 8,000 units. Since fixed costs do not vary with changes in volume, the flexible budget adjusts only the total variable costs—in this example, the materials costs. The materials costs are budgeted at $8,000 ($1/unit × 8,000). Column E shows the difference between the actual and the budgeted costs using a flexible budget. When the budgeted materials costs are adjusted for the decrease in production volume, actual materials costs are $2,000 higher than the budget.

The flexible budget is a better tool to assess management performance because it eliminates cost distortions created by differences between the planned and the actual volume levels. It shows management what their budgeted costs should have been for the actual volume produced during the period. Flexible budgets are very useful in industries where variable costs can be readily identified (e.g., materials, labor) and total costs fluctuate significantly with changes in volume.

In my experience, flexible budgets are not commonly used, for several reasons. One factor may be management's ability to distinguish clearly between fixed and variable costs. Some variable costs, such as direct materials or direct labor, are easy to recognize, but others, such as water, electricity, and maintenance, are often semivariable in nature. The identification of the fixed and variable portion of semivariable costs is often difficult and may be somewhat arbitrary. As a practical measure, some managers limit the definition of variable costs to those in which the cost-volume relationship is clear-cut (e.g., direct materials) and define all other costs as fixed. Although this simplifying assumption may create some cost distortion, managers should weigh the magnitude of the distortion in comparison to the potential benefits of adopting a flexible budget. If management can identify the cost-volume relationship of their semivariable costs in a reasonable manner, this identification will increase the accuracy of the budget model.

The identification of fixed and variable costs is not an accounting exercise. It must involve the operational managers to ensure that the flexible budget model reflects the cost structure and cost-volume relationships for the organization. At a major manufacturing subsidiary in Puerto Rico, the finance department adopted a flexible budgeting process. It defined the fixed, variable, and semivariable costs for each area with limited input from the manufacturing staff. It also determined the semivariable costs of the manufacturing operation as 50 percent fixed and 50 percent variable. Although the manufacturing managers disagreed with this definition, the flexible budget was implemented with this cost relationship. The manufacturing managers saw little value in the performance reports generated by the finance department because the established cost relationships did not reflect the reality of the manufacturing operations. They found the actual-to-budget comparisons meaningless and did not use these reports to measure the results of their operations.

Another obstacle to the widespread use of flexible budgets is system applications. Some accounting applications are not geared to handle anything other than a static budget. The accountants therefore tailor the budgeting preparation method to fit the systems that are available in the organization.

Zero-Based Budgeting

Another budget preparation method is **zero-based budgeting**. Zero-based budgeting breaks the cycle of continuous overhead growth by assuming zero resources; all resources must be justified. The mechanics of zero-based budgeting is beyond the scope of this book. It is very time-consuming and has fallen into disuse.

Some companies have implemented modified versions of zero-based budgeting. They identify specific cost categories that they want to control closely and require detailed justifications for these items. The categories are chosen because they have a significant impact on the company's cost structure, such as head count, or they are potentially controversial, such as travel, subcontractors, and entertainment.

Continuous Budget

Some organizations use a **continuous budget** (also known as a rolling budget) to obtain a dynamic view of the business.[3] The continuous budget adds a new budget period as the period just ended is dropped. Figure 4-5 illustrates this process. Suppose an organization budgets a 12-month period by quarter. At the end of each quarter, the budget information is revised, and a new quarter is added to replace the one just ended. For example, during the first quarter of the fiscal year (Q1 Y1), the company updates the remaining three quarters and plans the first quarter of the next fiscal year (Q1 Y2).

A continuous budget always reflects a specific time horizon, usually one or two years, as defined by management. Continuous budgets force managers to plan the future regardless of the accounting period at hand. This method recognizes that the organization is in a constant flux and plans must be updated periodically to reflect new information. The continuous budget always will reflect the most recent information about the external environment and the company strategies.

The continuous budget allows managers to incorporate changes to the business in an organized manner. A major drawback of the static budget is its inability to incorporate changes. The continuous budget corrects for this situation and provides management with a continuous view of the business. On the minus side, a continuous budget means that a company is in a constant planning mode. In larger organizations, the availability of information and the logistics

Figure 4-5. *Continuous Budget.*

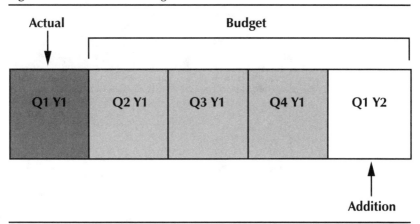

of implementation present formidable challenges that may hinder a more widespread use.

Forecasts

Some companies incorporate changes to the static or flexible budget through a monthly or quarterly forecast. A **forecast** projects the financial results of an organizational plan for a specific time period. In contrast to a budget, a forecast may or may not be used to measure management performance. As seen in Figure 4-6, a formal monthly or quarterly forecast does not extend beyond the fiscal year. In addition, the original budget remains unchanged. Some companies use forecasts to avoid unpleasant surprises at year-end. Management should clearly define what plan will be used to measure and evaluate operational results: the original budget or the forecast. Forecasts that are not used for measurement purposes may not have the same degree of accuracy as those that are.

Forecasts are often a necessity in companies that use static budgets. It is one of the few mechanisms available to understand the impact of internal and external changes on the financial results of the organization. It requires the involvement of all key managers and should not be an accounting exercise to satisfy a corporate requirement.

Choosing the Method

The choice of the budget preparation method depends on the size and complexity of the organization, the management information

Figure 4-6. *Forecasts and the Budget.*

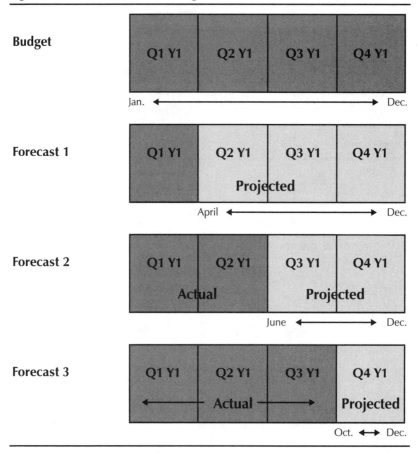

needs, and its stage of organization development. It is easier to implement a flexible budget in a company that has $5 million in sales and one location than a company that has $5 billion in sales and hundreds of locations. Moreover, a company with a high level of fixed costs or a stable operating environment will probably find a static budget perfectly adequate for its management information needs.

The state of a company's systems applications will also influence the choice of a budget preparation method. For example, some financial application packages can support only a static budget. The organization should ensure that its financial systems applications support the budget preparation method it chooses. Otherwise the development of alternate systems may be required to consolidate budget data, analyze information, and prepare management reports. Finally, the budget preparation method should support the long-term objectives of the company and provide managers with meaningful information to compare budgeted to actual performance.

Guidelines for a Smoother Budgeting Process

Regardless of the size and complexity of the organization, the budgeting process will take time and effort. However, certain actions make the process flow more smoothly:

1. *Ensure that top management has identified and communicated the strategies and priorities for the upcoming year.* This is the budgeting downfall for many companies. Priorities are not properly established at the start of the process or are not adequately communicated to the organization. When top management fails to communicate its priorities to the organization, each manager will prepare the budget according to his perceived needs, priorities, and expectations. This situation will inevitably result in changes during the management review process. It also creates a lot of rework and frustration for all parties.

2. *Encourage each unit or function to develop business objectives and specific action plans.* In many organizations that I have visited, managers develop the budgets for their areas but do not tie these to specific plans. The budget becomes a number-crunching exercise instead of a thoughtful planning process for the next fiscal year.

3. *Clearly define the expected results and the individuals or groups responsible for producing them.* Management should clearly set the expectations and requirements for the process. What information will be required? In what format? Who will be responsible for providing the information? By when? Are there specific financial targets that must be achieved? The finance department is usually responsible for coordinating the budgeting process so that both corporate and local management needs are satisfied.

4. *Communicate the requirements.* Communication is a key factor in the budgeting process. It is not enough to set expectations and requirements; management must communicate these to the key indi-

viduals in the process. The finance group is often assigned this communicator role.

5. *Establish budget guidelines.* Budget guidelines help ensure that the numbers submitted will fall within acceptable parameters. The guidelines can be at a macrolevel (the budget for Division A or Department B should not exceed last year's level or should not be greater than a specified amount) or microlevel (salary increases will be budgeted at 3 percent per year). By issuing these guidelines, management can avoid a great deal of rework at the end of the process.

6. *Hold an informational meeting.* Line managers frequently complain that the finance department does not allow enough time for the preparation of a well-thought-out budget. In defense of my fellow accountants, many deadlines are established by headquarters and are outside of their control. However, sometimes the deadlines are set arbitrarily and can be modified. When deadlines are unrealistic, managers submit the information late or incomplete. Since the finance department staff expects managers to submit the information late or incomplete, they make the deadlines tight to allow time to rework the numbers with the managers. It becomes a vicious cycle.

My recommendation is to have the finance group hold an informational meeting at the start of the process. In this meeting, deadlines, due dates, and responsibilities can be discussed and agreed on. Moreover, the finance group can review the budgeting guidelines and the information requirements and clarify any questions or issues about the process. This meeting then becomes a communication tool that can significantly facilitate the process for the entire organization.

7. *Provide training.* Accountants often assume that managers and supervisors know how to prepare and present a budget, when in fact many have never received any formal training in this area. They have learned by trial and error or years of accumulated frustration and experience. An organization can improve the quality and efficiency of its budgeting process by providing training to key personnel in this area.

Chapter Summary

The budget is a quantitative expression of a company's short-term plans and should tie in with its long-term strategic direction. Companies should tailor the budget process to meet their own particular needs for information and management control.

The budget process begins with a review of the company direction and the long-term strategies. In this review, management establishes short-term strategies and sets the priorities for the next fiscal year. These plans drive the allocation of resources within the organization. The plans are then quantified and summarized in an operating budget.

The budget is a tool to evaluate managerial performance. However, it should be used with caution. The budget, like any other management control system, has implications for human behavior in the organization. Managers should establish a budget process that motivates its employees to take the right course of action. As Charles Horngren and George Foster state in their classic cost accounting textbook, "Changing conditions call for changes in plans. The budget must receive respect, but it should not prevent a manager from taking prudent action."[4]

Notes

1. Reprinted from *How to Be the Life of the Podium* by Sylvia Simmons. Reprinted by permission of AMACOM, a division of American Management Association International, New York, NY. All rights reserved. http://amanet.org.
2. See Grant W. Newton, *Certified Management Accountant Review*, Part 3: *Management Reporting, Analysis, and Behavioral Issues* (Westlake Village, Calif.: Malibu Publishing Company, 1994), pp. 235–240 for a concise discussion on the behavioral aspects of the budgeting process. Other readings on this subject include Thomas A. Stewart, "Why Budgets Are Bad for Business," *Fortune,* June 4, 1990, and James A. Horsch, "Redesigning the Resource Allocation Process," *Management Accounting* (July 1995): 55–59.
3. For a discussion on how this concept is applied in practice, see Ralph Drtina, Steve Hoeger, and John Schaub, "Continuous Budgeting at the HON Company," *Management Accounting* (January 1996): 20–24.
4. Charles T. Horngren and George Foster, *Cost Accounting: A Managerial Emphasis,* 7th ed. (Englewood Cliffs, N.J.: Prentice Hall, 1991), p. 175.

Chapter 5

Budget Preparation
Procedures

Most organizations have a clear set of procedures for preparing the budget. These procedures outline the steps and relevant information involved in building the annual plan. The annual plan has two major components: the operating budget and the financial budget. The **operating budget** is a financial representation of the short-term plans of the organization across all functions. It consists of the income statement and all supporting budget schedules. Nonfinancial managers and supervisors are actively involved in the preparation of the operating budget. They define short-term plans and develop detailed budgets for their work areas or departments. The **financial budget** consists of the capital budget, the cash budget, the budgeted balance sheet, and the budgeted statement of cash flows. It shows the impact of the planned operations on the company's financial position at year-end. The accounting staff usually prepares the financial budget with some involvement from the line managers.

This chapter focuses on the preparation of the operating budget. It describes the basic steps in developing an operating budget and shows how to estimate each major element of the income statement: sales, cost of sales, and operating expenses. The chapter provides a practical approach to budgeting. A theoretical approach can be found in any good cost-accounting textbook.[1]

The Operating Budget

Nonfinancial managers are key players in the preparation of the operating budget. They determine the business strategies and define the key assumptions that will underlie the budgeted figures. Then they prepare and review the numbers that will ultimately be summarized in a budgeted income statement for management approval.

The operating budget is a set of budgets that are summarized into the three major elements of the income statement: sales, cost of sales, and operating expenses. Figure 5-1 shows the different budgets that are included in the operating budget and the sequence of steps in its preparation.

Sales Budget

The sales budget is a critical building block of the operating budget. It drives the resource allocation of other areas such as manufacturing and sales and marketing. It also determines the inflow of funds that will be available to support long-term investments in R&D and infrastructure. The sales budget should support the company strategies and reflect the desired sales growth, product mix, and customer base.

Sales are usually projected based on historical data. Although the past is not necessarily an indicator of the future, it provides a

Figure 5-1. *Operating Budget.*

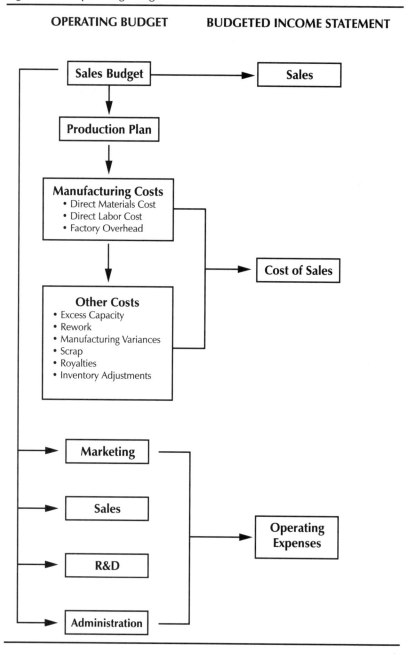

reasonable starting point to estimate future sales. If historical data is not available, you should gather data from other external sources such as industry surveys, trade journals, or research studies of similar companies in the area.

As you gather historical data, you should determine what information is available and for what time periods. Is the information available by month, quarter, or year? Is it by product, customer, or region? Often the raw data is available but not summarized in a useful manner. It may have to be reorganized in a format that meets your needs.

At a minimum, you should compile historical data for one year. This time frame will allow you to identify seasonal trends in the business and highlight unusual items, such as special orders or promotions that should not be considered in the current-year projections. It may also provide clues about pricing behavior. What has been the company pricing policy? Will a change in price have a significant impact on demand? What is history telling us?

Historical data should be analyzed in light of the internal and the external environment. Is the company growing or shrinking? Is the industry growing or shrinking? What uncontrollable aspects of the environment may affect sales (e.g., a rise in interest rates, environmental regulations, seasonal epidemics, a change in cultural values)? Performance expectations of outside interests such as bankers, investors, and shareholders should also be considered. Management should gather this information during the strategic review and analysis prior to the start of the budget process.

The sales budget should be expressed in tangible measures, such as units, pounds, billable hours, square feet, or number of clients serviced, and then given a monetary value based on an average price per unit of measure (UM). This UM should tie the financial results directly to the heart of the business. What was sold? What was the average price? How did the sales mix affect my operating results?

In simplest terms, the sales budget multiplies the estimated sales volume (expressed in a UM) by the average sales price per UM. Suppose Company X has two products, A and B. Figure 5-2 shows estimated demand for the upcoming year.

Based on this data, the sales budget is estimated at $1,500,000. The sales dollars, however, do not reflect the price and volume differences of the two products or the projected sales mix. The sales mix is the relative combination of quantities or dollars of products that compose total sales. Product A represents 75 percent of the sales volume but only 30 percent of the sales dollars. Product B, on the

Figure 5-2. *Sales Budget Example.*

Description	UM	Customer Demand	Price per UM	Sales Budget[a]
Product A	Each	300,000	$ 1.50	$ 450,000
Product B	Each	100,000	$10.50	1,050,000
Total budget				$1,500,000

[a]Product A = 300,000 each × $1.50 per unit = $450,000;
 Product B = 100,000 each × $10.50 per unit = $1,050,000.

other hand, contributes 25 percent of the volume but 70 percent of the total revenue. Changes in the sales mix can significantly affect the revenue projections. Let us return to the example in Figure 5-2. Suppose Company X sold 100,000 units of Product A and 300,000 units of Product B. Although the total units sold remain unchanged (400,000), the sales revenue is considerably different: $3,300,000 instead of $1,500,000.[2]

Companies with many products or customers should apply the 80/20 rule: Focus on the products that comprise 80–90 percent of sales dollars, and budget for these in detail. The remaining 10–20 percent can be extrapolated using simple math. Let us return to Products A and B above. Suppose these two products represented 80 percent of the total sales for the year. The remaining 20 percent consists of many products that are sold in very small amounts. We can calculate the total sales budget for the company as follows:

Total sales of Product A and B	$1,500,000
Percentage of total sales	80%
Total sales budget, Company X ($1,500,000 ÷ .80 = $1,875,000)	$1,875,000

This simple approximation method calculates the total budgeted sales without having to budget in detail all products or all customers.

Each organization must determine the appropriate measures to use as the basis for estimating revenue. In manufacturing organizations, this basis is typically units sold per period. In service organizations, it can be a variety of measures depending on the nature of the organization and the services provided—for example, number of customers, orders, patient hours, or service hours.

The preparation of a sales budget is far from an exact science.

The sales budget applies qualitative judgment to quantitative methods. After the numbers are crunched, the sales figures are adjusted up or down depending on what the manager is willing to commit and the expectations of the next level of management. This situation can have unforeseen consequences. At one of my former employers, the manufacturing organization was given two sales projections. The official budget was the number the sales division formally committed to the board of directors. In addition to the official budget, the sales staff provided a figure for "upside" sales. "Upside" was a term the sales division used to denote a potential sales figure that was higher than what was committed in the budget. For example, the division would commit to sell 1,000 units for a quarter and identify another 200 units of potential sales or "upside." Manufacturing was asked to be ready to produce to "upside" sales. This readiness implied purchase commitments and capacity investments that were not supported by the budgeted sales levels. Therefore, budgeted production costs were high relative to sales because they included investments to support a sales volume that was higher than the budget. In addition, if the upside did not materialize during the year, manufacturing got saddled with the excess capacity, the excess inventory, and top management wrath for failing to control costs!

The sales budget is based on a set of assumptions at a particular point in time. It is very important that all assumptions used to prepare it and any qualitative adjustments are well-documented. If sales do not materialize as planned, these differences can be traced to actual decisions made during the planning process. Because of the uncertainty in the external environment, managers should present at least three scenarios: a best case, a worst case, and a most likely case. Although the sales budget can be prepared based on the most likely scenario, the difference between the best case and the worst case measures in a quantitative manner with the level of risk and uncertainty in the budgeted figures. The organization can then prepare a contingency plan if either scenario materializes during the year.

If you work for a large, decentralized corporation, you may never have to prepare a sales budget in your entire career. Most managers prepare budgets only for their specific areas of responsibility. Nevertheless, it is important for everyone to understand the importance of the sales budget and how it drives the budget for the rest of the organization.

Production Plan

After top management approves the sales budget, manufacturing management develops the production plan, which details the quantities of each major product that will be manufactured during the year. It is expressed in physical terms, such as units, pounds, and cases. Cost analysts are sometimes (but not often) involved in the development of the production plan.

The production plan considers both the estimated sales units and the desired inventory levels in determining the production quantities for the upcoming year. The planned production for each major product is calculated as follows:

$$\text{Planned production} = \text{Sales} + \text{desired ending inventory} - \text{beginning inventory}$$

Let us return to the Company X example. The company has estimated the beginning inventory levels and the desired ending inventory levels for each product as shown in Figure 5-3. Beginning inventory must be estimated because the actual beginning inventory levels will not be known until the start of the new fiscal year. The desired ending inventory levels are determined by the company's inventory management policies. How much inventory does management want to maintain in relation to sales? What customer service level is required? What is the cost of an out-of-stock situation? How much time does it take to receive raw material inventory? Based on the data provided in Figure 5-3, Company X would produce 290,000 units of Product A and 135,000 units of Product B.

Some companies ignore inventory levels to simplify the budget preparation process and assume that the planned sales will equal the planned production volume. This approach could result in an under- or overallocation of manufacturing resources. If the current inventory levels are too high, management may choose to produce at

Figure 5-3. *Detailed Production Plan for Company X.*

Description	Sales Volume (in units)	Estimated Beginning Inventory	Desired Ending Inventory	Production Volume (in units)[a]
Product A	300,000	50,000	40,000	290,000
Product B	100,000	25,000	60,000	135,000
Total budget	400,000	75,000	100,000	425,000

[a]Planned production = Sales + desired ending inventory − beginning inventory.
Product A = 290,000 = 300,000 + 40,000 − 50,000.
Product B = 135,000 = 100,000 + 60,000 − 25,000.

a lower rate than the planned sales level and fill sales orders from inventory. If inventory levels are too low, management may want to build inventory and produce at a higher rate than the planned sales level. If managers do not consider inventory in the planning equation, manufacturing areas could have too many or too few resources to meet the production requirements during the year.

The production plan should also consider the capacity requirements of the plant. **Capacity** is the amount of output that can be obtained from a particular process during a given time period. Capacity can be constrained by people, facilities, or equipment. The budgeted production volume should not exceed the plant capacity unless capital investments are planned during the year that will expand the existing capacity.

Budgeted Manufacturing Costs

Many accounting textbooks describe the preparation of a direct labor budget, a direct materials budget, and an overhead budget to compute the cost of goods manufactured and the cost of goods sold. In reality, many manufacturing companies determine the cost of sales based on an estimated production cost per unit. In this section, we discuss how to calculate budgeted manufacturing costs in the simplest form. The impact of manufacturing yield and capacity utilization on product cost is discussed in Chapter 10.

Direct Materials Costs

Production costs consist of three major elements: direct materials, direct labor, and overhead. In manufacturing systems, the direct materials required to produce a product are found in the bill of materials or the product structure. The **bill of materials** (BOM) shows the components needed and the quantity required to manufacture a product or a batch of product. The quantities in the BOM are multiplied by the estimated costs for the next fiscal year to obtain the total materials cost per product. Generally an individual or a group of individuals is responsible for BOM maintenance. These individuals should review and approve the BOM at the start of the budget cycle. This review ensures that costs will accurately reflect the materials usage on the production floor.

The purchasing department generally supplies the estimated purchase prices for raw materials. These prices should consider possible price increases from vendors, changes in government regulations, and other factors that are discussed in more detail in Chapter 10. Figure 5-4 shows the budgeted materials cost per unit for Product B. The total budgeted materials cost for Product B is obtained by multiplying the unit materials cost of $3.85 by the planned production volume of 135,000 units, as follows:

1. Materials costs per unit $3.85
2. Planned production volume   135,000
3. Total materials cost, Product B $519,750
   (1) × (2) = $3.85 × 135,000

The estimated materials costs for Product A would be calculated in a similar manner. These costs would then be added to the total materials costs of Product B to obtain the total budgeted materials costs for Company X.

Direct Labor

Direct labor costs are calculated by multiplying the estimated or standard labor hours per unit by an average or standard labor rate. In manufacturing systems applications, the labor hours required by a work center or operation are typically found in the routing file. The **routing file** identifies the sequence of operations that are required to manufacture a product and shows the labor and machine hours required at each stage of the process. Manufacturing personnel are responsible for providing the labor hours required at operation. This information is based on engineering studies, actual production data, or experience.

The standard or average labor rate is calculated based on the

Figure 5-4. *Budgeted Materials Cost per Unit for Product B.*

Description	UM	Quantity per UM	Cost per UM	Total Cost[a]
Component X	Each	1	$1.25	$1.25
Component Y	Each	4	0.40	1.60
Component T	Feet	10	0.10	1.00
Total budgeted unit cost				**$3.85**

[a]Budgeted cost for Product B = (1 × $1.25) + (4 × $0.40) + (10 × $0.10)
                                                    = $3.85.

expected salary levels and the employee mix for the department or cost center. Let us suppose that Operation L has nine employees, each earning $5.15 per hour. Payroll taxes and fringe benefits are estimated at 15 percent of the base rate. Salary increases are projected at 3 percent of the base wages. The budgeted labor rate would be $6.10 per hour, as shown in Figure 5-5. The calculated labor rate should include all labor-related costs such as employer payroll taxes and fringe benefits.

This calculation methodology works well when all employees in a department are paid at the same rate. However, a cost center may have employees at different pay scales. In this situation, the average labor rate must be calculated in a different manner. Figure 5-6 shows the budgeted salary levels per employee for Operation S. The total labor expense (column F) is the sum of the base salary, projected salary increase, and the payroll taxes and benefits. This total figure is divided by the total hours paid, to obtain an average labor rate of $7.21.

Managers may plan the required head count for their area by comparing the total labor hours required to meet the budgeted volume levels to the total labor hours available in the department. The **total labor hours available** are the estimated number of hours that an employee has available to work after deducting legally mandated breaks, vacation, sick leave, training, and other nonproductive time. Appendix C explains this calculation in detail. This calculation will alert managers to an excess or shortage of labor so they may take the corresponding measures to manage the situation.

Figure 5-7 shows an example of this calculation, assuming total available labor hours per employee at 1,750 per year. Operation L will require 16,400 labor hours based on the budgeted production volumes. The number of employees required in this operation is rounded down to 9 (16,400 total labor hours ÷ 1,750 hours per employee = 9.37 employees). The difference between the total labor

Figure 5-5. *Budgeted Labor Rate for Operation L.*

Current labor rate per hour	$5.15
Expected salary increase (3% × $5.15)	0.15
Base labor rate with projected increase	**$5.30**
Taxes and fringe benefits (15% × $5.30)	0.80
Budgeted labor rate, including fringe benefits	$6.10

Figure 5-6. *Average Labor Rate Calculation for Operation S.*

Employee Name (A)	Current Wages (B)	3% Increase (C)	Projected Wages (D)	Taxes and Fringe Benefits (E)	Total Labor (F)
Doe, John	$ 10,712	$ 321	$ 11,033	$ 1,655	$ 12,688
Rivera, José	15,000	450	15,450	2,318	17,768
Pérez, Juana	15,500	465	15,965	2,395	18,360
Lee, Chan	11,000	330	11,330	1,700	13,030
Park, Kwon	10,712	321	11,033	1,655	12,688
Brown, Leroy	10,712	321	11,033	1,655	12,688
May, Cecil	10,712	321	11,033	1,655	12,688
Hunter, Lorna	17,000	510	17,510	2,627	20,137
Total, Operation S	**$101,348**	**$3,039**	**$104,387**	**$15,660**	**$120,047**

Sample Calculation for John Doe
3% increase = (Column B) × 0.03 = $10,712 × 0.03 = $321.
Projected wages = (Column B) + (Column C) = $10,712 + $321 = $11,033.
Taxes and fringe benefits = (Column D) × 0.15 = $11,033 × 0.15 = $1,655.
Total labor = (Column D) + (Column E) = $11,033 + $1,655 = $12,868.

Average labor rate, Operation S   **$ 7.21**

Detailed Calculations
Total hours   = Hours paid per period per employee × number of employees
paid   = (52 weeks per year × 40 hours per week) × 8
                 = 16,640 hours

Average labor = Total salaries + fringe benefits ÷ total hours paid
rate   = ($104,387 + $15,660) ÷ 16,640
              = $7.21

hours available and the total labor hours required represents the excess or shortage of labor that must be addressed as part of the budgeting process.

Fluctuations in production volume during the year may create an excess or shortage of labor during any given month. This situation is usually handled by working overtime, hiring temporary labor, or reassigning workers to other areas. A manager should evaluate whether this labor excess or deficiency is a permanent or temporary state of affairs before deciding how to manage this situation for the budgeted period.

Figure 5-8 shows the calculation of the direct labor costs per unit for Product B. The direct labor cost is determined by multiplying the labor hours required per unit by the average labor rate per hour at each stage of the process or operation. Total direct labor costs for Product B would be calculated as follows:

1. Direct labor costs per unit $1.04
2. Planned production volume   135,000
3. Total direct labor cost, Product B $140,400
   (1) × (2) = $1.04 × 135,000

The estimated labor costs for Product A would be calculated in a similar manner and added to the total costs of Product B to obtain the total budgeted labor costs for Company X.

Department Expenses (Overhead)

Department expenses (overhead) is usually budgeted at the cost center or departmental level. It includes all costs required to run

Figure 5-7. *Summary of Labor Requirements.*

Total labor hours available: 1,750

Operation L	Labor Hours per Unit	Production Volume	Total Labor Hours
Product A	0.01	290,000	2,900
Product B	0.10	135,000	13,500
Total labor hours			16,400
Number of			
employees required			9.37
Operation S			
Product A	0.02	290,000	5,800
Product B	0.06	135,000	8,100
Total labor hours			13,900
Number of			
employees required			7.94
Summary			
Product A	0.03	290,000	8,700
Product B	0.16	135,000	21,600
Total labor hours			30,300
Number of			
employees required			17.31

Figure 5-8. *Budgeted Unit Labor Costs for Product B.*

Operation	Labor Hours Required	Cost per Labor Hour	Labor Cost per Unit[a]
Operation L	0.10	$6.10	$0.61
Operation S	0.06	$7.21	0.43
Total	**0.16**		**$1.04**

[a]Budgeted labor cost = (0.10 × $6.10) + (0.06 × $7.21) = $1.04.

a particular operation except for direct labor and direct materials. (Chapter 2 discussed the major components of department expenses.) Because overhead costs are collected by the department or cost center, these overhead costs must then be assigned to the products on some reasonable basis.

Before deciding on the basis of assignment, management should determine which indirect and support costs will be included in the overhead pool. In theory, most costs incurred within a manufacturing facility can be considered overhead. These costs may include accounting, information systems, human resources, and other support departments such as building maintenance. In practice, many organizations report administrative support separately as an operating expense and do not include it as overhead. Some companies, however, allocate a portion of these support departments to the production areas based on a standard billing rate or some other agreed-on basis.

Factory overhead is assigned to individual products or services based on a predetermined **overhead rate**, derived by dividing the total overhead costs for the plant, department, or area by an appropriate activity measure. The **activity measure** (machine hours, labor hours, units) quantifies the frequency and the intensity of use of an operation by the product or service. It should bear a causal relationship to the costs being distributed. In Figure 5-9, management has determined that labor hours is the most appropriate measure because Operation L is a labor-intensive process. A company can use a single plantwide rate or multiple departmental rates to allocate overhead to products. For simplicity, I have chosen to use a single overhead rate in Figure 5-9. If your company manufactures diverse products, a single overhead rate is not recommended because it may distort your product costs.

When products are diverse, they require different levels of attention and effort as they move through the production process. Multi-

Figure 5-9. *Overhead Rate Calculation.*

Total factory overhead costs	$121,200
Total labor hours (per Figure 5-6)	30,300
Budgeted overhead rate per labor hour	**$ 4.00**
($121,300 ÷ 30,300)	
Overhead costs assigned to Product B	**$ 0.64**
(0.16 labor hour per unit @ $4.00 labor hour)	

ple overhead rates will allow you to differentiate these different patterns of resource consumption among products; a single overhead rate will not.

Some companies break down the overhead rate into its fixed and variable components. I would discourage this practice. As I noted in Chapter 2, the classification of fixed and variable costs is difficult and somewhat arbitrary. The use of a fixed and variable overhead rate adds complexity to the costing process and may provide no real value in terms of management information. (The assignment of overhead costs is discussed in more detail in Part III.)

The sum of the budgeted labor, materials, and overhead costs equals the budgeted manufacturing cost of a product. Typically these costs are calculated on a per unit basis and then multiplied by the projected sales volume to obtain the total cost of sales. The total budgeted manufacturing cost for Product B is calculated as follows:

Materials	$3.85	(from Figure 5-4)
Direct labor	1.04	(from Figure 5-8)
Overhead	0.64	(from Figure 5-9)
Total cost per unit	**$5.53**	
Total budgeted costs	**$746,550**	
($5.53 × 135,000)		

These costs would be added to the budgeted production costs for Product A to obtain the total budgeted manufacturing costs for Company X.

Cost of Goods Sold

Cost of sales can be budgeted in various ways. If the organization has determined the production cost or the merchandise cost per unit, budgeted cost of sales is obtained by multiplying the budgeted manufacturing cost per unit times the budgeted sales units. Figure 5-10 shows the budgeted cost of sales for Company X. For this example, we assume that the unit cost of Product A is $0.75; detailed calculations are not provided for this product. The unit cost of Product B was calculated in the prior section at $5.53 per unit.

Sales and cost of sales are usually calculated in detail by applying the 80/20 rule. Suppose the two products in Figure 5-10 represented 80 percent of the company's projected sales for the next fiscal year. We can calculate the total cost of sales budget for the company as follows:

Total cost of sales of Product A and B	$778,000
Percentage of total sales	80%
Total cost of sales budget, Company X	$972,500
($778,000 ÷ 0.80 = $972,500)	

A company may also elect to budget cost of sales based on a desired gross margin or as a percentage of budgeted sales. These methods are often used by retail organizations where the number of items sold is too extensive to warrant a detailed cost of sales calculation. The example shown in Figure 5-11 demonstrates this type of calculation.

Although both methods greatly simplify the cost of sales calculation, they have a distinct disadvantage: They do not tie the cost of sales to specific products, services, or customers. If the gross margin or cost of sales percentage is not achieved, it may be difficult to pinpoint the underlying causes. Was the variance caused by a drop in sales volume, higher production costs, or a change in the sales mix?

Figure 5-10. *Budgeted Cost of Sales, Company X.*

Description	UM	Sales Volume	Production Cost per UM[a]	Cost of Sales Budget[b]
Product A	Each	300,000	$0.75	$225,000
Product B	Each	100,000	$5.53	$553,000
Total budget				$778,000

[a]Cost of sale of Product A is $0.75; no detailed calculations have been provided for this number.
[b]Product A = 300,000 units × $0.75 per unit = $225,000.
 Product B = 100,000 units × $5.53 per unit = $553,000.

Figure 5-11. *Hot & Gooey Bakery Cost of Sales Calculation.*

Method 1. Cost of Sales Percentage

Hot & Gooey Bakery has budgeted sales of $500,000 for next year. Cost of sales has historically run at 45% of sales. Management plans to implement a new inventory control system that should reduce material losses. It agrees to budget cost of sales at 44.5 percent of sales to reflect the expected improvement in this area. Therefore, budgeted cost of sales for the year would equal $222,500 ($500,000 × 0.445).

Method 2. Gross Margin Percentage

Hot & Gooey management has set the desired gross margin at 55.5% of budget sales. Therefore, the cost of sales would be 45.5% (100% − 55.5%), or $222,500 (45.5% of $500,000).

When sales are tied to a UM, these questions can be answered more readily.

Service organizations generally do not report cost of sales, but show a breakdown of their most significant operating expenses by type (e.g., labor, fuel). However, some service organizations report the direct costs of providing services to a customer as cost of sales. This procedure allows them to separate the costs of revenue-generating functions from other operating expenses. Suppose you have a sales office that provides engineering support to end customers. This office prepares its revenue budget based on the projected support hours for each customer. Each support engineer has a fixed billing rate that is determined when the sales budget is established. Cost of sales can be calculated by charging the costs of the support engineers at a budgeted hourly rate. Figure 5-12 details this calculation.

The $36 cost rate is based on total available hours of 1,750. The available hours, as explained in Appendix C, adjust for vacation, sick leave, training, and other nonbillable time off. The calculated cost rate of $36 will recover all the labor costs associated with a support engineer if the company bills out 1,750 hours. Suppose the total billable hours for this engineer were budgeted at 1,600 hours. The budgeted cost of sales would equal $57,600 (1,600 hours × $36 per hour). The 150 unbilled hours could be reported as excess capacity under other cost of sales or as an operating expense. In addition to the labor cost, the company may opt to include as cost of sales any

Figure 5-12. *Calculation of Budgeted Cost Rate.*

Annual salary	$45,000
Payroll taxes and fringe benefits (40%)	18,000
Total labor costs	$63,000
Total available hours	1,750[a]
Budgeted cost rate per hour	**$36**
($63,000 ÷ 1,750 hours)	

[a]See Appendix C.

training, travel, and miscellaneous expenses that will be billed out to the customer.

Other Costs

Manufacturing and merchandising companies may incur costs that are generally charged as other cost of sales. These types of costs vary from company to company. Here I examine the most common ones.

Excess Capacity

These costs represent excess or idle capacity that cannot be reduced in the short run to reflect changes in customer demand. These figures tell management that the organization could support a higher sales or revenue volume than is currently provided for in the sales budget. In my experience, most organizations charge the cost of excess capacity to their current products or services, a practice that overestimates the costs of the products and services and distorts product profitability. (Excess capacity issues are discussed in more detail in Chapters 10 and 11.)

Royalties

Sometimes organizations are required to pay royalties for the use of a process, a product, or a specific technology. If the royalty payment is related to the product or service offerings, it should be included as other cost of sales.

Inventory Adjustments

Inventory adjustments reflect the dollar value of any adjustments made to the inventory balances. The most common inventory adjustment is the **book-to-physical-inventory adjustment**. This adjustment is the difference between the inventory dollars as recorded in the financial records compared to the dollar value of what is physically in the warehouse. If financial records reflect more than what is actually on hand, this inventory loss is reflected as an increase in other cost of sales. On the other hand, if the financial records show less than what is physically in the warehouse, this increase in inventory is reflected on the income statement as a decrease in other cost of sales. In general, inventory adjustments are not budgeted. The reason is both political and practical. No manager wants to plan for inventory adjustments. It sends the wrong message to the organization that a certain level of inventory adjustments is acceptable.

Manufacturing Variances

Manufacturing variances result from the use of a standard cost system to book inventory and cost of sales. If a company has a standard cost system, manufacturing variances are usually recorded as other cost of sales. (Standard cost systems are explained in detail in Chapter 12.) Most companies do not budget manufacturing variances. The assumption is that if the standard costs have been properly set, the manufacturing variances at year-end should equal zero.

Scrap

Scrap is defined as raw materials or products that are damaged during the production process and cannot be reused. It can also include finished products that are returned by the customer but cannot be reworked or sold. In manufacturing organizations, even the most efficient process will produce scrap. This type of scrap is considered normal and should be included in the manufacturing cost. Scrap is generally recorded as a separate line item when it is over and beyond what is expected from the normal manufacturing process. Scrap includes all manufacturing costs incurred up to the point at which the material or product was discarded. In my experience, although management acknowledges that scrap occurs, it certainly does not like to plan for it! My advice is as follows: If historically you have incurred a certain level of scrap, you should budget for it unless you have a clear action plan to reduce the current levels. This will make your budget more realistic and facilitate the explanation of budget to actual variances to the next level of management.

Rework

Products that do not meet manufacturing or customer specifications must be reworked before they can be sold. Some organizations have departments that are dedicated to rework. Others perform rework within the production floor. Rework should include all the labor, material, and overhead costs associated with remanufacturing the product. If rework is a significant cost in the organization, it should be included as other cost of sales in the budget.

*   *   *

Some companies choose not to budget other cost of sales items since some of these costs, such as inventory adjustments, rework, and scrap, are often the result of inefficiencies in the operating processes or breakdowns in the internal control procedures of the organization. My recommendation is to budget for these costs if they are significant unless there are specific actions in the business plan designed to reduce or eliminate these costs. Otherwise the budget will not represent a realistic projection of the financial results for the upcoming year.

Operating Expenses

Operating expenses contain all departments, areas, or cost centers that are not included as part of merchandise or manufacturing costs. These areas include research and development, sales and marketing, and general and administrative expenses.

Operating expenses are usually budgeted by department. Some areas such as R&D and marketing can be budgeted by major projects or promotions versus individual departments and then consolidated by department or functional area. Operating expenses are budgeted at the discretion of management. A manager uses her experience to estimate the resources required to accomplish the stated objectives for the area. Financial and nonfinancial indicators can be used to promote efficiency. For example, what is the cost per employee? How does it compare to last year? What is the cost per services rendered (per check, per purchase order, per invoice collected)? The identification of key performance indicators for nonmanufacturing areas can assist you in planning your departmental costs. (Chapter 6 explains in more detail how to prepare a departmental budget.)

Budgeted Income Statement

The operating budget is summarized in a budgeted income statement that shows the gross margin and the operating income from the pe-

Figure 5-13. *Budgeted Income Statement, Company X.*

Company X
Budgeted Income Statement
for the Year Ended December 31, XXXX

	Budget	**% of Sales**
Sales	$1,875,000	100.0
Cost of sales	972,500	51.9
Gross margin	902,500	48.1
Operating expenses		
Sales and marketing	200,000	10.7
R&D	150,000	8.0
Administration	100,000	5.3
Total operating expenses	450,000	24.0
Operating income	$ 452,500	24.1

riod. The **gross margin** is the difference between sales and cost of sales. Gross margin as a percentage of sales is an important performance indicator. It is commonly used to evaluate cost control and overall product or service profitability before deducting operating expenses. The gross margin percentage is also used to benchmark a company's performance against similar companies in the same industry. **Operating income** is the difference between gross margin and operating expenses. It is the income generated from the main business operations. Miscellaneous income and expenses would be reported below this number and are typically budgeted by the finance unit. Figure 5-13 shows the budgeted income statement for Company X based on the sales and cost of sales figures already computed in this chapter.

Chapter Summary

Nonfinancial managers are typically involved in the preparation of the operating budget. Although an individual or a group may be responsible for only a piece of the budget such as a department or particular product, everyone who participates in this process should understand how the pieces fit together. This chapter has covered all the important elements for building an operating budget. Most managers and supervisors will participate in the budget process by preparing the detailed budget for their department or work area. These budgets are then summarized as cost of sales or operating expenses in the income statement.

Notes

1. See Charles T. Horngren, George Foster, and Srikant M. Datar, *Cost Accounting: A Managerial Emphasis* (Upper Saddle River, N.J.: Prentice Hall, 1997). A more concise explanation for the experienced professional can be found in Jae K. Shim and Joel G. Siegel, *Modern Cost Management and Analysis* (Hauppauge, N.Y.: Barron's Educational Series, 1992).
2. Sales revenue $= (100{,}000 \times \$1.50) + (300{,}000 \times \$10.50) = \$150{,}000 + \$3{,}150{,}000 = \$3{,}300{,}000.$

Chapter 6

How to Prepare Your Departmental Budget

*"Of course they always tell you to make changes --
that's because you always tell them how easy it
is to make changes."*

The preparation of the departmental budget is the ideal time for a manager to question current procedures, look for alternative ways of accomplishing objectives, and redesign or improve existing processes. The departmental budget consists of five major elements: short-term strategies and plans; the organizational structure; departmental spending; the capital budget; and the documentation of assumptions, risks, and opportunities.

Short-Term Strategies and Plans

Top management defines the short-term direction of the organization at the start of the budget cycle. With this information, a manager and his team can define the department's short-term goals for the next fiscal year. Some departments also develop a departmental mission statement, which clearly states the purpose and the long-term direction of the organizational unit. This mission statement should not change from year to year. However, the management team should review this statement each year to ensure it is aligned with the overall direction of the organization.

The short-term goals of the organizational unit provide the framework for developing the tactical plan. The **tactical plan** identifies the specific actions or projects required to achieve the stated objectives. The tactical plan answers three basic questions:

- What will the organization do next year?
- Who will do it?
- When will it get done?

A manager should tie each major program, project, or action directly to the departmental objectives. She should establish the major milestones, the estimated due dates, and the individuals responsible for its execution.

The list of planned projects should be short and achievable within the budget time frame. The management team should obtain consensus on the department priorities and rank the projects accordingly. This ranking will simplify the decision-making process if budget cuts are required later.

Organizational Structure

Most large organizations require managers to submit a head-count plan as part of their budget package. The **head-count plan** usually details the current and future staffing requirements of the department by job classification. During the budgeting process, a manager has an opportunity to examine the current organization and ask some hard questions. How is the area currently organized? Is it performing according to expectations? What are the department's strengths? What are its weaknesses? Does the current organizational structure prepare me to meet the challenges of the future? What skills do we have? What do we need?

The manager should also consider alternative organizational models. Are there functions that can be consolidated, centralized, or eliminated? Are there tasks being performed that are not related to the purpose of the department? Can some processes be structured more efficiently?

After a thorough examination of the organization, a manager is ready to estimate staffing requirements for the next budget period. The head-count plan usually summarizes the type and the number of positions that are required to achieve the departmental objectives. It may or may not include the names of the current employees in the department and their specific job title. A manager may also be asked to provide additional written justification for any new positions. This head-count plan will drive the budget calculation for labor and labor-related expenses such as training, travel, and employee relations.

Departmental Spending

Once a manager has defined the objectives and staffing requirements, he is ready to quantify these plans into a budget. Some managers rely heavily on historical information to budget costs. However, the current management focus on cost reduction and downsizing requires a manager to understand his cost structure more thoroughly. Answering the following questions, which focus on the activities of the department, can yield a better understanding of costs:

- What are the principal activities of my department?
- What types of resources (e.g., people, equipment, supplies) are required by each activity? What do these resources cost?
- What factors drive the costs in these activities? Some examples are government regulations, good manufacturing practices, and customer requirements.
- Is there waste or inefficiency that can be eliminated?
- What alternatives are available to lower costs in these areas?

In preparing the budget, a manager should identify the type of expenses that are typically incurred in the work area. **Recurring expenses** are incurred on a regular basis and can be estimated based on historical data. Examples are payroll-related expenses, utilities, and depreciation. **Nonrecurring expenses** are incurred infrequently, often due to a special circumstance such as a government fine, the implementation of a new computer system, or a new product introduction. Because of their infrequent and unpredictable nature, these expenses are often difficult to budget. **Discretionary costs** are incurred at the discretion of the department manager—for example, training, travel, and supplies. There is no mechanism to determine the optimal amount in these areas, and the benefits are difficult to quantify. **Committed costs** result from contractual obligations (e.g., a maintenance contract or purchase agreement) or are a consequence of past decisions (e.g., depreciation). Generally these costs cannot be altered in the short term and represent fixed amounts that can be calculated precisely.

The classification of departmental costs facilitates the preparation of cost estimates and ensures that no significant expenses are overlooked. In the next sections, we examine how to estimate costs for major expense categories.

Labor

Labor often represents 60–70 percent of the total departmental spending. Labor costs are derived from the head-count plan. These costs include salaries, payroll taxes, vacation and sick pay, commissions, bonuses, fringe benefits, overtime, and temporary employees. There are two ways to estimate the total labor expense:

- *By employee.* This method lists the employees by name, position, and salary (actual or proposed). The payroll-related expenses are calculated based on the specific salary of each employee.

- *By position.* This method estimates payroll expenses using the average salary and the number of employees required for each budgeted position. It is an appropriate method to use when the department has a large number of employees or when detailed salary information is not available.

The integration of computer technology has greatly facilitated the calculation of budgeted labor expenses. At one of my former employers, the finance department provided managers with a file that showed all the relevant payroll information for each area. The manager would modify the worksheet as appropriate, adding or deleting positions according to his plan. The human resources department provided the salary estimates for new positions. Once the manager entered this information, the program would automatically calculate the total departmental salaries and fringe benefits and put this information into another spreadsheet that summarized the departmental spending by cost category.

Budgeted labor costs should also include projected salary increases. There are different ways to incorporate salary increases into the budget. Some companies establish a fixed percentage as part of the budget guidelines; for example, all managers should budget salary increases at 5 percent of base salaries. Others require managers to budget salary increases by employee based on their expected performance (merit) or some other basis (e.g., a raise in the minimum wage or union negotiations).

Depreciation

An organization owns buildings, machinery, and equipment that it uses to generate income over a number of years. Accountants classify these items as **capital assets** (they are also known as fixed assets). Capital assets are reported as property, plant, and equipment on the balance sheet. Accountants allow only a portion of the total cost of such assets to be charged as expenses in a particular period. This charge is called depreciation expense. Suppose you have a truck that may produce income for five years. Accountants require you to charge the cost of that truck against income over a five-year period.

Depreciation expense is a systematic method that accountants use to spread the cost of an asset over the number of periods it is expected to benefit the company. The finance department usually provides the budgeted figure to the department manager. It should include the depreciation charges for all existing equipment and any new equipment that will be purchased in the upcoming year. The cost of any new equipment should be included in the capital budget.

Department managers often take the budgeted depreciation figure provided by the finance department as a given. However, sometimes the budgeted depreciation calculation is based on outdated or incomplete information. Managers should request a detailed fixed asset listing for their area that ties to the budgeted depreciation figure provided by the finance department. They should use this listing to verify that all assets in the department have been accounted for and that any new capital purchases have been included in the budgeted depreciation expense. Managers should be particularly attentive to equipment that has been transferred, sold, or discarded that appears on the asset listing. These assets continue to accumulate depreciation costs even though the equipment is no longer physically in the department. A manager who detects this situation should notify the finance department immediately.

Other Expenses

Other expenses may include water, electricity, travel, training, supplies, maintenance, and subcontractor fees. There are several ways to estimate these types of expenses:

- *Use historical costs.* Historical costs are the actual costs incurred in prior periods as shown on the financial reports. Although historical costs may not be indicative of future spending levels, they provide a solid basis for estimating expenses. If your department has historically spent an average of $1,000 in office supplies for the past two years, you could safely budget the same amount for the following year given no significant changes in the future operating environment. Moreover, historical data can be modified to consider the impact of future events such as a price increase or a new equipment purchase.

- *Obtain vendor quotes.* Vendors can provide estimated costs for a product or service. This cost estimation method is useful when there is no historical data or when a price change is expected.

- *Make estimates based on expected usage.* Some costs can be directly related to the use of a particular resource. The total cost of the resource will vary depending on its expected usage during the budget year. Suppose you have estimated the electricity consumption for your department at 181,000 kilowatt-hours per month based on the next year's production plan. The cost per kilowatt-hour has averaged $0.08 for the past year and is not expected to increase. The budgeted electricity cost for the year would be $173,760 (181,000 kilowatt-hours per month × 12 = 2,172,000 × $0.08 = $173,760).

An **activity measure** is the tangible factor that describes how the resource is consumed. In the example, the activity measure is kilowatt-hours. Some common activity measures are the number of employees, the units produced or sold, machine hours, labor hours, and kilowatt-hours. The manager must identify the appropriate activity measure and then estimate the cost per activity measure.

Suppose you are budgeting training expense. You have 10 employees in the department and would like each employee to attend a minimum of two training sessions per year. Based on prior experience, each training session costs an average of $500. Therefore, you would budget $10,000 (10 employees × 2 training sessions × $500 per session) for training.

Cost estimation based on expected usage assumes a direct relationship between the costs and expected usage of the resource. Therefore, a manager must ensure that the cost-volume relationship established is appropriate to estimate future costs. Suppose we use head count to budget supplies. Supplies are estimated at $500 per person per year. This cost estimate assumes that the supplies expense will vary directly and proportionately with the number of employees in the department. Although this assumption may be reasonable to budget for office supplies, it may be totally inappropriate for production supplies. (The concepts of activity measure and activity cost are explained in Chapter 14.)

- *Obtain comparative data.* Sometimes it is possible to obtain spending data from companies in similar industries. This method is particularly useful when starting a new project or department and no historical data is available for projecting operating expenses. The comparative data serves as a starting point for estimating departmental spending. This data should be adjusted as necessary to reflect the reality of the local operating conditions.

The comparative data can also serve to test the reasonableness of the budgeted figures. If the budget figures are significantly higher or lower than similar operations in other parts of the organization, the manager must be prepared to justify this disparity during the budget review process.

In sum, a manager has various alternatives to estimate departmental spending. I strongly recommend that managers document the cost estimation methods for these items since significant expenses are usually carefully examined during the management review process. Managers should support these cost estimates with historical data, industry data, vendor quotes, or other pertinent information. If the cost estimation method is not documented properly, the budget review process may become a discussion of the estimation methodology instead of the business issues at hand. A finance expert can greatly assist in this process.

Pay particular attention to those expenses that are management "hot buttons" in your organization—for example, travel, overtime, temporary labor, and subcontractors, which are usually discretionary costs. These expenses tend to draw a lot of management attention regardless of their importance to the department. Therefore, management may find these items easy to cut because they seemingly have no visible impact on the operations.

Capital Budget

The capital budget identifies long-term projects that will require a significant outlay of funds and will benefit future periods. It is an integral part of the annual budgeting cycle and should be reviewed with the same diligence as the head-count plan or the departmental expense budget. Traditionally the capital budget has focused on investments in property, plant, or equipment. However, major investments in training, marketing, sales promotions, or R&D should also be analyzed as capital projects. These types of projects are often long term in nature and require a significant disbursement of funds. Therefore, they should be evaluated as capital projects even though accounting regulations may require that these projects be considered operating expenses. (Chapter 7 discusses the capital budget and investment analysis process in detail.)

Documentation of Assumptions, Risks, and Opportunities

The budget is based on key assumptions about the company's operating environment at a specific point in time. These assumptions should be documented as part of the budget package that is submitted to the next level of management. In addition, a manager should highlight any potential risks or opportunities in the budget. For example, suppose there is a 50 percent chance that the government will impose stricter environmental regulations next year that would require a significant capital investment for the organization. Due to the uncertainty of the legislation, the manager opts not to include this amount in his budget. However, he should explicitly discuss this risk and its potential financial impact in this section. Project delays, foreign exchange risk, and supplier relationships are examples of items that should be discussed in this section.

Risks and opportunities should be included in the budget narrative when there is a reasonable chance that the situation will materialize in the upcoming year. They should also be quantified whenever possible. It will be easier for a manager to explain a budget deviation during the year if he foresaw and documented the situation as a possible risk or opportunity during the budget process.

Chapter Summary

As you prepare the budget for your area, do not lose sight of your goal: to present a realistic assessment of your resource requirements for the next fiscal year. This chapter provides some tools and suggestions to facilitate the budget preparation process. Budget procedures and requirements vary from company to company and are a function of the size and complexity of the organization as well as the unique style of its management team. In the final analysis, you will have to adapt this material to fit your own particular situation.

Appendix D shows a detailed departmental budget for the purchasing department of a fictitious company. Appendix E shows the capital budget for this department. These appendices illustrate the five major elements of a departmental budget discussed in this chapter.

Chapter 7

Capital Investment Analysis

ROBOTICS INSTITUTE

© 1983,1991 HARLEY SCHWADRON

SCHWADRon

C apital investments are long-range decisions that usually involve large sums of money and have uncertain outcomes. Should we use the most advanced technology in our products? Should we invest in a companywide training program? Should we upgrade our voice and data communications system? The significance of the investment is directly related to the expected outcome and its potential impact on the organization. A $100,000 equipment purchase may be considered a minor investment for a large multinational company such as IBM but may be tremendously significant for a small to medium-size corporation.

This chapter discusses capital investment analysis and its integration into the planning cycle. It examines the nature of capital investments, the typical capital investment cycle, and how to identify and classify project costs. It also discusses how to evaluate capital investments and explains the most common techniques for financial analysis.

The Nature of Capital Investments

Most people generally view capital investments as tangible projects related to facilities, machinery, or equipment. A capital investment, however, can be any long-term project that is expected to yield benefits over time. Under this definition, research and development (R&D) programs, marketing campaigns, and product transfers could also be considered capital investments.

In practice, capital investment analyses generally emphasize asset purchases (land, machinery, equipment, or furniture). They usually do not include investments in training or marketing programs that may have a long-term impact (e.g., changing the warranty policy) and do not require the purchase of capital equipment. These types of projects, however, meet the criteria of a capital investment: (1) they are long term in nature, (2) they require a significant outlay of funds, and (3) they are expected to yield benefits over time. Therefore, they should be analyzed as a capital investment with the same rigor as an asset purchase.

A capital investment is similar to a bank loan. When a bank makes a loan, it expects to recover the principal amount plus interest. When a company makes a capital investment, it expects to recover the initial cash committed plus some additional cash in the future. Capital investments usually involve large amounts of money. These investments may commit the company to a certain course of action over a considerable period of time and therefore can affect the company's flexibility to adapt to new market conditions or new technology. Capital investments can also have a significant impact on product cost. The long-term impact of capital investment decisions requires that these projects be analyzed in the context of the company's overall strategic direction and the long-term financial objectives.

The Capital Investment Cycle

Figure 7-1 shows the typical capital investment cycle in a medium-size to large organization. Planning is the most critical element in this cycle. It involves the identification and quantification of major investment decisions and their projected benefits to the organization. Capital investment decisions should tie directly to the strategic direction of the organization and to the short-term corporate objectives. For example, does your company want to be a technology leader or invest only in proven technologies? This strategic decision dictates the type of R&D projects funded by the company.

The identification of capital investments culminates in a capital budget, which is an output of the annual planning cycle. The approved capital budget provides a blueprint for authorizing capital expenditures during the year. After the capital budget is approved, a

Figure 7-1. *The Capital Investment Cycle.*

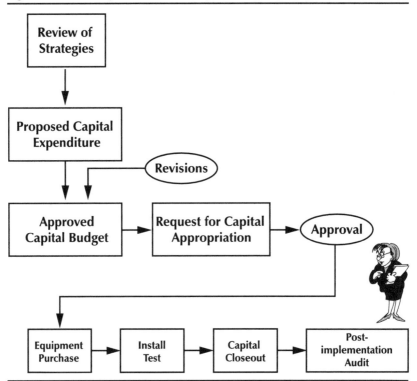

manager generally submits an authorization form (e.g., capital appropriation request form) to request the disbursement of funds. This form describes the nature of the project and provides detailed information on costs, benefits, risks, and opportunities. In some companies, this form expands on the information submitted during the budgeting cycle. Several levels of management usually approve the request for capital appropriation depending on the monetary value of the investment. The magnitude of some projects may require approval by the board of directors.

Once the appropriation has been approved, the project manager is authorized to select vendors, obtain vendor or supplier commitments, and disburse funds against this project. The finance department typically provides a project tracking number and monitors the expenditures to ensure that the actual amounts spent do not exceed the approved levels. On completion of the project, the project manager notifies the finance department, which closes out the project. Once the closeout process is completed, no further charges are permitted against the project. A postimplementation audit should be conducted to monitor how well the organization has executed the investment project. Because a capital project may cut across fiscal years, many companies have developed specific guidelines to handle multiyear projects. You should familiarize yourself with your own company guidelines in this area.

Cost Classification

One important step in the capital investment process is the identification and classification of project costs. This classification is important because generally accepted accounting principles require that the cost of assets whose benefits extend over a period of time be charged against future income. A **capital asset** is an economic resource that provides benefits to a company over one or more years beyond the period of acquisition. **Capital costs** are the expenditures incurred in the acquisition of capital assets. These costs are shown on the balance sheet and systematically charged against operating income over the estimated useful life of the asset. This systematic method is called **depreciation**. Therefore, the capital investment proposal should identify those costs that will be **capitalized** and charged to future accounting periods and those that will be **expensed** and charged against current operating income.

Capital assets typically include land, machinery, furniture, and

Figure 7-2. *Capitalization Policy Example.*

The purchase of an asset is considered a capital expenditure when:

1. It is an item costing at least $1,000 and having a useful life of at least three years.
2. Items costing less than $1,000 are treated as capital assets if their useful life is at least three years and they are part of:
    (a) a number of items forming a larger unit whose total value is greater than $1,000; or
    (b) a number of items of a permanent nature whose total aggregate value is greater than $1,000. An item that routinely falls in this category will be treated as a fixed asset even though only one is bought at a time; for example, a chair.

---

equipment. The capital costs consist of the purchase price of the item and all other costs incurred to make the asset ready for use, such as freight, duties, insurance, sales tax, installation charges, and brokerage fees. Figure 7-2 shows an example of the capitalization policy of a major Fortune 500 corporation.

Costs are also considered capital expenditures if they prolong the life of the property, increase its value, create a permanent improvement, or make the asset adaptable to a different use. Suppose you overhaul your computer system and increase its speed and capacity. This expenditure has permanently improved the performance of the equipment and should therefore be accounted as a capital cost.

Costs that are ordinary and necessary to maintain the property in efficient operating conditions should be expensed. These expenditures do not add value to the property or equipment nor do they appreciably prolong its life. They merely keep the asset in good operating condition. Maintenance and repairs are examples of such expenditures. Figure 7-3 shows commonly incurred costs for capital projects and their recommended classification. Although these classifications may vary from company to company, this list can serve as a guide to ensure that all project costs are properly accounted for.

Capital Budgeting Process

The capital budget identifies long-term projects that require a significant outlay of funds and will benefit future years. It is an integral

Figure 7-3. *Classification of Common Capital Project Costs.*

Machinery and Equipment	Capital	Expense
Purchase price	X	
Broker's commission	X	
Duties	X	
Sales taxes	X	
Insurance	X	
Freight and transportation	X	
Site preparation	X	
Installation	X	
Maintenance supplies		X
Maintenance contract		X
Ordinary repairs		X
Upgrade/overhaul of asset	X	
Add-ons to original asset	X	
Operating supplies and minor tools		X
Labor costs related to machine setup, validation, testing, or training (e.g., mechanics, engineers)	X	
Business travel incurred to review, validate, test, or install equipment	X	
Outside consultants hired to review, validate, test, or install equipment	X	
Training costs for new equipment (preinstallation)	X	
Training costs (postinstallation)		X
BUILDING		
Ordinary repairs		X
Painting an area		X
Building and leasehold improvements	X	
Upgrade electrical or water installations	X	
Install heat or air-conditioning	X	
Maintenance contract		X
Maintenance supplies and minor tools		X
CONSTRUCTION		
Permits and licenses	X	
Municipal taxes	X	
Engineering design	X	
Construction costs	X	
Engineering charges (corporate)	X	
Insurance cost during construction	X	
Install new partitions, doors, walls	X	
Remove/relocate partitions, doors, walls		X
Patch/paint existing partitions and walls		X
Paint new partitions and/or walls	X	

part of the annual budgeting cycle and should be reviewed with the same diligence as the head-count plan and the expense budget. Traditionally the capital budget has focused on investments in property, plant, or equipment; however, major investments in training, marketing, sales promotions, or R&D should also be analyzed as capital projects even though these costs may be reported as operating expenses on the income statement. These types of projects are often long term in nature and require a significant disbursement of funds. Therefore, they should be analyzed with the same rigor as capital asset purchases.

The capital budget describes the major projects that will be funded during the next fiscal year and itemizes their cost. It should detail all the costs of a project, capital and expense. Some projects may require the purchase of capital assets and result in increased operating expenses such as labor, utilities, or supplies. Top management should understand the total project costs when choosing among alternatives. If the project will affect more than one area or department, the incremental costs for all areas should be identified and summarized in the capital budget proposal. The incremental expenses associated with capital projects should also be included in the departmental spending budgets where they will be incurred.

Organizations usually issue budget guidelines on the level of documentation that will be required for capital projects. These guidelines are issued as part of the budget package at the start of the process. Although each company has its own particular needs and formats, a good capital budget proposal should contain the following elements:

- *Description of the project.* The capital budget proposal should clearly describe the nature of the project and how it ties to the departmental goals and the company objectives.

- *Estimation of the project costs.* The requester should identify all direct and indirect costs of the project even if these costs will be incurred in another department or division. The cost breakdown should separate capital costs from operating expenses by area or department. For example, if the project requires a group of engineers from the corporate office, these costs (salary, fringe benefits, travel expenses) should be included in the project estimate regardless of which organizational unit pays for them. In this manner, management has a complete picture of the total investment required and can make better trade-off decisions among competing alternatives.

- *Identification of projected benefits.* This section should address what benefits will be obtained from this investment. Will it increase quality, flexibility, or customer service? Will it reduce costs? Is it required by law? The requester should quantify, if possible, the financial impact of the expected benefits. Some companies may require a financial evaluation during the budget process. Others may postpone the detailed financial analysis until the budget has been approved and a formal capital appropriation request is submitted.

- *Risks and opportunities.* The requester should clearly identify the risks and opportunities associated with a project. These may be financial or operational. For example, the project may commit the company to a technology platform for the next three to five years, or it may provide an opportunity to increase market share by 10 percent. This discussion of risks and opportunities will provide management with a better understanding of the uncertainties involved in the project.

After the costs and benefits have been quantified, the manager should incorporate these numbers into the budget. For example, if a project will result in lower material costs due to increased scrap recovery, these cost savings should be incorporated into the budgeted cost of sales figure. Because the project may affect areas that are not under the immediate control of the requester, she should coordinate with the finance department to ensure that all project costs and benefits are accounted for in the budget. Management may take a conservative approach and opt not to incorporate the estimated benefits of a project into the budget. However, this approach should be a conscious decision of the management team and not a budget oversight. Appendix E shows an example of a capital budget justification form using the guidelines discussed here.

Managing the Capital Budgeting Process

The capital budget is a useful tool for identifying and approving major investment projects. Unfortunately, it too often is an afterthought in the budget preparation process. Managers may place a significant amount of time and effort in reviewing and analyzing cost of sales and operating expenses, but then put together the capital budget without adequate documentation or justification. Projects may be inconsistent with the company's strategic objectives or conflict with a project in another department or area.

I have seen companies manage the capital budget in two ways. In the **detailed item approach**, only projects that are approved in the capital budget can be implemented. Although substitutions are allowed during the year, these must replace a specific item in the capital budget and must be justified to the next level of management. Moreover, any incremental funds beyond the budgeted amount usually require additional authorizations by one or more levels of management. This approach, although slightly rigid, motivates managers to incorporate capital investment decisions into the annual planning process. It communicates a strong message that any capital investments not included in the annual budget will be subject to a high level of scrutiny. Moreover, it encourages managers to perform a thorough analysis of the proposed expenditures since they know deviations from the budget will be carefully examined.

Under the other method used to manage capital budgets, what I call the **big bucket approach,** the organization assigns a specific amount of money (the big bucket) to a list of loosely defined projects. During the course of the year, managers submit capital appropriation requests for a portion of this money. Once all the money has been appropriated, no further projects are approved. The bucket approach may work for small organizations, but it has some significant drawbacks, particularly for large organizations. First, it disassociates capital investment decisions from the annual planning process. Projects may be approved that do not support the company's short- or long-term direction. Second, because projects are reviewed on a piecemeal basis, it is difficult to evaluate the big picture and make trade-off decisions among various alternatives. It encourages a "first come, first served" attitude, with those projects that are submitted early during the year having a better chance of approval.

Capital investment priorities should be set during the review of the strategic plan prior to the start of the annual budget. The capital budget is an integral part of the annual planning cycle and should be reviewed with the same rigor as department expenses. A capital budget request should provide management with enough details to understand the questions: How? What? Where? and Why? The formality of this process may vary depending on the size of the organization. In a small organization, the process may be less formal because the decision makers are directly involved in the day-to-day management or are very close to the business. In larger organizations, where the decision maker does not have personal knowledge of the business unit, a more formal process is required. This process allows managers to evaluate alternative investment proposals using a consistent presentation format and clear-cut evaluation criteria for approval.

Evaluating Capital Investments

The formal evaluation of a capital investment project may occur during the annual budgeting cycle or when a formal capital appropriation request is submitted to management for approval. The rigor of this process depends on the magnitude of the investment. During the evaluation process, management assesses the long-term impact of a project on the company's financial and operational well-being. They identify the incremental costs and weigh these against the expected benefits that will be obtained over the life of the project. They also take into account other qualitative factors that cannot be quantified into a monetary figure but are important considerations in the decision-making process.

The evaluation of a capital project typically involves five major steps:[1]

1. The identification of the relevant cash flows
2. The financial Analysis of the project
3. An assessment of the project risk
4. A sensitivity analysis or "what if" analysis
5. The evaluation of other qualitative factors

After these five steps are completed and documented, management makes a decision on the project. The final decision may require several layers of management approval depending on the size of the investment and its potential effects on the financial condition of the corporation.

Step 1. The Identification of Cash Flows

Managers who are making capital budget proposals often have difficulty identifying the relevant cash flows to include in their analysis. A **cash flow** is the cash that enters or leaves the business. A **cash inflow** is the cash that enters the business or, conversely, the cash that does not leave the business. Examples of cash inflows are the additional cash generated by sales, cash savings due to head-count reduction or a decrease in operating expenses, or cash savings due to a reduction in the level of inventory. A **cash outflow** is all the cash that leaves the business, such as the acquisition of machinery or equipment, additional inventory purchases, or incremental operating expenses. Cash flows are not affected by the accounting treatment of the underlying business transaction. For example, depreciation expense is not considered a cash outflow. The cash outflow occurs when the equipment is purchased.

Several types of cash flows should be considered in a capital investment analysis:

- *Initial investment.* This is the initial amount required to start the project. For property, plant, and equipment, it represents the purchase price plus all normal expenditures to get the asset in place and ready for use. It is treated as a cash outflow in the year that the project is started. This time period is known in accounting terms as Year 0.

- *Inventory.* A capital investment may require the purchase of additional inventory. This situation may occur when a company introduces a new product or opens a new retail outlet. This incremental inventory purchase is considered a cash outflow. On the other hand, the project may result in an inventory reduction. This situation generally occurs when a company consolidates operations or reduces the inventory levels in its warehouses. The reduction is treated as a cash inflow because the company will have to purchase less inventory in future years, resulting in a net cash saving. Changes in inventory levels are treated as one-time cash inflows or outflows in the year that the expected increase or decrease is expected to occur.

- *Operating expenses.* Capital projects often affect operating expenses such as support personnel, maintenance, operating supplies, and utilities consumption. The project initiator should determine the increase or decrease in operating expenses that will occur as a result of the project.

- *Disposal of existing equipment.* If existing equipment is to be sold, the estimated cash proceeds should be included in the analysis as a cash inflow in the year of sale. If the equipment is to be discarded, the incremental expenses incurred for disposal should be included as a cash outflow in the year of disposal. If the equipment is donated, the tax benefit of the donation should be included as a cash inflow.

- *Future disposal price or costs.* If the project includes equipment that will be sold at the end of its useful life, the estimated market value of the equipment is an increase in the cash flow in the year of disposal. The project initiator must estimate the projected market value of the equipment at the time of its disposal and incorporate it into the cash flow analysis. Any future disposal costs should also be estimated and included.

- *Depreciation on the new equipment.* Depreciation is relevant because of the income tax effects on cash. Remember that depreciation is an expense that is deducted to arrive at net income. Therefore, the depreciation deduction shields a certain portion of net income from taxes. This tax saving is called the **depreciation tax shield** and is included as a cash inflow.

- *Book value of the existing equipment.* The net book value of the existing equipment is a sunk cost and has no impact on cash flow.[1] It is relevant to the financial analysis because it is used to calculate the net capital gain or loss for tax purposes. The tax savings or the additional taxes that result from the disposal of the asset (through a sale, donation, or write-off) should be accounted for as a cash flow in the year of disposition.

After all cash flows have been identified, the attractiveness of the investment is evaluated from a financial perspective.

Step 2. The Financial Analysis of the Project

The financial analysis is an important aspect of the evaluation process. Some companies reject a project that does not meet some minimum established acceptance criterion. The acceptance criterion is usually defined in terms of time (how much time will it take to recover the original investment?), money (how much additional cash will the company earn from this investment?), or both.

Several methods can be used to analyze the financial return of a capital investment: the return on investment (ROI) method, the payback method, and the discounted cash flow method. Because each method has its advantages and limitations, companies typically use more than one method to evaluate a capital project.

Return on Investment Method

The **return on investment method**, also called the **accounting rate of return**, measures the incremental operating income that will be generated per dollar of investment. It is calculated by dividing the incremental operating income by the required initial investment and presenting this figure as a percentage of the initial investment. The formula for calculating ROI is as follows:

$$\text{ROI} = \frac{\text{Annual incremental operating income}}{\text{Initial investment}} \times 100$$

Let us assume that Beachwear, Inc. plans to purchase a $100,000 computer system. The system has a useful life of five years and is expected to generate cash savings of $40,000 per year. Depreciation expense is recorded using the straight-line method.[2] The annual incremental operating income and ROI would be calculated as follows:

Cash savings	$40,000
Less depreciation expense	20,000
Expected increase in annual operating income	$20,000
Return on investment	**20%**
($20,000 ÷ $100,000)	

Managers regard projects with a high ROI as more attractive than those with a low ROI. Some companies set a minimum ROI level below which they will not consider the project. Suppose Beachwear, Inc. has set the minimum ROI level at 25 percent. The capital investment in the example would be rejected because it fails to meet the minimum criteria.

The ROI method is simple and easy to understand. It is based on the accounting values of the required investment and the operating income and therefore can be easily tied to the numbers reported in the company's financial statements. The major drawback of the ROI method is that it does not consider the changing value of money over time. It assumes that a dollar today is worth the same as a dollar received sometime in the future despite the company's ability to invest current funds at a positive return. Moreover, it is difficult to calculate the ROI when the operating income over the life of the investment varies from year to year. For these reasons, the ROI method by itself is not viewed as an acceptable way to evaluate capital investments. Nevertheless, companies often present the ROI calculation in addition to other measures of financial return.

The Payback Method

The **payback method** measures the time that it will take to recover the total funds invested in a project. It shows the time required for the total cash inflows to equal the total cash outflows. The payback period is usually expressed in years and is calculated as follows:

$$\text{Payback period } = \frac{\text{Amount of initial investment}}{\text{Annual net cash inflows}}$$

The net cash inflows are the sum of the cash inflows (revenue or cost savings) and cash outflows (incremental operating expenses such as labor or utilities). Let us return to Beachwear, Inc. The payback period in this example would be 2.5 years, as shown below:

$$\text{Payback period } = \frac{\$100,000}{\$40,000} = 2.5 \text{ years}$$

A project is considered attractive if it has a short payback period. Projects with short payback periods allow managers to recuperate their investment quickly and give them more flexibility to reinvest these funds in the future. They also have fewer risks than projects with longer payback periods.

The payback period is a popular method to evaluate capital investments. Managers like this approach because it is simple to understand and explain: The shorter the payback period is, the more desirable the investment. Because the payback period focuses on short-term results, it does not require managers to predict cash flows far out into the future. This situation minimizes possible manipulation of figures in the preparation of capital investment requests. Managers sometimes inflate cash flows in later years to make an investment appear more desirable than it actually is. The payback period exposes this situation by focusing on only the time it takes to recover the original investment.

The payback approach has two major limitations. First, like the ROI method, it ignores the time-dependent value of money. Second, it ignores cash flows after the investment is recovered. An example will illustrate this point. Suppose you have two projects costing $500,000 each. Project A will yield net cash inflows of $250,000 for three years, for a total of $750,000. Project B will yield $250,000 for five years, for a total of $1,000,000. Although the payback period of

Figure 7-4. *Payback Method, Nonuniform Cash Flows for a High-Speed Copier.*

Year	Year 0	Year 1	Year 2	Year 3	Year 4
Initial investment	$(20,000)				
Cash savings		5,000	10,000	15,000	15,000
Net cash flows	**$(20,000)**	**$ 5,000**	**$10,000**	**$15,000**	**$15,000**
Cumulative cash flows	$(20,000)	$(15,000)	$ (5,000)	$10,000	$25,000
Payback period[a]	**2.33**				

[a]Payback period = 2 years + $5,000/$15,000.

both projects is the same, two years ($500,000 ÷ $250,000), Project B produces a higher total amount of cash for the same amount of investment.

The payback formula is designed to handle uniform cash flows. When cash flows are not uniform, the payback calculation takes a cumulative form: Each year's net cash inflows are accumulated until the initial investment has been recovered. Let us assume you plan to purchase a new energy-efficient, high-speed copier for $20,000. This machine is expected to produce cash savings of $45,000 over the next five years. The cash savings occur in a nonuniform manner, as shown in Figure 7-4. The original investment is $20,000. At the end of Year 3, the investment has been fully recovered. Therefore, the payback period is greater than two years and less than three years.

The exact payback period of 2.33 years is calculated by dividing the cash investment yet to be recovered at the end of Year 2 ($5,000) by the annual cash savings in Year 3 ($15,000). This ratio identifies the point between Years 2 and 3 when the investment will be fully recovered.

Discounted Cash Flow Methods

Discounted cash flow (DCF) methods measure the cash inflows and outflows as if they occurred at a single point in time. These methods recognize that money has a cost: the interest forgone. A dollar today, because it earns interest with the passage of time, is worth more than a dollar received sometime in the future. In contrast to the ROI and the payback method, the DCF methods explicitly consider the time value of money. There are two main DCF methods: **net present value** (NPV) and **internal rate of return** (IRR). A variation of the payback method, the **discounted payback period**, can also be used to consider the time value of money. All methods require the identification of a **required rate of return**. This rate is the minimum acceptable rate of return on an investment. It is also known as the **hurdle rate**, the **cost of capital**, or the **discount rate**.

The Discount Rate

Cash received today can be invested to generate additional cash in the future. Therefore, a dollar today is worth more than a dollar received tomorrow. The discount rate allows the company to adjust cash flows received in the future to their value in the present. In DCF analysis, the discount rate or required rate of return is a critical variable because it can significantly affect the financial desirability of a capital project. Projects with a high discount rate must generate a greater amount of cash than those with a low discount rate to recover the original investment.

In large organizations, the discount rate is usually set by the corporate finance or treasury function. In smaller organizations, the manager or financial analyst must determine the appropriate discount rate for each major project. Several factors influence the choice of a discount rate:

- *Cost of capital.* What is the current cost of funds? Will the project be financed with internal or external capital? Because of the complexities of estimating the cost of capital, some companies use the cost of debt financing to determine the discount rate (e.g., the prime rate plus 1 percent). This approach assumes that the project will be financed through external borrowing and estimates the interest rate that the company will be charged for these funds. A project should return enough to recover the original investment and the interest paid on borrowed funds.

- *Alternative uses of capital.* Another way to determine the discount rate is to evaluate the alternative uses of these funds. If the company did not invest in this project, how would it invest this money, and what would it earn on this investment? Suppose the best alternative is to invest in low-risk treasury bills at a 6 percent interest rate. You would want your project to return at least 6 percent above your original investment; if not, the company could buy treasury bills, earn 6 percent interest, and be no worse off for this decision.

- *Project risk.* The discount rate should be adjusted for risk. A $50,000 equipment purchase in proven technology does not carry the same degree of risk as a company expansion or the development of a new product. The discount rate should reflect the level of risk associated with the project: The higher the risk, the higher the discount rate that should be used to evaluate the project. The adjustment of the discount rate for project risk is usually a judgment call by management and should be well-documented.

After evaluating these factors, the manager or financial analyst should choose an appropriate discount rate for the project. Different projects will be evaluated using different rates depending on the situation of the company at the time of the evaluation and the degree of risk associated with the project. The finance group should ensure that the discount rates are consistent for projects with similar risk factors.

Discounted Payback Period

The discounted payback period is a variation of the payback method that considers the time value of money. The **discounted payback period** is the time required for the discounted cash flows to equal the original investment. Let us return to the high-speed copier example. Figure 7-5 shows the discounted payback period using a discount rate of 6 percent. The discount factor can significantly affect the payback calculations: The higher the discount rate, the greater the difference between the simple and the discounted pay-

Figure 7-5. *Discounted Payback Method for a High-Speed Copier.*

Year	Year 0	Year 1	Year 2	Year 3	Year 4
Initial investment	$(20,000)				
Cash savings		5,000	10,000	15,000	15,000
Net cash flows	**$(20,000)**	**$ 5,000**	**$10,000**	**$15,000**	**$15,000**
Discount factor	1.000	0.943	0.890	0.840	0.792
Discounted cash flows[a]	**(20,000)**	**4,715**	**8,900**	**12,600**	**11,880**
Cumulative discounted cash flows	$(20,000)	$(15,285)	$(6,385)	$ 6,215	$18,095
Discounted payback period[b]	**2.51**				

[a]Discounted cash flows = Net cash flows × discount factor (6%).
[b]Payback period = 2 years + 6,385/12,600.

back methods. In the example shown in Figure 7-5, the difference between the payback period (2.33 years) and the discounted payback period (2.51 years) is not significant due to the low discount rate and the small size of the initial investment.

Net Present Value

Net present value (NPV) calculates the expected monetary gain or loss on a project by discounting all the projected cash flows to the present using the required rate of return. If the present value is positive, the project is accepted; if it is negative, the project is rejected. Figure 7-6 uses the high-speed copier example to illustrate the concept of NPV. The NPV is calculated by multiplying the net cash flows for each period by the appropriate discount factor. This project would be accepted because the NPV of $18,095 is significantly higher than the amount of the original investment. Figure 7-7 (see page 118) shows the detailed NPV calculations for this example.

The discount rate has a significant impact on the present value calculation. For example, the present value of $1.00 received a year from today is $0.91 at a 10 percent discount rate but only $0.83 at a

Figure 7-6. *Net Present Value for a High-Speed Copier.*

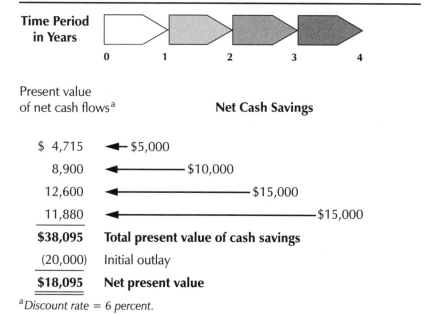

Present value of net cash flows[a]	**Net Cash Savings**
$ 4,715	◄— $5,000
8,900	◄——— $10,000
12,600	◄———— $15,000
11,880	◄———— $15,000
$38,095	**Total present value of cash savings**
(20,000)	Initial outlay
$18,095	**Net present value**

[a]*Discount rate = 6 percent.*

Figure 7-7. *Detailed Net Present Value Calculations for a High-Speed Copier.*

Year	Annual Cash Flows	Discount Factor @ 6%	Annual Cash Flows (Discounted)[a]
1	$ 5,000	0.943	$ 4,715
2	10,000	0.890	8,900
3	15,000	0.840	12,600
4	15,000	0.792	11,880
Present value of cash flows			$38,095
Initial investment			$20,000
Net present value[b]			$18,095

[a]Annual cash flows $\times$ discount factor = $5,000 $\times$ 0.943.
[b]NPV = Present value of net cash flows − original investment
    = $38,095 − $20,000.

20 percent discount rate. The higher the discount rate is, the lower the present value of the cash flows. Higher discount rates are used when the project is considered extremely risky or the projected cash flows are very uncertain. In Figure 7-7, a discount rate of 16 percent would reduce the present value of the cash savings from $38,095 to $29,635 and the net present value from $18,095 to $9,635.

Internal Rate of Return
    Some managers find it easier to use a percentage measure of value. The **internal rate of return** (IRR) is the interest or discount rate at which the present value of the estimated net cash inflows, including the initial investment, is equal to zero. The IRR can be interpreted as the growth rate of the investment. A higher growth rate is viewed as more desirable than a lower one. It can also be interpreted as the highest rate of interest an investor could pay for borrowed funds and still break even on the project. Therefore, projects with high IRRs are preferred to those with low IRRs.
    Let us return to the high-speed copier example. The IRR for this project is 34 percent. Does this mean the project should be accepted? The desirability of this project would depend on the company's minimum required rate of return for capital investments. If the minimum return were 25 percent, then the project would be accepted; if the rate were 50 percent, the project would be rejected.

The IRR rate can be calculated by trial and error, but it is most easily computed using a hand-held calculator or a computer application.

Comparison of NPV and IRR

In theory, the NPV method is preferred over the IRR for several reasons.[3] The NPV method shows the end result in dollars, not as a percentage, and therefore allows the company to evaluate the expected benefits of the project in absolute monetary terms. The use of the IRR method to compare different projects may produce results that are inconsistent with the NPV analysis, as shown in the example in Figure 7-8. In this example Projects A and B have the same IRR. However, Project B is superior to Project A because the company earns more cash by choosing it. If only the IRR figures were used, the company would be indifferent between the two alternatives.

NPV has two additional advantages over IRR. First, it allows a company to add the NPV of several proposed projects and select the group that returns the highest total NPV. Second, it allows a manager to use different discount rates in the evaluation of a project when the rate of return is not constant from year to year.[4] IRR, on the other hand, assumes a constant rate of reinvestment each year.

Most calculators and computer spreadsheets are equipped with programs that calculate NPV and IRR. The manager or analyst enters the key variables: the initial investment, the number of periods, the

Figure 7-8. *Comparison of Net Present Value and Internal Rate of Return.*

Project A	Year 0	Year 1	Year 2
Initial investment	$(150,000)		
Cash savings	—	$100,000	$100,000
Net cash flows	$(150,000)	$100,000	$100,000
NPV @ 15% discount	$ 12,571		
IRR	22%		
Project B			
Initial investment	$(300,000)		
Cash savings	—	$200,000	$200,000
Net cash flows	$(300,000)	$200,000	$200,000
NPV @ 15% discount	$ 25,142		
IRR	22%		

interest or discount rate, and the net cash flows for the project. The program then calculates the NPV or the IRR accordingly.

Step 3. Risk Assessment

Risk factors should be explicitly identified and documented as part of the capital evaluation process. Four types of risk factors should be considered:[5]

■ *Economic risks*—the external nontechnological risks that are a cost of doing business, such as a change in government regulations, the rate of economic growth, or a rise in interest rates.

■ *Commercial risks*—factors such as changing social values, competitive actions, and trade barriers that can affect the amount of revenues or cost savings realized from the project.

■ *Technological risks*—the failure to meet technological goals. They assess factors such as vendor support, equipment performance, technological obsolescence, compatibility with existing technologies, and new technologies.

■ *Implementation risk*—the failure to meet project plans due to human behavior or organizational factors. Some factors that may contribute to implementation risk are reorganizations, employee compensation systems, employee morale, and training.

Managers should evaluate the potential impact of the risk factors on the financial viability of the project. If possible, they should redo the financial analysis, taking these factors into consideration. This technique is known as a sensitivity analysis and is discussed in the next section. Managers should also discuss risks that cannot be quantified as a monetary figure but may jeopardize the company's quality, customer service, flexibility, or image in the community.

Step 4. Sensitivity Analysis

Sensitivity analysis is a what-if technique that shows how the financial outcome of a project will change as a result of a change in an underlying assumption. It allows a manager to examine alternative scenarios by changing a key variable in the analysis. What if the project costs exceed the approved amount by 10 percent? What if sales are underachieved by 20 percent? What if the cost savings do not materialize as expected?

Sensitivity analysis provides an indication of the risks and opportunities that are associated with a project. For example, suppose a company is evaluating two projects to increase production capacity at its main manufacturing facility. Both projects provide additional production capacity for the organization. Management decides to analyze the two projects under three alternative scenarios. The best case assumes the organization will fully use the additional production capacity and significantly increase revenues for the company. The most likely case assumes that the additional capacity will eliminate back orders and generate some increased sales. The worst case assumes that the additional capacity will alleviate the back order situation but will not produce increased sales. The results of the financial evaluation are shown in Figure 7-9.

The NPV of Project A ranges from a negative $400 to $2,000, whereas the NPV of Project B goes from $200 to $1,000. Which project is better for the company? If a manager presented only the most likely case, Project A would seem more attractive than Project B because, all other things being equal, it generates a higher financial return. However, if risk is factored into the equation, Project B may seem a more attractive alternative because even in the worst-case situation, it remains a profitable investment. Although Project A has the potential of generating the higher return, it also has a greater degree of risk. The range between the worst-case and the best-case scenario may indicate the level of volatility and risk associated with the project.

Sensitivity analysis helps managers focus on decisions that may be very sensitive to changing business conditions. It allows them to determine in a quantitative manner the risks and opportunities associated with a project. A more sophisticated analysis, changing several variables at the same time, would be a quantitative uncer-

Figure 7-9. *Sensitivity Analysis Example.*

Scenario	Project A Net Present Value (in 000s)	Project B Net Present Value (in 000s)
Best case	$2,000	$1,000
Most likely	$ 900	$ 800
Worst case	($ 400)	$ 200

tainty analysis.[6] This more complex option is not necessary in many cases.

Step 5. Evaluation of Other Qualitative Factors

Measures of ROI and the accompanying sensitivity analysis are tools to assist management in the decision-making process. However, some outcomes of a project cannot be measured in a quantitative manner. How do you value an increase in employee morale or the loss of customer goodwill? Regulatory agencies may also require investments in people or technology that cannot be financially justified. In this step, managers should explore those qualitative factors that cannot be assigned a dollar value but are important to the decision-making process. These qualitative factors at times may override an unfavorable financial result.

Capital Projects Administration

Once a capital project is approved, the project manager is authorized to commit company funds. Medium-size to large firms typically have formal procedures to track and monitor capital projects. When the approved capital appropriation request is received in the accounting department, it is typically assigned a project reference number, which is placed on all purchase orders issued against the project. The monetary values of these purchase orders are called **committed funds**. Once funds have been committed, they are deducted from the total funds available for the project.

An accountant is assigned the responsibility of tracking the funds committed and paid for a capital project. The accountant also ensures that disbursements are properly authorized and recorded on the company books. She prepares monthly or quarterly reports that list the status of all capital projects; the total dollar amount approved; and the disbursements on a quarter to date, year to date, or project to date as may be required by management.

The project manager is ultimately responsible for the dollars charged against a capital project. Upon completion of the project, he is responsible for notifying the accounting department to close out the project formally. Once a project is closed, purchase orders cannot be issued and invoices cannot be paid against a project.

The Postimplementation Evaluation

Some organizations use a **postimplementation evaluation** to evaluate their investment decisions. The purpose of this audit is to determine how well the company has executed the project in the light of the original analysis. The postimplementation evaluation can trigger procedures for corrective action if a project is not achieving the desired results. Management can also use this information to improve investment decisions in the future.

In my experience, the postimplementation audit is the weakest link in the capital investment process. Although most companies exert tight control over capital projects during their implementation, they rarely go back and analyze the expected performance against the actual results. Therefore, no one can benefit from the learning opportunities and process improvements that could be uncovered by reviewing the results of past investment decisions.

Companies involved in reengineering and continuous improvement efforts should view the postimplementation audit as an important feedback mechanism on their capital investment process. By understanding what was done well and what was done poorly, management can avoid future mistakes, such as budget overruns, delays in implementation, and the installation of mismatched technology.

Chapter Summary

Management should review proposed capital investments as an integral part of the company's planning cycle. Capital investment priorities should be set during the strategy review prior to the start of the annual budgeting process. The capital budget requests should support the organization's strategic direction and reflect organizational priorities. They should be reviewed with the same rigor as the departmental-spending budgets. Capital investment decisions that are made in a vacuum ultimately result in wasted resources and lost opportunities.

The techniques and tools available to analyze capital investment vary depending on the complexity of the organization and the nature of the investment. A $5,000 equipment purchase should not merit the same amount of time and effort as a $1,000,000 plant relocation. The basic tools for financial analysis—the ROI rate, the payback period, the NPV, and the IRR—were discussed in this chapter, as well as the benefits and limitations of each approach.

Managers should explicitly consider qualitative factors and risk factors in any capital investment decision. Although a project may produce a high rate of return, a company may choose not to pursue it for qualitative reasons such as employee morale or negative publicity. Managers should also assess the economic, commercial, technological, and implementation risks in any project. These risk factors should be incorporated into a sensitivity analysis, which allows a manager to estimate the financial impact of these risks.

Organizations should have procedures to track and monitor capital investments. The formality of the procedures will vary with the size and complexity of the organization. Medium-size to large organizations generally have fairly sophisticated procedures to track capital investments. The postimplementation evaluation remains a weak link in the capital administration process. Major projects should undergo a postimplementation evaluation to evaluate the results and improve future investment decisions.

Notes

1. The net book value of a capital asset = Historical cost − accumulated depreciation.
2. The straight-line depreciation method calculates depreciation expense by dividing the cost of the asset by its estimated useful life. In the Beachwear, Inc. example, the depreciation expense is $20,000 ($100,000 ÷ 5)—the initial investment of $100,000 divided by the estimated useful life of 5 years.
3. See James C. Van Horne, *Financial Management and Policy* (Englewood Cliffs, N.J.: Prentice Hall, 1989), pp. 131–136, for a more detailed comparison between NPV and IRR.
4. In my experience, companies rarely use different discount rates in an NPV analysis. Only one discount rate is typically used per project, though the discount rate may vary from project to project depending on the project's risk factors.
5. See Thomas Klammer, *Managing Strategic and Capital Investment Decisions* (Burr Ridge, Ill.: Irwin Professional Publishing, 1994), pp. 83–95.
6. See M. Granger Morgan and Max Henrion, *Uncertainty: A Guide to Dealing With Uncertainty in Quantitative Risk and Policy Analysis* (New York: Cambridge University Press, 1992).

Chapter 8

Performance Measurement and Reporting

"I just wanted to get your reaction to that."

C urrent management philosophies emphasize the use of key performance indicators to monitor organizational well-being. These indicators focus on critical success factors such as quality, customer service, cost, and innovation as defined in the company long-term strategies. Because they reflect the core processes of the business, management uses this information to improve overall company performance.

Most organizations have some type of performance measurement system to monitor the results of their operations. This system completes the planning loop by providing a systematic mechanism to measure the organization's performance against the established plans (see Figure 3-1). Traditionally performance measurement has focused on a comparison between actual and budgeted performance, primarily expressed in monetary terms and reported at regular (usually monthly) intervals. Actual financial results are compared to the budgeted plan, and variances are analyzed and explained. Although some organizations may include nonfinancial performance indicators (e.g., head count, units produced, units sold, percentage of completion), performance reports that are prepared by the finance department generally reflect only the financial results of the operation.

This chapter discusses performance measurement and reporting as an integral part of the planning cycle. It examines traditional approaches to performance measurement and their limitations in the current business environment. It discusses the current approaches to performance measurement, presenting the characteristics of an effective performance measurement system and showing how it provides a critical link to the organization's long-term strategies and objectives. It also discusses how to define the key performance indicators and integrate these measures into the performance reporting structure. Finally, it presents guidelines to assist managers in the development or redesign of a performance measurement and reporting system.

Traditional Approaches to Performance Measurement

Hammer and Champy talk about the notion of discontinuous thinking that lies at the heart of business reengineering. They state that discontinuous thinking involves "identifying and abandoning the outdated rules and fundamental assumptions that underlie current business operations."[1] Traditional approaches to performance measurement clearly fall into this category. Many organizations have not redesigned their performance measurement systems to meet the needs of today's business environment.

Responsibility Accounting

In general, traditional performance measurement systems are financially oriented and use responsibility accounting to evaluate the results of their operations. **Responsibility accounting** is the system that measures in monetary terms the plans and actions of each **responsibility center**, an organization, group, division, department, or work area for which a manager is held accountable. Figure 8-1 shows the four types of responsibility centers that are generally used in organizations:

- *Cost centers*—units whose managers are accountable only for costs. A cost center typically controls the inputs to the process (e.g., manpower and supplier relationships) but has no control over sales or the generation of revenue. Manufacturing facilities of large corporations are often evaluated as cost centers. Support areas such as accounting, human resources, and purchasing are other examples of cost centers. In Figure 8-1, the administration, the field operations, and the customer service departments are evaluated as cost centers.

- *Revenue centers*—units evaluated solely on the basis of sales. Managers of these units should exert significant influence over pricing decisions, sales and marketing strategies, and any other factors that may affect their ability to generate sales. Revenue centers do not control the cost of sales. A field sales office or the sales division of a corporation is an example of a revenue center.

Figure 8-1. *Examples of Responsibility Centers.*

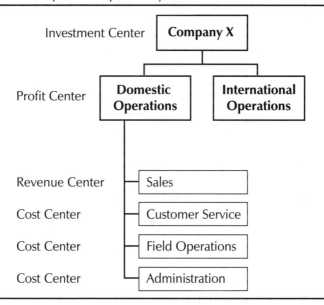

■ *Profit centers*—units evaluated based on the operating income or net income of the organization. A true profit center manager should control all major factors affecting revenues and costs, such as pricing, sales and marketing strategies, and sources of supply. A business unit or a geographical region is a common example of a profit center. In the example in Figure 8-1, the domestic and international operations are considered profit centers.

■ *Investment centers*—units evaluated based on profitability and return on capital invested. Most publicly traded companies are evaluated as investment centers. They measure profits and the return on investment through some established measure, such as return on assets or return on capital.[2] In Figure 8-1 the company as a whole is considered an investment center.

Top management must decide how they want to set up the responsibility centers in their organization. Although the company as a whole will usually be evaluated as an investment center, individual subunits can be measured as profit centers, revenue centers, cost centers, or investment centers. Ideally, responsibility accounting systems should focus on **controllable costs**: costs that can be significantly influenced by a particular individual for an area or department over a period of time. A manager is held accountable for only those costs that he can significantly control. Responsibility reports often segregate or exclude noncontrollable costs.

Responsibility accounting is financially oriented. It shows how much was earned or spent in dollars compared to a planned amount. However, it provides no data on the operational performance of the organizational unit. Operational performance data monitors the execution of a company's key business processes. It provides the business context to understand the financial results for a particular time period. Operational performance information is obtained through the use of nonfinancial performance indicators and is usually reported by nonfinancial personnel.

Nonfinancial Performance Indicators

Traditional performance measurement systems use nonfinancial indicators as well as financial reports to monitor and control their operations. These measures are used to manage the day-to-day operations and are summarized at the end of a reporting period by work area or department. Some examples of these measures are units produced, units sold, pounds of scrap, yield percentages, defect rates, processing time, overtime hours, orders served, and customers serviced per time period. Some organizations hold daily, weekly, or monthly review meetings to discuss these nonfinancial indicators, identify potential problem areas, and determine corrective action.

Nonfinancial performance indicators are usually reviewed and reported by operations personnel and reported separately from the financial results. The finance department is typically not involved in the preparation of these numbers.

Limitations of the Traditional Approach

Traditional approaches to performance measurement provide financial, operational, and physical measures for local activities. However, they may fail to move the organization in the right direction, for several reasons.[3] First, these measures are usually developed from a bottom-up perspective and do not necessarily measure the core processes and critical success factors as defined in the company strategy. Therefore, they may not provide a coherent set of performance measures that move the organization in the desired direction.

Second, traditional methods are focused on the historical performance of internal operations. They can report what happened last period within the organization but provide no information on how managers can improve performance in the following period. In many cases, they are retrospective rather than proactive. They tell the score at the moment but cannot provide early warning signals to change a poor outcome.

Third, financial and operational performance indicators that should be linked are reported in separate places. It is difficult to see the big picture or understand financial results when the operational data is in one place and the financial data is in another. Financial reporting should incorporate key performance indicators as an integral part of the management reporting system.

Fourth, in many cases, organizations have excessive measures that can become dysfunctional. Sometimes the measures are too detailed or encourage local optimization at the expense of what is best for the company as a whole. For example, suppose a purchasing manager is evaluated based on her ability to buy parts at the budgeted cost. She may be reluctant to buy a higher-quality part that results in lower scrap costs because it would result in an unfavorable price variance for her department.

These limitations of traditional performance measurement approaches have caused organizations to develop new approaches to performance management.

New Approaches to Performance Measurement

New approaches to performance measurement focus on the links among company strategies, business processes, and performance indicators. They emphasize an integrated approach, using a consistent set of performance measures derived from the company's long-term strategy to manage the organization.

Kaplan and Norton have proposed a comprehensive framework for developing an integrated performance measurement system called the **balanced scorecard**. The balanced scorecard is a four-quadrant model that allows managers to view the business from four different perspectives: customer, internal, innovation and learning, and financial. Kaplan and Norton write:

> It [the balanced scorecard] provides answers to four basic questions:
>
> - How do our customers see us (the customer perspective)?
> - What must we excel at (the internal business perspective)?
> - How can we continue to improve and create value (the innovation and learning perspective)?
> - How do we look to our shareholders (the financial perspective)?[4]

The balanced scorecard provides financial and operational performance measures on these four critical dimensions. It includes not only the financial measures that tell what has already happened, but also the key operational measures that will determine future financial performance. The balanced scorecard model is summarized in Figure 8-2.

The balanced scorecard overcomes many limitations of traditional performance measurement systems. First, it minimizes information overload by limiting the number of measures used. Second, it brings together in a single management report different elements of a company's competitive strategy. Finally, it guards against suboptimization by forcing senior managers to consider important opera-

Figure 8-2. *Balanced Scorecard.*

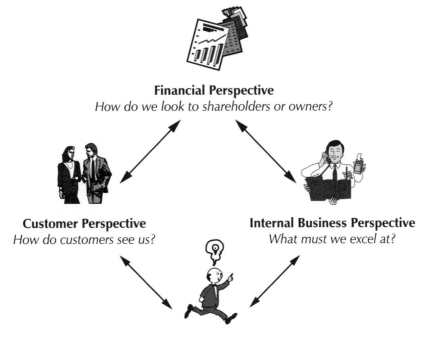

Financial Perspective
How do we look to shareholders or owners?

Customer Perspective
How do customers see us?

Internal Business Perspective
What must we excel at?

Innovation and Learning Perspective
How can we continue to improve and create value?

tional measures together and understand the trade-offs of one area versus another.

The Institute of Management Accountants has also proposed a structured approach for designing and implementing an integrated performance measurement system (I-PMS). An I-PMS "can be envisioned as an enterprisewide management system that links strategic objectives, core business strategies, critical success factors, and key performance indicators."[5] It relies on an integrated set of key financial and nonfinancial performance measures that manage performance at all levels of the organization. These systems have an external focus on the business environment, the marketplace, and the competition and an internal focus on the key business processes that will create sustainable competitive advantage and generate long-term growth. It includes nonfinancial indicators such as market share, customer satisfaction, and quality, as well as the more traditional financial measures, such as net profits, revenue growth, and return on investment.

There is no single set of performance measures that can be applied to all types of businesses. Each organization must develop its own performance measures to support its business strategies and satisfy management needs for information. Nevertheless, current approaches to performance measurement generally agree that effective performance measurement systems should have the following common characteristics:[6]

■ *Clear strategic objectives.* Whatever the organization believes is the key to its long-term success must be clearly communicated throughout the organization. Some examples of companies that have accomplished this objective are Motorola and its Six Sigma quality initiative and Wal-Mart's emphasis on low, everyday prices.

■ *A focus on core processes.* Core processes are the fundamental aspects of a business that are key to its overall success. The measurement system should focus on the key processes that provide a competitive advantage. For example, in a service environment, employee training may be a core process. Managers should identify performance measures that capture the important dimensions of this process (e.g., training hours per employee per quarter) and their end results (e.g., increased sales or improved customer service levels).

■ *The identification of critical success factors.* **Critical success factors** (CSFs) focus on the key performance dimensions a company must excel at if it is to achieve its strategic goals.[7] Suppose the strategic objective for your company is to provide premium service to its customer base. Management recognizes that the quality of the service and the timeliness of its delivery are two critical areas to achieve this goal. They then establish specific measures, such as the number of service calls per customer order (quality) and service cycle time (delivery), to monitor the performance in these areas. Figure 8-3 provides an example on how to link the strategic objectives, the CSFs, and the key performance indicators to create an integrated performance measurement system.

■ *The ability to provide early warning signals.* Effective performance indicators should signal where the performance is headed regarding the critical success factors. A performance indicator presented in a vacuum does not provide any meaningful information about the business. It must be compared against another relevant number, such as historical results, competitor data, or a targeted goal, to detect significant trends that may require management attention. For example, managers could compare the key performance indicators for quality and timeliness with the same data for prior periods. This comparison would allow them to detect deteriorating service levels that could ultimately affect future revenue growth. Management could also compare the company's performance in these areas to that of major competitors. This comparison could enable them to assess how well they are performing relative to the competition and whether they are falling short of customer expectations.

■ *Integration to the compensation and reward system.* Compensation systems should motivate and reward employees for moving the organization forward in the desired direction. Performance indicators can serve as a basis for rewarding the organization's key contributors by tying employees' compensation packages to one or more tangible goals. This linkage provides employees with a strong incentive to focus on the variables that are critical to the success of the firm. For example, management could tie 75 percent of the service technicians' annual bonus to their achievement of the quality and timeliness targets throughout the year. The other 25 percent could be linked to other factors that the company might deem important, such as costs or absenteeism.

Performance indicators must be aligned throughout the organization starting from top management's goals and objectives down through the core business processes to the specific objectives of teams and individual employees. The performance measurement system can significantly affect how managers and employees behave, particularly if this behavior is directly tied to the compensation and reward system. Management must ensure that the performance measurement system provides employees with the direction and motivation to advance the organization's long-term goals.

Defining Performance Indicators

Key performance indicators (KPIs) provide a tangible mechanism to measure the critical success factors. They are quantifiable measures

Figure 8-3. *How to Link Strategic Objectives to Critical Success Factors and Key Performance Measures.*

Strategic Objective	Critical Success Factors	Key Performance Indicators

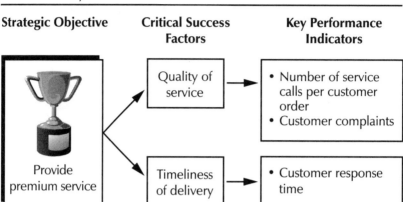

that the organization uses to evaluate and communicate performance against expected results. KPIs generally should have the following attributes:[8]

- They should be *strategically linked* and *integrated* throughout the organization. Performance measures should be linked to specific strategic objectives and aligned throughout the organization. They should be compatible with the key business processes or functions.

- They should be *controllable*. Individuals or teams should have the ability to change or influence the measured results significantly. They should be able to act on the measured dimension to improve performance in that area.

- They should be *measurable*. The performance measures should be realistic and should be quantified in a meaningful manner. The management team should ensure that an adequate mechanism is in place to gather the information in a timely manner.

- They should be *simple*. The measures should be easy to understand and explain to employees, and their relevance for achieving the organizational objectives should be readily apparent. They should not require complex computations or mathematical formulas that only an expert can analyze and interpret.

- They should be *limited in number*. Performance measures should contain only those measures needed to direct attention and action in the appropriate areas. In my experience, when an organization has too many performance indicators, measurement becomes an end in itself. Significant resources are tied up measuring performance that does not provide actionable information on the CSFs of the company.

■ They should be *credible.* Users should believe that the measures are good indicators of performance in the desired dimension. Credibility is attained when the measures are objective, resistant to manipulation, and applied fairly throughout the organization. Selective application of performance measures can seriously undermine the credibility of a performance measurement system.

KPIs should present a balanced view of the organization. The concept of balance requires that all key dimensions of performance, as defined by the CSFs, are measured and reported in such a manner that managers can understand the trade-offs and interrelationships among the different areas. For example, achieving a 100 percent on-time delivery objective may result in unacceptable financial results. The concept of balance also suggests that each CSF should have a reasonable number of measures relative to other CSFs. A company that has 10 financial indicators and 2 customer satisfaction indicators does not have a balanced set of performance measures. This situation may also send the wrong message to the organization in terms of the importance of one dimension over another.

A balanced set of measures does not imply that all performance dimensions are equally important. At times, one dimension of performance may outweigh another in terms of importance for the organization. How you balance these dimensions is a management judgment call and requires a healthy dose of common sense. The balance among performance measures is a dynamic process and will change according to the needs and the strategic objectives of the organization at a particular point in time.

Each company must develop a unique set of performance indicators tailored to its particular needs and operating environment. In general, the key performance indicators will be related to the following categories:[9]

■ *Environmental indicators* ensure that the organization is achieving its environmental objectives.

■ *Market and customer indicators* track what is happening in the marketplace and with specific customers. These may include measures of customer satisfaction, customer acquisitions, customer retention, and the profitability of specific markets and customers.

■ *Competitor indicators* track the competition on many of the same dimensions with which they track their own business. This information may be difficult to obtain, particularly for privately held companies.

■ *Internal business processes* track the key business processes among critical dimensions such as quality, speed, flexibility, customer satisfaction, productivity, and innovation.

■ *Human resources indicators* track the effectiveness of the human resources management process.

■ *Financial indicators* assess financial performance and shareholder value.

Figure 8-4 shows examples of performance indicators within each major category.

Reviewing Your Performance Measurement System

Most likely your company has a performance measurement system in place. If this is the case, you must determine if it provides an integrated approach to managing the organization. Do the performance measures track the critical processes? Are they linked to strategic objectives?

Employees who are involved in the development or redesign of performance measurement systems should ask a series of fundamental questions during the design process:

■ What important aspects of the business need to be tracked, and why?

■ What will the information be used for? How will it change the decision-making process?

■ Who should receive this information?

■ Is the information currently accessible? If not, how will it be collected?

Figure 8-4. *Examples of Performance Indicators.*

Environmental
- Fines/violations of government regulations
- Hours of community service
- Use of recyclable material
- Amount of toxic waste produced
- Quality of indoor air/ environment

Market and Customer
- Company market share
- Percentage of sales from new customers
- Customer returns
- On-time delivery
- Customer complaints
- Customer satisfaction indices

Competitor
- Competitors' market share
- Financial performance
- Manufacturing or service response time
- Number of new products
- Quality
- Customer satisfaction indices

Internal Business Processes
- Time to market
- Number of new products
- Manufacturing or service cycle time
- Number of products reworked
- Scrap
- Manufacturing efficiency percentage
- Capacity utilization

Human Resources
- Length of service
- Employee turnover
- Training hours per employee
- Applicants-to-acceptance ratio
- Number of formal employee complaints
- Number of overdue performance evaluations

Financial
- Sales growth
- Gross margin percentage
- Net income as a percentage of sales
- Market/customer profitability
- Cash flow
- Excess obsolete inventory value

Adapted from "Developing Comprehensive Performance Indicators." *Statements on Management Accounting, Statement No.* 4U, Canada: Society of Management Accountants of Canada, 1995.

■ At what frequency will the information be reported, and in what format?

Performance measures should be aligned to the company's strategic objectives and cascade down to the rest of the organization. They should provide different levels of feedback for different levels of management. For top management, the measures should be at a macrolevel and may lead to corrections in goals and strategies. At lower levels, these measures should provide specific feedback on business processes that may prompt short-term corrective action.

Figure 8-5 shows an example of this cascade effect. In this example, the company has a strategic objective to stimulate market growth through the introduction of new products. Each level of management has a different set of performance indicators. Top management has a set of broad-level indicators to evaluate their success. How much did new products contribute to total revenue? What is the percentage of total unit sales generated by new products? Middle managers are more concerned about the implementation mechanics: ensuring that the right product is at the right place, at the right time. Their measures focus on managing the organization to achieve the expected results. First-level managers are engaged in the actual execution of the strategy. Their measures provide feedback on the key business processes that can ultimately affect sales, such as quality (defect rates), customer satisfaction (customer returns), and time to market (cycle time). Hence, as performance measures cascade down the organization they move from a macro- to a microperspective.

Performance Reporting

Performance reporting focuses on how the results of the operation are communicated to the organization. In a traditional performance measurement system, the financial results are typically reported separately from the KPIs in operational areas. Herein lies one of the problems with the current state of management reporting: The financial data is in one place, the operational data in another. It is difficult to see the big picture when critical information that should be linked is reported in separate places.

Performance reporting should merge the operational and financial results in a single management document. This merger of information has a twofold advantage: (1) it summarizes key operational and financial data in one place, and (2) it allows managers and employees to link operating data to the financial results. This integration should take place at all levels in the organization, not just in the summary reports prepared for division or group management. This integration is a fundamental aspect of current approaches to performance measurement.

Performance reporting should also quantify the financial impact of nonfinancial performance indicators whenever possible. This calculation may reveal hidden costs and opportunities that are other-

Figure 8-5. *The Cascade Effect in an Integrated Performance Measurement System.*

Top Management

Strategic Objective:
Stimulate market growth through the introduction of new products.

Middle Management

Key Performance Indicators

- Percentage of sales revenue
- Percentage of total sales units
- Market share

First-Level Management

Key Performance Indicators

- Inventory levels
- Customer order rate
- Order lead time
- On-time delivery rate
- Customer returns

Key Performance Indicators

- Manufacturing cycle time
- Defect rate
- Units sold
- Units produced

wise not visible in the accounting records. For example, suppose a company has a manufacturing efficiency of 85 percent. What does this mean in terms of cost? It means that the company could have manufactured more products with the same amount of resources. Therefore, the inefficiencies in the manufacturing process resulted in higher costs for the organization. Figure 8-6 shows one way to capture the financial impact of the manufacturing efficiency.

The cost of manufacturing inefficiency, $37,500, is an estimate of the additional cost that the company has incurred to produce the required output. It puts a tangible dollar figure on a nonfinancial performance indicator. Armed with this information, managers can focus on those areas that will result in higher financial returns for the organization.

The financial quantification of a performance indicator helps identify cost improvement opportunities only if it is meaningful to the users. The users should understand how the number is calculated, agree with the calculation methodology, and understand its

Figure 8-6. *Example of Financial Quantification of a Nonfinancial Performance Indicator.*

1. Expected production (in units)	50,000
2. Actual production (in units)	42,500
3. Manufacturing efficiency [2 ÷ 1]	85%
4. Total production cost	$250,000
5. Actual production cost per unit [4 ÷ 2]	$5.88
6. Expected cost based on 100% output	$5.00
7. Cost of manufacturing inefficiency	**$37,500**
(7,500 units @ $5.00)	

significance for their area. This calculation allows managers to relate nonfinancial performance goals to their impact on the organization's financial results. It can become a useful management tool to understand the trade-offs among the critical performance dimensions as identified in the company's strategic objectives.

In the future, performance reporting will gradually replace traditional financial reporting. Traditional financial reporting focuses on only one dimension of a company's performance and ignores other dimensions that are critical to the organization's long-term success. Moreover, traditional financial reporting has become excessively detailed, generating thousands of reports on a regular basis that require a review (and often a response) from the pertinent management team. Integrated performance measurement systems provide companies with an opportunity to overhaul their financial reporting practices. The evolution from financial reporting to performance reporting will lead to a greater integration between the financial results and the other key dimensions of the business.

From Financial Reporting to Performance Reporting

Traditionally, financial reports have been an integral part of the performance measurement system. Many organizations prepare financial reports that show monthly and year-to-date actual results compared against the budget or the latest forecast. These reports, which are prepared for internal use only, generally include a company income statement and a financial performance report for each major responsibility center. The responsibility center reports may be the same for all areas or customized by major functions, such as manufacturing, R&D, sales, marketing, and administration. Once the formats are established, they are rarely revised. Each month after the books are closed, the finance department runs the financial performance reports for each area and hands them to the appropriate managers. The reports are very detailed, often showing the revenue and costs by general ledger account number. Accountants often require managers to explain budget variances above or below a fixed percentage.

In my experience, this type of financial reporting focuses managers on achieving the financial targets, often at the expense of strategic objectives. It may block them from changing plans and shifting resources that the business requires but may result in a budget overrun for either the department or a specific cost category (e.g., office supplies). In addition, the level of detail presented in these reports may cloud their ability to see the real business issues as reflected in the financial figures.

Performance reporting should highlight potential problems or areas of opportunity in ways that are meaningful to users. It should be a management tool for decision-making purposes and not a yardstick for determining reward and punishment. Managers should understand the financial results in light of the current business environment and determine the implications for the future. These implications should be incorporated into budgetary revisions or periodic financial forecasts.

Accountants should prepare performance reports so that they are meaningful to the users and reflect the unit's operational and financial performance. Traditional financial reports are designed to meet the needs of external users such as corporate or group headquarters, banks, or government agencies. They are not tailored to the needs of the internal users. Financial reporting needs to evolve into performance reporting, where the financial and operational results for each area are reported together in a simple, user-friendly document.

This evolution requires an assessment of current management reporting practices. Although this reevaluation should be part of a concerted, companywide effort, you can improve the performance reports for your area by asking yourself some key questions:

- What financial and operational reports do I currently receive? With what frequency?
- Do I understand the information contained in the reports? Is it useful to me? Is it relevant to the business? Does it support the company's strategic objectives?

- Can the format be modified to present the information in a simpler or more meaningful manner?
- Do I need more detail or less? Is there any supplemental information that I would like to have reported?
- Can I integrate the financial and operational data in one summary report?

Your finance organization can assist in this assessment process and help you redesign the reports to meet your needs. The finance department should ensure that a general uniformity is maintained throughout the company while meeting the particular needs of the users. Multiple reporting formats can create confusion if they do not have a similar appearance for all areas. It is analogous to the Macintosh or Windows operating systems. Regardless of the type of hardware or the particular software application, all programs that run on these operating systems have the same general appearance. This feature makes it easier to learn and use these programs. Knowledge gained in one application is transportable to another. The same concept applies to financial reporting. While reports can be tailored to meet the particular needs of a user or area, they should maintain the same general appearance and format as the other reports in the organization. Moreover, the amount of resources consumed in the preparation of more custom-tailored financial reports should be balanced against the benefits of the additional information provided.

Appendix F shows examples of a performance report for a manufacturing cost center that applies the concepts discussed in this section. This type of report would be prepared for middle management and would substitute the traditional month-end reports, both financial and operational. The report has two major sections: the operations summary, which shows the KPIs for the area, and the cost summary, which shows the costs incurred by major expense category. In a one-page summary, management can see the unit's performance for a particular reporting period in both financial and operational terms.

Performance reporting is unique to each organization; there is no standard format that will satisfy every company's needs. However, the following guidelines may help you in the redesign of your current performance reporting system:

- *Involve key users.* It is important to identify and involve the key users to establish the content and the format of the reports. Key users go up and down the corporate hierarchy. At a minimum you should have a senior financial person working with the supervisor or manager of the area, group, or division.

■ *Define user requirements.* What are the users' expectations? What information do they require? How much detail? In what format? By what date?

■ *Develop a sample reporting format.* What are the current key performance indicators? What is their purpose? What information do they provide to management? Are they consistent with the organizational strategies? Do they measure the critical processes of the areas? Can they be translated into dollars? What information is already available? Based on this information, develop a sample reporting format for discussion with the key users.

■ *Obtain consensus.* Key users should agree on the performance indicators and reporting formats for their areas. The end result should be a management report, not a finance report. The finance group should ensure that the overall appearance and format are consistent for the entire organization.

Users should review the content (what is reported) and the format (how it is reported) of their performance reports at least once a year. Organizations can change dramatically from year to year: New products are added, production lines are shut down, divisions are merged, and managers come and go. A periodic review of the management reports ensures that the information presented is relevant to the current operating environment and reflects the needs of the user community.

Chapter Summary

An effective performance measurement system provides a beacon to the organization. It ensures that everyone knows where the organization is at and where it needs to go to achieve its long-term plans. It is an integral part of the planning cycle because it provides a systematic mechanism to evaluate the company's performance. Management can then use this information to revise the company strategies or change how these strategies are being implemented.

An effective performance measurement system should have clear strategic objectives and identify the critical success factors that are essential to attain the organization's long-term goals. KPIs are tangible measures that the organization uses to monitor the critical success factors. Key performance measures should be strategically linked to organizational objectives and be integrated throughout the organization. They should be simple, few in number, and provide information that can be acted on by managers and employees. Performance indicators should present a balanced view of the organization. They should be measured and reported in a manner that shows the potential interrelationships among the key performance dimensions and can help managers understand the trade-offs of one dimension versus another.

Performance reporting focuses on how the results of the operation are communicated to the organization. It should integrate all relevant aspects of a company's performance and present this information in a user-friendly format to management. It should combine the operational and financial results into one integrated management report. Although financial information is the end result of the company's strategies and actions, it shows only one dimension of its performance. It cannot measure quality, customer service, flexibility, or other factors that are critical to its long-term success. Performance reporting can correct for the deficiencies of traditional management reporting by integrating the financial results of the operation with other key aspects of an organization's performance.

Notes

1. Michael Hammer and James Champy, *Reengineering the Corporation* (New York: HarperCollins, 1993), p. 3.
2. **Return on assets** is calculated by dividing net income by total assets. It measures the amount of profit received for every $1.00 invested in assets. **Return on capital** is calculated by dividing net income by owner's capital. It measures the amount of profit generated for every $1.00 of the owner's investment in the business.
3. See *Statements on Management Accounting 4U*, "Developing Comprehensive Performance Indicators," May 31, 1995, pp. 1, 7, and *Statements on Management Accounting 4DD*, "Tools and Techniques for Implementing Integrated Performance Management Systems," May 15, 1998, p. 3.
4. See Robert S. Kaplan and David P. Norton, "The Balanced Scorecard—Measures That Drive Performance," *Harvard Business Review* (January–February 1992): 71–79; and Robert S. Kaplan and David P. Norton, "Putting the Balanced Scorecard to Work," *Harvard Business Review* (September–October 1993): 134–142.
5. See *Statements on Management Accounting 4DD*, p. 4.
6. See *Statements on Management Accounting 4U*, pp. 4–6.

7. See *Statements on Management Accounting 4DD*, p. 24.
8. See *Statements on Management Accounting 4U*, pp. 24–25.
9. Ibid., pp. 15–9, and Appendix B on p. 51. I have included in Figure 8-4 other performance indicators based on my experience in addition to those listed on the pages referenced here.

Part III

Costing Principles and Systems

Chapter 9

The Costing Process

EASTER BUSINESS

DYE

PROFIT

DELIVERY

EGGS

osts represent the estimated dollar value of the resources consumed by the organization in providing a product or service;
they are a critical element of many business decisions. Detailed cost information can provide a company with useful data on
its resource spending and how each product or service contributes
to profitability. An example illustrates this point.

The Meneer Company has three products, J, K, and L, that are sold in boxes of 24 units each. The three products are sold for the same price, $10, but have different manufacturing costs. Figure 9-1 shows the detailed price and cost information for each product, the average cost per unit, and the average gross margin per unit.[1]

The average cost and average gross margin figures are important performance indicators. However, they do not provide management with enough detailed information to make well-informed marketing and sales decisions. Management must understand how each individual product contributes to profitability to make strategic choices. Product L, with a gross margin of $7.00 per unit, is far more profitable than Product K, with a gross margin of $3.00. By understanding the cost of each product and its contribution to profits, management can explore changes in the product mix, the manufacturing process, or marketing strategies to improve overall profitability. Suppose the Meneer Company wants to increase its $9,000 total gross margin. One possibility is to change the sales mix. For example, if it sold 1,250 units of Product J, 250 units of Product K, and 500 units of Product L, its total gross margin would increase to $10,500.[2]

This chapter provides an overview of the costing process. It starts with a discussion of the different types of manufacturing and service organizations and explains how their particular characteristics affect the systems used to collect and calculate costs. It also ex-

Figure 9-1. *Product Cost and Price Information, Meneer Company.*

Product	Unit Price	Unit Cost	Gross Margin per Unit	Sales (units)	Total Cost[a]	Total Gross Margin[a]
J	$10	$5	$5	$1,000	$ 5,000	$5,000
K	$10	$7	$3	750	5,250	2,250
L	$10	$3	$7	250	750	1,750
Total				$2,000	$11,000	$9,000

Average cost per unit
$$= \text{Total cost} \div \text{unit sales}$$
$$= \$11,000 \div 2,000$$
$$= \$5.50$$

Average gross margin per unit $= \text{Total gross margin} \div \text{total sales}$
$$= \$9,000 \div 2,000$$
$$= \$4.50$$

[a]Total cost $= \text{Unit cost} \times \text{sales (units)}.$
Total gross margin $= \text{Gross margin per unit} \times \text{sales (units)}.$

plains the two major cost accumulation systems, job order and process costing, and discusses the types of organizations for which they are most appropriate. The chapter then provides a systematic framework that can be used to approach any costing exercise. The detailed procedures for developing product and service costs are discussed in Chapters 10 and 11, respectively.

Types of Manufacturing Organizations

There are two basic types of manufacturing organizations. **Process manufacturers** build like products in a continuous manner following a uniform sequence of production operations. Process industries include steel, plastic, chemicals, distilled spirits, and petroleum. **Discrete manufacturers** make different products, either as a single unit or as a distinct, identifiable batch or job. Examples of discrete manufacturing industries are electronics, printing, construction, and furniture. Discrete manufacturers track their products through the manufacturing operations using **work orders** or **production orders**. A work order contains information on the product, the operations required, the quantity ordered, the quantity completed by operation, and other important tracking information. Some manufacturers have hybrid operations. For example, pharmaceutical companies manufacture their product in large batches of like units. Although the process is continuous, each batch is tracked using a unique lot number. The Food and Drug Administration (FDA) requires this lot number in the event of any problem with the manufactured lot that could result in a product recall. When the product reaches the packaging operation, work orders are used to capture the specific labor, material, and overhead associated with each packaging presentation (e.g., bottles of 50 tablets, 100 tablets).

The type of manufacturing operations determines how product costs are calculated. In discrete manufacturing, labor and material can be more easily tied to a specific product or batch of products using work orders. In processing manufacturing, costs are based on averages since all units go through the same manufacturing process.

Types of Service Organizations

Service organizations cover a broad spectrum of operations, including entertainment, health care, banking, and public utilities. Because service processes are so diverse, it is useful to classify these processes along two key dimensions: the degree of labor intensity and the level of customer contact and customization that are required to deliver the product. **Labor intensity** describes the quantity of labor and the skill level of the workforce that are required to perform the service. In low-intensity service systems, such as professional service firms, investments in capital equipment can improve the productivity and the quality of the service delivery significantly. In high-intensity labor systems, such as professional search firms, the expertise of the workforce is critical to deliver a high-quality product. **Customer contact and customization** is the level of customer interaction or the degree of customer customization that is involved in providing the service. In high-contact systems, such as hospitals, the customer can affect the timing, the nature, and the quality of the service because he is directly involved in the delivery process itself. In low-contact systems, such as department stores, the customer interaction is short or infrequent and therefore the customer has a minimal impact on the service delivery process.

Figure 9-2 shows a matrix that classifies service organizations according to the degree of labor intensity and the level of customer contact.[3] Four distinct types of organizations emerge:

- *Service factory.* These organizations, also called **quasi-manufacturing service**, are characterized by low labor intensity and a low

Figure 9-2. *Types of Service Organizations.*

Key Dimensions		Customer Contact and Customization	
		Low	High
Labor intensity	Low	**Service factory** • Airlines • Fast foods • Hotels • Data processing	**Service shop** • Auto repair • Hospitals • Computer repair • Print shops
	High	**Mass service** • Department stores • Schools • Supermarkets • Retail banks	**Professional service** • Engineers • Consultants • Accountants • Lawyers

Source: Service Operations Management by Schmenner, Roger W., © 1990. Adapted by permission of Prentice-Hall, Inc., Upper Saddle River, NJ.

degree of customer contact and customization. Some examples are transportation companies, hotels, and fast food chains.

- *Service shop.* As the customer contact increases, the service becomes more customized. Decisions made by the customer can affect the output of the services provided. This type of service organization resembles a discrete manufacturer or job shop operation. Some examples are auto repair shops and computer repair services.

- *Mass service.* Mass service organizations have a high degree of labor intensity and a low level of interaction with the customer. There is little customization for the consumer. Department stores and supermarket chains are some examples.

- *Professional service.* This type of organization is highly specialized. It requires high labor intensity and a high degree of customer contact. Customization is a key element of the service delivery process. Some examples are accounting firms, law firms, and consulting groups.

The type of service operation will largely determine the complexity of the costing process. For example, the similarity of service factories to assembly-line operations allows the implementation of industrial engineering tools such as process flow diagrams, task analysis, and time and motion studies. This data can be used to improve the flow of operations and greatly facilitates the development of cost information. Mass services or highly customized services present greater challenges because process controls are more informal, capacity is loosely defined, and work standards may be difficult to establish.

Moreover, some services cannot be easily placed in this four-dimensional matrix. For example, a computer distributor may offer a variety of services—some with characteristics of service shops, such as equipment installation and repair, and others with the characteristics of professional services, such as software service and support. The diversity of service operations increases the complexity of the costing process within an organization. Ultimately the costing system for a service organization will be a function of the type of operations, the size of the organization, and the resources that management is willing to invest in improving cost data.

Job Order–Costing and Process-Costing Systems

There are two major types of product costing systems: job order and process costing. **Job order costing** accumulates the costs of an individual job, contract, or customer order. It is appropriate for companies that manufacture products in identifiable batches or provide customized products or services, such as law firms, aircraft manufacturers, shipbuilders, and auto repair shops. In these types of organizations, each individual product or service consumes different amounts of resources. Therefore, the cost of a particular item should reflect the specific resources consumed in its manufacture or delivery.

Job order accounting systems track all costs by job or work order number. Direct costs such as materials and labor are charged to a job based on the actual or the standard usage. Service organizations may charge other costs directly, such as travel, telephone, supplies, or freight. Indirect costs such as factory overhead, occupancy expense or technology costs are assigned based on a predetermined overhead or cost assignment rate. The calculation of this rate is discussed in more depth in subsequent chapters.

In **process costing**, all units produced within a given time period are assigned the same cost. Process-costing systems are generally used by industries that provide like products or services in a continuous manner, such as food processing, plastics, chemicals, data processing, and transportation services. These systems accumulate costs by departments or processes. Unit costs are calculated by dividing the total costs of these areas by some measure of output (e.g., units produced, customers served, or patients attended). Process costing assumes that all units of a product or service consume the same amount of labor, materials, and indirect costs. It makes no attempt to assign these costs to individual units.

Both job order and process costing involve some averaging of costs. Job order costing averages costs over a small quantity of units, and process costing does its averaging over a much larger number. Job order and process costing are at opposite ends of a broad continuum. Some companies use both job order–and process-costing systems for different aspects of their business. Most companies use **hybrid systems** that combine elements of both job order and process costing. For example, pharmaceutical companies generally trace material costs to specific batches of production. Labor and overhead costs, however, are assigned to each batch based on a predetermined rate. Unit costs are obtained by dividing the total costs of the batch by the number of units produced.

Hybrid systems allow companies to tailor the cost accumulation system to meet their particular needs. For example, in the health care industry, the labor and supplies administered to each patient may differ significantly, but the use of indirect resources such as facilities, administration, or information systems is similar for all patients. A heath care facility may choose to track the cost of labor and supplies by individual patient (job order) and charge indirect costs based on a flat rate per patient (process costing).

In determining the most appropriate costing approach for the organization, a manager must decide the level of detail desired, the cost of obtaining the data, and whether the perceived benefits of the information will outweigh the cost of measurement. In a hospital, for example, it is technically possible to determine the treatment costs for each patient by recording in the medical record the labor and medical supplies consumed. However, the data collection of the time spent by the doctors and nurses on a particular patient may be cumbersome and encounter a lot of resistance. A hybrid system may trace some items, such as medical supplies or diagnostic tests, by patient and assign other costs, such as labor and occupancy costs, on an average basis. This type of data collection is less burdensome to maintain and has less potential for employee resistance. Therefore, a hospital administrator may chose to implement a hybrid costing system even though a pure job order costing system would provide her with more accurate and detailed information.

Figure 9-3 summarizes the characteristics of job order–and process-costing systems and provides some examples of industries that may use these systems.

A Costing Approach

Costing is not simple and many times, not straightforward. Information is often unavailable, and the company's business processes can be complex. Managers and accountants are often at a loss on how to approach a particular costing exercise. They lack general costing guidelines that can be applied to a variety of situations across many different industries.

This section provides an eight-step approach for developing costs. It presents some general costing guidelines that can be applied in any company or industry. When combined with the detailed costing procedures described in Chapters 10 and 11, this approach will result in the availability of more accurate cost information for management decision-making purposes.

Figure 9-3. *Job Order and Process Costing.*

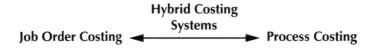

Job Order Costing	Hybrid Costing Systems ↔	Process Costing

Types of Organizations

- Professional services
- Auto repair shops
- Shipbuilding
- Aircraft manufacturers

Types of Organizations

- Chemicals
- Plastics
- Food service
- Postal delivery

Key Characteristics

- Custom products or services
- Produced or delivered in small quantities
- Each item consumes different amounts of resources

Key Characteristics

- Like items
- Produced or delivered in large quantities
- All items consume equal amounts of resources

Step 1. Define the Item to Be Costed

The definition of the **cost object** or item to be costed is a critical first step in any costing exercise. The cost object can be almost anything in an organization: a product, a service, a business process, or a marketing campaign, among many others. It can be defined in very narrow terms, such as the cost of a specific surgical procedure, or in very broad terms, such as the average cost of all surgical procedures. A clear definition of the cost object defines the scope of the costing exercise. It sets limits on the data collection process and allows information to be gathered more efficiently. The scope and the availability of information will determine the organizational resources required to develop the desired costs.

Step 2. Understand the Purpose of the Costing Exercise

An organization uses different costs for different purposes—for example, to value inventory, determine product profitability, make contract bids, or choose a manufacturing site. All participants in a costing exercise should understand how the information will be used. For example, if your purpose is to value inventory for financial statement preparation, you would probably calculate full manufacturing costs as required by generally accepted accounting principles. However, if you are bidding on a special project and have excess capacity in your facility, you may want to consider only the incremental costs of production. The purpose will also determine the key cost elements that should be included in the analysis. In the excess capacity example, the cost analyst would probably include labor and material in the analysis and exclude all overhead costs that would not change as a result of this decision.

Step 3. Determine the Cost Basis

Costs can be estimated on an actual or a projected basis. **Actual costs** show what has happened in the past based on historical data; therefore, they may provide a more accurate representation of the business. **Projected costs** are estimated future costs that are based on historical data, industry forecasts, supplier quotes, management estimates, and other sources of information. Projected costs are used in the preparation of budgets, capital investment analysis, and other key management decisions. Historical data should not be used to develop cost projections if the business is undergoing or is expected to undergo significant change.

Step 4. Gather Information on the Business Processes

Obtain as much information as possible on the product or service to be costed. What is its nature? How will it be produced or delivered? Are incremental resources required? Does it involve a new technology? Examine historical records. Determine other sources of information such as engineering studies, consultants' reports, and process flowcharts. Get information from different sources. These sources will allow you to have a broader business perspective on the costing process. If possible, validate information through independent sources such as suppliers, trade journals, or industry analysts. You can use this information to identify key cost elements, develop cost estimates, and assess the financial risk in your numbers.

Step 5. Identify the Major Cost Components

There are three major cost components in any cost analysis: labor, materials, and indirect costs. Indirect costs can be treated as a single category called overhead or can be classified by cost type, such as support labor, utilities, facilities costs, or depreciation. For example, in a highly automated facility, you may want to isolate the depreciation costs, the engineering support costs, and the maintenance costs associated with automation. In the discussion of service costs, we classified overhead into technology costs, occupancy expense, and other costs.

Labor, materials, and overhead are what I call "hard numbers"; at some point, they will represent cash outlays by the company. How you estimate and report these costs will be discussed in the next two chapters. There are other costs, however, that do not represent cash outlays but are lost opportunities for the firm. Opportunity costs were discussed in Chapter 3. These costs are rarely included in the cost of the product or the service but should be considered in the management decision-making process.

Step 6. Calculate the Cost

Based on the information gathered in Steps 2–5, you are now ready to calculate the product or service costs. Individual costs are calculated for each key cost component and then added together to obtain the total cost of a product or service. The detailed calculation procedures are discussed in the next two chapters.

Step 7. Document Your Assumptions

All costs are based on assumptions. Even calculations of historical costs make some assumptions about how the product or service consumes indirect costs or overhead. These assumptions allow us to distribute indirect costs in a reasonable manner. For example, traditional cost-accounting systems assume a direct relationship between labor or machine hours and overhead costs; the more hours are used, the more overhead costs are charged to a product or service.

Cost projections are based on assumptions about the future. Even if you use historical data to estimate costs, you have still made an assumption: that the future will be the same as the past. Typically when managers use historical data to estimate costs, they consider potential changes in the business environment and adjust the data accordingly. Key managers should discuss and agree on the costing assumptions prior to the cost calculation. If they do not, they may be tempted to manipulate the assumptions until they reach an acceptable number. Costs are only as accurate as the assumptions that underlie their calculation. If the assumptions do not reflect the nature of the business processes, the costs will not be accurate. In addition, unpredictable events, such as accidents, fires, hurricanes, and political changes, may render prior cost assumptions invalid. In these situations, cost should be recalculated to reflect the changes in the operating environment.

Step 8. Perform Reasonableness Tests

Reasonableness tests assess the validity of the cost model and can be done on a subjective or quantitative basis. **Subjective reasonableness tests** rely on the individual judgment of experts. Experts are knowledgeable individuals who can often detect inconsistencies or errors in an item's cost based on their understanding of the business processes. An expert's "gut feel" raises a flag that further investigation of the operating assumptions or the calculation methodology is required. Any changes to the cost model made on the basis of subjective judgment should be documented as part of the costing exercise.

Quantitative reasonableness tests are statistical analyses that can be done on an absolute or relative basis. **Absolute reasonableness tests** match like with like. They compare the calculated cost figure to a historical cost, a standard cost, or a prior cost estimate of the same product or service. A **relative reasonableness test** compares the calculated cost of an item with historical, standard, or estimated costs of similar items. For example, suppose a company produces two types of plastic glasses: a 4-ounce and a 6-ounce version. Since both products go through the same manufacturing processes, their costs should be similar except for a small difference in the material costs. If the costs of the 4-ounce glass are higher than the 6-ounce glass or if the cost differential is greater than expected, there may be an error or inconsistency in the costing process that should be investigated immediately. In quantitative reasonableness tests, significant differences should be reconciled and explained; an unexplained difference raises questions about the validity of the cost model.

Figure 9-4 summarizes the costing approach. In the next two chapters, we focus on how to calculate product and service costs in more detail.

Chapter Summary

Good cost information is vital for planning and controlling your business. However, cost information is never an exact calculation of

Figure 9-4. *General Costing Guidelines.*

---

1. Identify the item to be costed.
2. Understand the purpose of the costing exercise.
3. Determine the cost basis.
4. Gather information on the business processes.
5. Identify the major cost components.
6. Calculate the cost.
7. Document your assumptions
8. Perform reasonableness tests.

---

the resources consumed in manufacturing a product or delivering a service. Cost information, whether historical or projected, is based on a set of assumptions that determine the accuracy of the cost calculation. A very precise methodology will produce inaccurate costs if the underlying assumptions of the business processes are not correct. Inaccurate cost information can result in poor business decisions and, ultimately, can be quite costly to your company. This chapter discussed the different types of costing systems that organizations use and provided some general costing guidelines that can be applied in a variety of costing situations.

The preparation of cost information is only one step in the management decision-making process. Cost information should highlight problems or present opportunities to manage the business more effectively. However, for cost information to be useful, management must act on the information provided. Costing is only a means to an end. Do not lose sight of this goal as you develop and analyze the costs of your organization.

Notes

1. Gross margin is the difference between the sales revenue and the full manufacturing cost in total or on a per unit basis. It represents the amount of revenue available for covering operating expenses after all production costs have been recuperated.
2. The $10,500 total gross margin is calculated as follows: Total gross margin = (1,250 units $\times$ $5) + (250 units $\times$ $3) + (500 units $\times$ $7) = $10,500.
3. See Richard B. Chase and Nicholas J. Aquilano, *Production and Operations Management: A Life Cycle Approach* (Homewood, Ill.: Richard D. Irwin, 1989), pp. 98–107 and Roger W. Schmenner, *Service Operations Management,* Englewood Cliffs, New Jersey, Prentice Hall, 1995, p. 11.

Chapter 10

How to Cost a Product

P roduct costs are the costs to manufacture or build a tangible
product. They can be reported in total or on a per unit basis
and are typically divided into three major cost categories: materials, labor, and overhead. Although there are general guidelines
on what type of costs should be included in each category, a company has considerable latitude in what it classifies and reports as a
product cost.

Product costs should accurately reflect the resources consumed in the manufacturing process. Managers use these costs to evaluate product profitability, identify cost reduction opportunities, determine the optimal sales mix, evaluate special orders, and decide which products to subcontract. Costs for these types of decisions require a level of precision at the individual product or product family level that is not required for inventory valuation and financial accounting purposes. Financial statements prepared for external users are concerned with the accuracy of the aggregate inventory and cost of sales figures reported. The individual breakdown by product is not important as long as the aggregate figure is fairly and accurately stated.

As I have noted throughout this book, there are different costs for different purposes. This chapter focuses on product costing for management decision-making purposes. It explains how to calculate the labor, materials, and overhead costs for a product. It discusses how manufacturing yield and capacity utilization affect the product cost. The discussion also covers some basic concepts of production and operations management. This understanding is key to the product-costing process. You cannot analyze or calculate product costs accurately unless you have a thorough understanding of the operations on the production floor.

Materials Costs

All products are made up of a list of parts or components called a **bill of materials**. The bill of materials (BOM) or the **product structure** contains a listing of all the parts that are required to manufacture a product. It shows how a product is put together and contains information to identify each item and the quantity required per unit or batch. Figure 10-1 shows a BOM for Product 12-999, a box of frozen bread. This product has a **subassembly**, item 12-999-01, which is a pound of frozen bread. A subassembly is an intermediate product that is used to manufacture another product. Generally subassemblies are not sold to end customers, but are produced for internal use only. A subassembly also has a BOM—in this example, the list of ingredients required to produce a pound of frozen bread. Therefore, a BOM can have several levels, starting with level 0 for the end item or **parent part**, then level 1 for the next level, and so on. This is called the **product hierarchy**. Figure 10-2 shows the product hierarchy for Product 12-999.

Figure 10-1. *Sample Bill of Materials, Freshly Baked, Inc.*

Freshly Baked, Inc.
BILL OF MATERIALS

Product Number: 12-999

Product Description: Frozen White Sandwich Bread

Unit of Measure: Per Box

Item Number	Item Description	UM	Quantity Required
12-999-01	Sandwich Bread, Frozen	LB	12
C33295	Box, Model 33295	BX	1
LINER	Box liner	EA	1

The BOM usually contains a provision for material losses that normally occur during the production process. Companies have different names for this type of loss such as the **scrap factor** or the **materials usage factor**. The scrap factor is expressed as a percentage of the materials dollars or the materials quantity. Some inventory systems isolate the scrap factor and incorporate it into the BOM; others add this amount to the quantity required to manufacture the product. You should know and understand the materials usage or scrap provision in the BOMs of your company. The scrap factor represents an opportunity for improvement: The lower the scrap factor is, the lower your materials costs.

Engineering, production personnel, or both, maintain the BOMs,

Figure 10-2. *Product Hierarchy for Frozen Bread, Freshly Baked, Inc.*

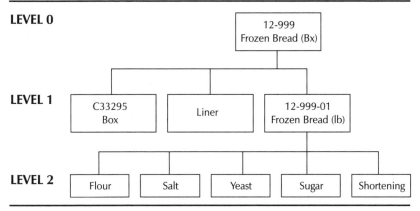

which should be reviewed at least once a year or whenever there is a significant change in the business. Changes in the manufacturing process or the product design can affect the material usage reflected in the BOM. BOMs are usually updated through a formal request called an **engineering change order** (ECO). Accurate BOMs are critical to obtain reliable cost data. Actual and projected material costs are usually based on the information contained in the BOM. In some manufacturing organizations, inventory is automatically relieved from the warehouse based on this information. Inaccurate BOMs can have serious negative consequences for a manufacturing organization: inaccurate costs, incorrect inventory balances, product rework, and inefficiencies on the production floor.

Materials cost is estimated by multiplying the quantities required in the BOM by the cost of each component. Components can be costed using one of the following four methods:

■ *Average actual cost.* Under this method, the inventory cost is updated each time an inventory purchase is made. Figure 10-3 shows the average actual cost of flour for Freshly Baked, Inc. for December. Each time a purchase is received, the average actual cost per pound is recalculated. A company that does not have an automated costing system may calculate average actual costs only once a month.

■ *Standard cost.* Standard costs are expected costs that serve as goals to be achieved. They are usually expressed on a per unit basis. Standard material costs are based on a standard material quantity as defined in the BOM and a standard price. Standard costs are gener-

Figure 10-3. *Average Actual Cost Example, Freshly Baked, Inc.*

Date	Purchases (lbs)	Cost per Pound	Total Cost	Average Actual Cost (lbs)
12/01	10,000	$0.205	$2,050	$0.205
12/15	5,000	0.180	900	0.197[a]
12/31	20,000	0.190	3,800	0.193[b]

[a]0.197= (Prior purchase + new purchase)/Total purchases
 = ($2,050 + $900) ÷ (10,000 + 5,000)
 = $2,950 ÷ 15,000
 = $0.197

[b]0.193= ($2,050 + $900 + $3,800) ÷ (10,000 + 5,000 + 20,000)
 = $6,750 ÷ 35,000
 = $0.193.

ally set once a year during the standards-setting process; they are not changed unless the difference between the actual cost and the standard cost is very large and significant.

■ *Last cost.* Last cost is the most recent cost. This valuation method is appropriate when the last cost is the most representative of the actual or projected cost of the item. If costs have been following an upward or downward trend consistently, the last cost may be a more accurate representation of the item cost than the average actual or the standard.

■ *Projected cost.* A projected cost is an estimated future cost based on the best available information. Projected costs are appropriate when estimating product costs for future time periods. Projected costs differ from standard costs in that they can be updated continually as more information becomes available.

Let us put all this information together to calculate the materials cost for Product 12-999-01, a pound of frozen bread based on the average actual cost. The average cost of a particular item can usually be found in the item master of the inventory management system. The **item master** is the heart of any inventory control system. It contains purchasing and other general information about a part including its actual, standard, and last cost. Organizations that do not have an automated inventory control system can manually calculate the average actual cost for each component from the inventory purchases made during the period, as shown in Figure 10-3.

Figure 10-4 shows a costed BOM for Product 12-999-01. A **costed bill of materials** shows the quantity and the cost of each component and adds these together to obtain the materials cost per unit or batch. For discrete manufacturers, the costed BOM represents the materials cost per unit of measure. For process manufacturers, the costing process is more complex because it must take into account the manufacturing yield, covered later in this chapter.

Figure 10-5 summarizes the discussion on estimating materials cost. It shows the elements of the formula, the parties responsible for providing and updating information, and a list of factors that could affect the quantity required or the cost of a component. Typically personnel from engineering or production are responsible for updating the BOM on a periodic basis. Any major change in the product design, the production process, or the manufacturing technology

Figure 10-4. *Costed Bill of Materials for Product 12-999-01,*
                Freshly Baked, Inc.

Item	Item Description	UM	Quantity	Average Actual Cost per UM	Total Cost[a]
Flour	Flour	Pound	.833	$0.30	$0.250
Yeast	Yeast	Pound	.018	.60	0.011
Shortening	Shortening	Pound	.009	.15	0.001
Sugar	Sugar, white	Pound	.003	.55	0.002
Salt	Table salt	Pound	.024	.10	0.002
Cost per pound					**$0.266**

[a]Total cost per ingredient = Quantity used × average actual cost per UM.

should trigger a review of the BOM. The estimated or actual cost of
a component is affected by a number of factors, such as worldwide
purchasing contracts, foreign exchange rates, volume discounts, the
number of suppliers, the general economy, government regulations,
and marketing strategies. Government regulations can affect materials costs if a certain percentage of local material content is required
to do business in that country. Marketing strategies may also require
a company to purchase materials from local suppliers to penetrate
an otherwise closed market. These factors should be considered in
developing unit cost estimates for the components of a product.

Figure 10-5. *Estimating Material Costs.*

Formula:	**Quantity Required** ×	**Cost per UM** =	**Materials Costs per Unit**
Who Is Responsible	• Engineering • Production	• Purchasing	
Factors to Consider	• Production process • Technology • Product design	• Purchasing contracts • Foreign currency rates • Purchase volumes • Number of suppliers • Government regulations • The economy • Marketing strategies	

Labor Costs

Direct labor costs are the wages, salaries, and fringe benefits of those manufacturing employees who work directly on the product. **Indirect labor costs** are the total compensation costs of employees who support the manufacturing process but do not work directly on the product. Indirect labor employees include maintenance personnel, line supervisors, and industrial engineers. Indirect labor costs are generally included as part of manufacturing overhead.

Traditional estimation of labor costs is based on **labor standards**, the estimated time a direct labor employee should take to complete an operation. Labor standards are based on engineering studies, historical data, or management estimates. A company that has a production control system to monitor the manufacturing operations usually keeps labor standards in the routing file. The **routing file** contains the sequence of operations that will be performed on the product and the detailed labor hours, machine hours, and setup time that will be required by each operation.[1]

The costing process is fairly simple in companies that use labor standards. The labor costs are calculated by multiplying the standard labor hours required for each operation by an average wage rate. The average wage rate should include the base salary, the payroll taxes, and the fringe benefits. The labor costs incurred in each operation are added to obtain the total labor costs for the product. Figure 10-6 summarizes the traditional method for assigning labor costs to products. It also shows the parties responsible for providing and updating the information and the list of factors that could affect the labor standards or the average wage rates. Production managers affect the average wage rate by determining the employee mix. Some operations require employees with higher skill levels, and therefore these operations will have a higher average wage rate.

Highly automated companies have eliminated the use of labor standards and detailed labor tracking for costing and control purposes. In the past, elaborate labor vouchering systems would trace direct labor hours to specific work orders or products. These hours would be compared and reconciled to the actual hours paid through payroll. Differences between actual and standard hours would be analyzed and reported in detail each month. When I worked at a major electronics manufacturer, we had one cost accountant whose sole job was to analyze, reconcile, and report direct labor hours and costs.

In the mid-1980s, many companies realized the significant loss

Figure 10-6. *Determining Labor Costs.*

Formula:	Labor Standard	×	Average Wage Rate	=	Labor Costs per Unit
Who Is Responsible	• Engineering • Production		• Human resources • Finance • Production		
Factors to Consider	• Production process • Technology • Product design		• Collective bargaining • Skill level required • Wage increases • Government regulations		

of time and misdirected resources involved in labor tracking for highly automated operations. These companies have eliminated labor tracking and reporting since labor represents an insignificant portion of the total manufacturing cost. These companies generally include labor costs as part of factory overhead costs. Labor standards are used for planning purposes only.

Some companies charge direct labor to products without using labor standards or labor tracking. Let us return to Freshly Baked, Inc. to illustrate this point. Freshly Baked is divided into two major product families: breads and pastries. Each product family has its own employees, space, and equipment. Freshly Baked has 10 employees in the bread area, including one supervisor. The total payroll is $12,000 per month, and the average production volume is 60,000 pounds per month. The labor costs are calculated at $0.20 per pound ($12,000 ÷ 60,000 pounds = $0.20/pound). In this calculation, we do not differentiate between direct and indirect labor; it is all charged to the product as labor. A company, however, may choose to include the indirect labor as part of the overhead calculation.

The labor calculation can be done on a monthly, quarterly, or year-to-date basis, using actual, standard, or projected costs; it is straightforward and simple. However, this method assumes that all products consume the same amount of labor resources per unit. If one product requires significantly more labor time than another does, this assignment method is not appropriate and could distort product costs. This issue is covered in more depth in Chapter 14.

Overhead Costs

Overhead costs are all manufacturing costs that cannot be directly traced to a product in a cost-effective way. Overhead costs include expenses such as minor tools, supplies, training, depreciation, electricity, and telephone. This category also may include charges allocated from departments that provide support services, such as quality assurance, warehouse, engineering, and information systems. These costs are collected by departments, work centers, or production areas and are called **cost pools.** Figure 10-7 shows the overhead allocation process where indirect costs collected in departments or work centers are traced to the product.[2]

Overhead costs are assigned to products using an **activity measure** such as direct labor hours, machine hours, or units produced. The activity measure characterizes the nature of the production process and should bear a causal relationship to the incurrence of the overhead costs. For example, the use of direct labor hours is an inappropriate activity measure for a highly automated factory since the indirect manufacturing costs bear little relationship to the amount of direct labor hours used.

The **overhead rate** establishes a relationship between the indirect manufacturing costs and the activity measure that characterizes the production process. Overhead costs are assigned to a product by multiplying the overhead rate by the quantity of the activity measure used or produced during the period. The overhead rate can be calculated based on actual, expected, or budgeted quantities. Figure 10-8

Figure 10-7. *Overhead Allocation Process.*

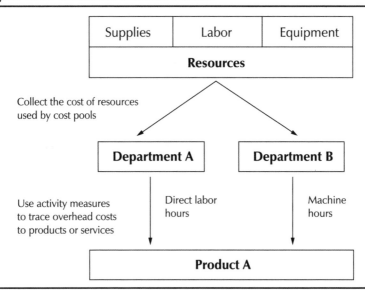

shows the formula for calculating the overhead rate and how to use the overhead rate to assign indirect costs to a product.

Let us return to Product 12-999-01 and apply the information in Figure 10-8 to calculate the overhead rate and assign the indirect overhead costs for this product. Because the manufacturing process is highly automated, the finance department has determined that machine hours are a reasonable basis to distribute the factory overhead costs. The total overhead costs for the plant are $30,000: $18,000 in the bread area and $12,000 in the pastries area. The machine hours consumed in each area totaled 150 and 120 hours, respectively, for this time period. The overhead rate for the bread area of $120 per machine hour is calculated by dividing the overhead costs of $18,000 into the 150 machine hours used.

However, before we can assign these indirect costs, we must know how many machine hours this particular product consumes. Suppose the engineering department determines that each pound of bread consumes .001 machine hour. The total overhead costs per pound of bread would equal $0.12 (0.001 machine hour × $120/machine hour). Figure 10-9 shows the calculation of the overhead rate and the overhead costs assigned to product 12-999-01. In this example, actual machine hours for the period were the basis for calculating the overhead rate.

Very few companies use one overhead rate. Most companies have different overhead rates for each department or work area, as shown in Figure 10-9. Only products that flow through the area are charged with the overhead costs for that area. In this example, the total overhead rate for all activities combined of $111 is not appropriate because the bread area has higher indirect costs ($120 per machine hour) than the pastries area ($100 per machine hour). If we use

Figure 10-8. *How to Assign Overhead Costs.*

Activity Measure Consumed	×	Overhead Rate per Activity Measure[a]	=	Overhead Costs Applied
• Machine hours				
• Direct labor hours				
• Kilowatt-hours				
• Material costs				
• Units of production				

[a]Overhead rate $= \dfrac{\text{Total overhead costs}}{\text{Actual or expected activity levels}}$

Figure 10-9. *Overhead Rate Calculation and Assignment of Overhead Costs, Freshly Baked, Inc.*

Overhead Rate Calculation	Total	Bread	Pastries
Total overhead costs	$30,000	$18,000	$12,000
Actual machine hours	270	150	120
Machine rate per hour[a]	111	120	100

Assignment of overhead costs to product 12-999-01
Overhead costs = .001 machine hour per pound × $120 per machine hour
= $0.12 per pound

[a]Machine rate per hour = Overhead costs (total or per area) ÷ machine hours (total or per area). The machine rate for bread = $18,000 ÷ 150 hours = $120.

the total or aggregate overhead rate to assign these costs, the cost of pastry products will be overstated because they will be absorbing a portion of the indirect costs related to bread products.

If a cost is significant and can be specifically identified to a product or service, it should not be included as an overhead cost. For example, most costing systems include depreciation as part of the overhead rate. Yet one of my clients charges depreciation directly to the product on a per unit basis. This client, a manufacturer of plastic products, can identify the specific molds that are used to produce a product or a group of products. Under a traditional cost system, the depreciation charge associated with each mold would be included in the overhead rate and allocated across all products. Therefore, products that require very expensive molds subsidize those that require less expensive ones. In our cost system redesign, we identified which products were manufactured with a particular mold and calculated a depreciation charge per unit. A product now receives the depreciation charges for the specific mold used in its manufacturing process. This change has not only resulted in more accurate costs but also highlighted some interesting business issues related to capital investments.

Cost Rollup

Once the individual cost elements of a product are calculated, we are ready to perform a **cost rollup**, an accounting process that sums

Figure 10-10. *Cost Rollup for Product 12-999-01, Freshly Baked, Inc.*

Cost Element	Cost	Reference
Materials	$0.266	See Figure 10-4
Labor	0.200	$12,000 ÷ 60,000 pounds
Overhead	0.120	See Figure 10-9
Total unit cost	**$0.586**	

the significant cost components of a product and calculates a total unit cost. In traditional cost systems, these components are defined as labor, materials, and overhead. If a product has subassemblies, these costs are rolled up into the unit cost of the end item or parent part. This process is generally done by a computer application at a user's request. Figure 10-10 shows a cost rollup for Product 12-999-01.

The calculated unit cost should be compared against a budgeted, expected, or actual cost for reasonableness. If the unit cost seems out of line with prior experience, the calculation of each cost element should be verified. The manufacturing management should review and approve all costs. If a manager believes that the calculated cost is not accurate, the assumptions that underlie the cost calculations, such as scrap, yield, cycle time, and labor hours, should be reexamined. The manufacturing managers should agree that the costing methodology and the operational measures (e.g., materials usage, labor hours, cycle time) on which the cost calculations are based provide a fair representation of the resources consumed to produce a product.

Manufacturing Yield and Product Cost

Process manufacturers that produce baked goods, paper, chemicals, or soft drinks do not produce their products in discrete units. These industries manufacture their products in lots or batches and have an expected level of output for each formulation. This expected output is known as the **standard yield**. The **expected cost per unit** is the total actual or estimated cost divided by the standard yield.

Let us return to Freshly Baked, Inc. Figure 10-11 (see page 174) shows the total labor, materials, and overhead cost for one batch of Product 12-999-01. Note that the BOM is expressed per batch, not per unit. The standard yield based on historical data is 330 pounds per batch. The expected cost per pound is obtained by dividing the total expected cost of the batch by the standard yield. The actual cost per pound is obtained by dividing the total batch costs by the actual yield. The **actual yield** is the actual output obtained from the manufacturing process. Suppose in the example that the actual yield is 300 pounds. The actual costs per pound are $0.46 versus an expected cost of $0.42. Although the total batch costs remain the same at $138.90, the actual unit cost is higher because the company could have produced 30 pounds more of frozen bread with the same amount of resources, resulting in lower unit costs and higher profits. These 30 pounds of bread that were not produced are lost forever; these costs will never be recovered through sales.

The relationship between cost and manufacturing yield is very important. Manufacturing yield represents a cost improvement opportunity. In the example in Figure 10-11, the cost of manufacturing inefficiency is calculated at $12.60 per batch, or $0.04 per unit. If Freshly Baked produces 7,000 batches per year, this inefficiency represents a cost reduction opportunity of $88,200 per year (7,000 batches × $12.60 per batch). The manufacturing yield can be improved through changes in the manufacturing process, product formulation, or production technology. A manufacturing yield of less than 100 percent represents a lost opportunity because more units could have been produced and sold with the same level of resources.

Capacity and Product Cost

Capacity is the amount of output that can be obtained from a process. It is measured in units of output per unit of time. Output can be defined in units, labor hours, machine hours, sales dollars, or other measures; time can be defined in years, months, days, hours, minutes, or seconds.[3] *Capacity* is an upper limit or constraint; it can be bound by people, space, machinery, or capital.

The definition of capacity seems fairly straightforward. However, in practice, capacity measurement can be quite difficult. Managers place different interpretations on the term *capacity*. There are also problems identifying appropriate measures of capacity for a specific situation. Suppose you have a production line that can manufacture several different products, and the maximum production capacity of this line is 24 hours a day. However, the output of the line will vary depending on the product that is being manufactured. What output will you assign as the maximum capacity of the line?

Figure 10-11. *Manufacturing Cost per Batch and per Unit, Product 12-999-01, Freshly Baked, Inc.*

Material Costs per Batch

Item	Item Description	UM	Quantity per unit	Cost	Total Cost[a]
Flour	Flour, Regal Type	Pound	250	$0.30	$75.00
Yeast	Bread yeast	Pound	6	0.60	3.60
Shortening	Halo shortening	Pound	3	0.15	0.45
Sugar	Sugar, Snow White	Pound	1	0.55	0.55
Salt	Salt	Pound	8	0.10	0.80
Total materials cost					**$80.40**

Total Costs per Batch

Materials	Per BOM				$ 80.40
Labor	Labor hours	Hours	2.70	7.00	18.90
Overhead	Machine hours	Hours	0.33	120.00	39.60
Total manufacturing costs per batch					**$138.90**

Expected unit cost[b]   (Standard yield = 330 pounds)   **$0.42**
Actual unit cost[c]   (Actual yield = 300 pounds)   **$0.46**

Cost of manufacturing inefficiency[d] = $12.30 per batch or $0.04 per unit

[a]Total materials cost = ΣQty used × average actual cost per unit of measure
                 = Σ(250 × $0.30) + (6 × $0.60) + (3 × $0.15) +
                   (1 × $0.55) + (8 × $0.10)
                 = $80.40.

[b]Expected cost   = Total costs per batch ÷ standard yield per batch
                 = $138.90 ÷ 330
                 = $0.42.

[c]Actual cost   = Total costs per batch ÷ actual yield per lot
                 = $138.90 ÷ 300
                 = $0.46.

[d]Cost of manufacturing = Expected cost × (standard yield − actual yield)
inefficiency   = $0.42 × (330 units − 300 units)
                 = $0.42 × 30
                 = $12.60 per batch
                 = $0.04 per unit ($12.60 per batch ÷ 300 units).

The answer to this question is not easy and illustrates some of the subtleties of capacity measurement.

There are several definitions of capacity. **Maximum capacity** or **theoretical capacity** is the maximum output that can be attained when the resources are used to their maximum potential. Theoretical capacity assumes that the company operates at a 100 percent output level all the time. It does not consider holidays, weekends, scheduled shutdowns, or any other possible constraints on production. The following example illustrates the calculation of theoretical capacity.

Suppose Plasticor, Inc., a manufacturer of plastic products, can produce 1,500 pounds per hour on Line Number 1. The maximum capacity of this line would be calculated as follows:

Maximum capacity = 1,500 pounds/hour × 24 hours/day
per day   = 36,000 pounds

Maximum capacity = 36,000 pounds/day × 7 days/week
per week   = 252,000 pounds

Maximum capacity = 252,000 pounds/week × 52 weeks/year
per year   = 13,104,000 pounds/year

This calculation assumes that there are no legal restrictions to running three 8-hour shifts per day, 365 days per year. **Practical capacity** (also called **design capacity**) is the output that a company would like to produce under normal operating conditions and for which the production system was designed. It is the maximum possible output given holidays, scheduled shutdowns for maintenance, and other unavoidable interruptions. Assume that Plasticor normally operates three 8-hour shifts, 5 days a week for 50 weeks each year. The plant shuts down 2 weeks during the year to perform scheduled maintenance on its production lines. The practical capacity would be calculated as follows:

Practical capacity = 1,500 pounds/hour × 24 hours/day
per day   = 36,000 pounds

Practical capacity = 36,000 pounds/day × 5 days/week
per week   = 180,000 pounds

Practical capacity = 180,000 pounds/week × 50 weeks/year
per year   = 9,000,000 pounds/year

The **planned** or **scheduled capacity** is the level of activity projected for a particular time period. This activity level is usually the basis for the annual business plan. The planned capacity can be above, below, or at practical capacity.

Capacity utilization is the extent to which a company uses its production capacity and is expressed as a percentage of the expected output. It is calculated using the following formula: (Actual output ÷ expected output) × 100. Capacity utilization can significantly affect unit cost and the perceived profitability of a product. When a company establishes a manufacturing plant, it has recurring costs that are independent of the volume produced, such as rent, depreciation, and facility maintenance costs. In addition, it may wish to maintain a fixed level of employees to manage the monthly fluctuations in the sales demand. When a plant operates at the desired capacity level, it is making maximum utilization of these resources; if it operates below this capacity, the cost of this excess capacity will be charged to its current products.

The example in Figure 10-12 shows the impact of capacity utilization on the unit cost. Suppose Plasticor produced 1,521,000 pounds and incurred overhead costs of $900,000 during the previous quarter. The actual overhead cost is $0.592 per pound. Plasticor, however, has a practical capacity of 180,000 pounds per week or 2,340,000 pounds per quarter (180,000 pounds/week × 13 weeks per quarter). If the organization had operated at practical capacity, the overhead cost per unit would have decreased to $0.385 per pound. The difference of $0.207 is the cost of excess capacity that is being charged to the product.

As shown in the example, some companies hide the cost of excess capacity in the overhead cost of their products. This practice distorts the true profitability of a product because it charges the product for resources it did not consume. This situation may cause profitable products to appear as unprofitable or uncompetitive in the

Figure 10-12. *Capacity and Unit Cost Example, Plasticor.*

Total overhead costs	$900,000	
Practical capacity (in pounds)	2,340,000	
Actual production (in pounds)	1,521,000	
Capacity utilization	65%	(2,340,000 ÷ 1,521,000)
Actual overhead cost/unit	$0.592	($900,000 ÷ 1,521,000)
Overhead cost/unit @ practical capacity	$0.385	($900,000 ÷ 2,340,000)
Total cost of excess capacity	**$315,315**	($0.385 × 819,000)
Excess capacity cost per unit	**$0.207**	($0.592 − $0.385) or ($315,315 ÷ 1,521,000)

marketplace. Based on this information, management may decide to remove these products from its sales offerings, thinking this action will improve the company's bottom line. However, fixed overhead costs do not go away with decreases in production volume. As uncompetitive products are dropped, the fixed overhead costs that had been assigned to these products are distributed among the remaining products, so their reported costs increase. Now other products become uncompetitive and are either outsourced or dropped. The cycle repeats itself in a downward spiral, reducing profits and competitiveness, until eventually the facility is closed. This phenomenon is known in accounting circles as the *death spiral*.[4]

Some accountants argue that all manufacturing costs should be included in the unit cost and reported as cost of sales when the products are sold. Cost management experts disagree with this approach.[5] They maintain that excess capacity is a continuing cost of running the business and is not related to the products manufactured during the period. These costs should be classified not as product costs but as period costs. Period costs, as you may recall from Chapter 2, are charged against income in the period incurred and cannot be inventoried. Under this method, excess capacity would be reported as a period expense under cost of sales.

This accounting treatment has several advantages. First, it provides a better representation of the true manufacturing costs by eliminating the cost of excess capacity from the unit cost. Second, excess capacity, which is typically beyond the control of the plant manager, becomes a visible item on the income statement. I recommend that excess capacity be reported as a separate line item under the cost of goods sold section of the income statement. This type of reporting would clearly show the cost improvement opportunities for the plant if more sales volume could be generated. In Figure 10-12, the $315,315 of excess capacity costs would be reported as a period cost under the heading of "other cost of sales" in the income statement.[6]

Chapter Summary

Product cost models should reflect the resources consumed in the manufacturing processes of the company. Labor, material, and overhead are the major cost components of a product in a traditional cost-accounting system. However, overhead costs such as electricity, maintenance, and depreciation have also become significant as factories continue to automate their production processes. A company may choose to isolate these costs in its cost structure, particularly if these can be identified with a particular product or group of products.

Manufacturing efficiency and capacity utilization can significantly affect product cost. They represent major cost improvement opportunities for the organization. These costs, however, are not always visible to production management. Manufacturing inefficiencies can be hidden in the labor and materials costs required to build the product. Excess capacity is buried in the overhead costs. Accountants should make these costs visible to management. They should quantify the cost savings that would result from improved manufacturing yields and estimate the impact of a higher capacity utilization on the bottom line. Product cost information can provide invaluable insight into the business when it accurately reflects the manufacturing processes and is presented in a format that is useful and understandable to nonfinancial managers.

Notes

1. Setup time is the time required to prepare a machine for use. Examples are the time spent on the installation and removal of equipment, cleaning time, the time spent entering the machine parameters, and the time running the machine before the first good unit of output is produced.
2. For an ample discussion on the two-stage allocation procedure that forms the basis of most modern cost systems see Robin Cooper, "The Two-Stage Procedure in Cost Accounting: Part One," *Journal of Cost Management* (Summer 1987): 43–51, and "The Two-Stage Procedure in Cost Accounting: Part Two," *Journal of Cost Management* (Fall 1987): 39–45.
3. Richard B. Chase and Nicholas J. Aquilano, *Production and Operations Management: A Life Cycle Approach* (Homewood, Ill.: Richard D. Irwin, 1989), p. 273.
4. Peter B. B. Turney, *Common Cents* (Hillsboro, Ore.: Cost Technology, 1991), pp. 39–40.
5. Thomas Klammer, ed., *Capacity Measurement and Improvement* (Burr Ridge, Ill.: Irwin, 1996), pp. 69–71; Robert S. Kaplan and Robin Cooper, *Cost and Effect* (Boston: Harvard Business School Press, 1998).
6. The Consortium for Advanced Manufacturing-International has proposed a new and innovative framework for analyzing capacity measurement and understanding its implications for product costs. The discussion of that capacity model is beyond the scope of this chapter. Thomas Klammer's *Capacity Measurement and Improvement* is highly recommended reading for those individuals who wish to increase their understanding of the issues surrounding capacity measurement.

Chapter 11

How to Cost a Service

"I don't use anesthetics anymore. I just give them an estimate of their hospital bill."

S ervice companies need accurate and relevant cost information to survive in the increasingly competitive business environment. Cost information is tied to cost control, performance evaluation, pricing, and ultimately, profitability. However, cost accounting has traditionally focused on the manufacturing industry. Although there is a wealth of accounting literature on how to develop and analyze costs in a manufacturing setting, there is significantly less information on costing practices in a service environment.[1] The underlying assumption is that manufacturing terms and cost concepts can be readily applied to the service industry.

The rise of the service economy, deregulation, and a changing competitive environment have required accounting professionals to place more attention on service costs. Service companies have increasingly become the subject of accounting articles and case studies on cost practices, and more service sector examples have been incorporated into cost-accounting textbooks. The rising interest in service costing among accounting professionals is closely tied to the popularity of activity-based costing (ABC) which has provided a useful framework to analyze and understand service costs. (ABC is discussed in Chapter 14.) Nevertheless, traditional costing procedures can also be applied to service organizations quite successfully.

This chapter discusses the major differences between manufacturing and service organizations and the implications of these differences for developing cost information. It describes specific procedures for developing service costs that can be adapted to different types of service organizations. The chapter builds on the service costs concepts presented in Chapter 2 and shows how these can be applied in a practical setting.

Manufacturing vs. Service Organizations

Manufacturing and service organizations are similar in several ways.[2] First, both provide something of value to the customer. Manufacturers produce a tangible product, such as a computer, an automobile, a bicycle, or a microwave oven—something that we can see and touch. Service providers offer a service package that is a mix of tangible and intangible products. For example, an airline not only physically transports passengers from one place to another, but also provides amenities, such as food and entertainment, that are part of the total service package.

Second, manufacturing and service organizations make design and operating decisions to determine the best way to deliver value to the customer. For example, a manufacturer may decide the size and location of a production facility; a service provider such as a bank may decide how big a branch office is required to meet local demand.

Third, both types of organizations plan and allocate scarce resources. They have procedures in place to schedule, measure, and control their operations.

Manufacturing and service organizations, however, have key differences that pose unique costing challenges for managers and accountants, which are discussed next.[3]

Nature of the Product

The major difference between service and manufacturing organizations revolves around what they offer to the customer. Manufacturing delivers products that are consumed; service delivers an interaction that is experienced. In manufacturing, the item to be measured, the cost object, can be easily defined. The products are tangible and clearly identifiable. In service, the identification of the cost object is often more difficult because of the intangible nature of the product. Consider the services provided by a hospital. A hospital offers multiple services: emergency care, outpatient clinics, inpatient care, and pharmacy, among others. How do you determine the specific services to be costed? For inpatient care, is the service provided the hospital stay, the medical procedures performed, the drugs administered, or a combination of all of these items? Should these services be costed on an individual basis or as an average cost per patient-day?

The identification of the cost object is a key first step in any costing exercise. In service organizations, this first step is typically more difficult than in manufacturing.

Input-Output Relationship

In general, manufacturing organizations have well-defined input-output relationships for their production operations. Specific product and process specifications determine the resources required to achieve a certain output at each stage of the manufacturing operation. The materials required to produce an item or batch are found in the bill of materials (BOM) file, and labor and overhead requirements are contained in the routing file. The identification of the input-output relationship facilitates the costing process because the labor, material, and overhead resources are clearly identified and can be readily costed.

Professional service and mass service organizations generally do not have the equivalent of a BOM or a routing file for their offerings. Although these organizations may have detailed process specifications and even labor standards for operational control, these are often not tied to cost information. In service factories or service shops where expected labor or materials inputs have been clearly defined or where work measurements exist for key processes, the costing process is greatly simplified.

Service organizations are generally more labor-intensive than manufacturing. While some service organizations have invested a significant amount of resources developing labor performance standards, it is often not feasible or cost-effective to define a precise input-output relationship in a service environment.

Consider the services provided by the branch officials of a retail bank. These employees offer multiple services to customers, such as opening and closing accounts, handling customer inquiries, and processing loan applications. How would you measure the time it should take a bank officer to provide each type of service? How do you incorporate the importance of the interaction with the customer in a work standard? Different customers have different needs. Some customers want the service to be performed quickly and efficiently; others want to share their life experiences or comment on the events of the day. This difference in customer needs and expectations makes it difficult to establish precise measurements for many service activities.

High-contact service activities also have a higher degree of variability than manufacturing operations do. These service providers encounter many different situations that may place varying demands on the organization's resources in terms of space, people, and materials. The resources required to treat a gunshot wound are very different from those required to mend a broken arm, even though both involve a bone fracture. In some service organizations, the specific problem must be identified before the service can be performed. Medical personnel must first diagnose a patient's condition before determining the appropriate treatment.

The high labor content and the variability of customer demands make it difficult to establish clear input-output relationships for many service activities. This situation makes the costing process for service organizations more complex than for a manufacturing organization. Often managers and accountants must learn to think differently. They must break away from the traditional manufacturing costing models to define the input-output relationship in a service environment.

Capacity Utilization

All service organizations have some level of customer involvement that may affect when, where, and how a service will be performed. A service organization is analogous to a just-in-time manufacturer: It must have the right product, at the right place, at the right time. Service companies cannot inventory their time or services and therefore cannot buffer fluctuations in customer demand as a manufacturing organization does. In the short run, their resources are fixed; a significant variation in customer demand will result in an over- or underutilization of company resources.

While service organizations can have a planned level of service or capacity, how this capacity is used is determined in large part by customer demands and needs. Therefore, service costs will always include a portion of unused capacity that is necessary to manage the variability of customer demand.

Manufacturing organizations, on the other hand, have more direct control over their scheduling and production operations. They are not dependent on the end customer to determine when and how the product will be manufactured. They can maximize their production capabilities and minimize costs by managing inventory levels to handle fluctuations in customer demand. In service organizations, unused capacity is lost forever; in manufacturing, it can be used to build inventory, which can be sold at some future date. In manufacturing, the cost of excess capacity is an opportunity for cost improvement; in service organizations, a portion of unused capacity is a necessary cost of doing business.

* * *

Service organizations represent a more complex costing environment than manufacturing organizations do. The cost object is more difficult to define, and the input-output relationships are often not well-established. Nevertheless, the same costing principles that are used in manufacturing organizations can be applied to service companies.

How to Develop Service Costs

The general costing approach described in Chapter 9 is a good starting point to develop service costs. It will help you understand what services need to be costed and why. What will the information be used for? How much precision is required? Service costs have the same basic elements as their manufacturing counterparts: labor, materials, and overhead. Labor and overhead are usually significant cost components. Materials may or may not be significant, depending on the type of service provided. In the food service industry, materials can be a significant cost; in other service industries, such as banks or insurance companies, materials may not be considered as significant.

Although service costs can be divided into labor, materials, and overhead, these categories may not be particularly meaningful to managers in a service organization. Our costing framework summarizes service costs into five major components: service labor, materials and supplies, technology costs, occupancy costs, and other service overhead costs. This classification allows managers to focus on those cost categories that are most significant for their organizations. Figure 11-1 summarizes a six-step costing procedure for service organizations.[4]

Step 1. Identify the Item to Be Costed

This step is the most critical one of the costing process. It defines exactly the service that is to be costed. As in manufacturing, this item is known as the **cost object**. In services, a precise definition of the cost object is required for determining its costs. For example, a hospital may choose to cost its emergency room based on the individual services provided or on an average per patient basis. The choice of the cost object depends on the management information needs and the purposes of the costing exercise.

Step 2. Classify Costs by Major Cost Categories

This step summarizes the available cost information by major cost categories: service labor, materials and supplies, technology costs,

Figure 11-1. *Summary of Service-Costing Process.*

1. Identify the item to be costed.
2. Classify costs by major cost categories.
3. Determine the direct costs.
4. Identify the indirect costs.
5. Assign the indirect costs.
6. Calculate the total service costs.

occupancy costs, and other service overhead costs. For example, the costs of a hospital emergency room could be classified into the following categories:

■ *Service labor* would include the medical and support staff. It could be subdivided into frontline labor (the medical and nursing staff) and support labor (administrative personnel).

■ *Materials and supplies* would consist of the hospital supplies used in the emergency room. Laboratory and other medical tests such as X-rays may be included in this cost category. However, if these costs are significant, they should be identified as a separate cost category.

■ *Technology costs* include the depreciation and maintenance expenses on the equipment used in this area. These costs may be broken down into medical equipment and office equipment.

■ *Occupancy costs* are the costs directly related to the space occupied by the emergency room, such as rent, depreciation, repairs, and maintenance.

■ *Other service overhead costs* would summarize all costs not included in the other four categories. If this category is very large, its significant cost components should be analyzed and included in a separate cost classification.

The cost classification by major category is a way to summarize detailed cost information in a meaningful format. It provides management with a general overview of the service cost structure and highlights which costs will require further analysis.

Step 3. Determine the Direct Costs

Direct costs are all the costs that can be directly identified with the service: labor (the people providing the service), materials, parts, supplies, telephone, and any other cost that can be traced directly to the service provided. In the emergency room, the direct costs are the salaries of the staff, the supplies, and the diagnostic tests performed on the patients. Sometimes it may be possible to identify a direct cost, but it is not economically viable to trace it to a particular service. For example, a hospital may be able to identify the particular medical supplies used for routine treatments such as gauze and cotton swabs. However, it is not cost-effective to trace these to a particular patient or treatment. These types of costs are treated as indirect and are assigned to the cost object in some reasonable manner.

Step 4. Identify the Indirect Costs

Indirect costs are common costs that cannot be directly traced to a particular service, such as occupancy costs, information systems, administrative support, and office management. The manager or cost analyst should identify the indirect costs that will be charged to the particular service or customer. An emergency room receives general administrative support from the hospital staff, such as human resources, accounting, information systems, and legal services. The hospital management must decide which indirect costs will be charged to the emergency room area. Management may choose not to charge an area for its fair share of indirect costs depending on the purpose of the costing exercise and the nature of the indirect cost. Costs that are seen as necessary business expenses, such as the salary of the hospital administrator, may not be assigned to a particular service area.

Step 5. Assign the Indirect Costs

Indirect costs must be assigned to the cost object to obtain the total cost of providing a service. This cost assignment should reflect a causal relationship between the service provided and the demands it places on shared resources. The **allocation base** is the factor that establishes a relationship between the cost of common resources and how these are consumed by the item being costed. The **cost allocation rate** is used to assign these indirect costs. This rate is analogous to the manufacturing overhead rate that is used to assign indirect factory costs to a product. It is calculated by dividing the total cost of the common resources by the allocation base.

Suppose the total occupancy costs for the hospital are $100,000. The hospital has a total area of 10,000 square feet. The total square footage is chosen as the allocation base for occupancy costs. The cost allocation rate would be $10 per square feet ($100,000 ÷ 10,000). If the emergency room uses 1,000 square feet of the space, the indirect costs assigned to the emergency room would be $10,000 ($10 per square foot × 1,000 square feet). The selection of the appropriate allocation base is critical in the assignment of indirect costs. Cost allocation is discussed in more detail in Chapter 12.

Step 6. Calculate the Total Service Costs

The sum of the direct and indirect costs is the total service costs. These costs are summarized by the five major cost categories: labor, materials and supplies, technology, occupancy costs, and other service overhead costs. This classification facilitates the presentation of cost information for management decision-making purposes.

Let us walk through a service-costing example to demonstrate how this costing approach can be applied in practice.

Service-Costing Example

Linda Banks owns Fast Food, Inc., a fast-food franchise outlet. The company operates in two shifts: a day shift and an evening shift. After reviewing the income statement in Figure 11-2 for the three months ending on August 31, Linda is concerned about profitability. She believes that a better understanding of her cost structure per shift would allow her to identify opportunities that will improve the bottom line. She uses the six-step costing process to develop the service costs for each shift.

Step 1. Identify the Item to Be Costed

Linda identifies the cost object as the number of customer orders per shift. She feels that this item establishes an appropriate input-output relationship for her business. The inputs are the cost of the resources as shown in Figure 11-2. The output is the number of customer orders served during each shift. The cost per customer order will allow her to make a meaningful comparison between the two shifts that takes into account the differences in cost and volume.

Step 2. Classify Costs by Major Cost Categories

As the second step in the analysis process, Linda summarizes the operating expenses by major cost categories, as shown in Figure 11-3. As a result of this analysis, she decides to focus on the most significant cost items: service labor, materials, and occupancy costs. She combines technology and other costs with occupancy costs because the small dollar amounts in these categories do not justify a separate classification for these costs. She labels this cost category "occupancy and other costs."

Figure 11-2. *Service-Costing Example, Fast Food, Inc.*

Fast Food, Inc.
Income Statement
For the Three Months Ended August 31, XXXX

	Actual	% Sales
Sales	**$150,000**	100.0
Cost of sales (materials)	67,500	45.0
Gross margin	**82,500**	55.0
Salaries hourly	29,458	19.6
Salaries supervisory	7,200	4.8
Payroll taxes	4,692	3.1
Fringe benefits	2,199	1.5
Insurance	650	0.4
Utilities	9,450	6.3
Telephone	954	0.6
Repairs and maintenance	2,502	1.7
Licenses	900	0.6
Rent	9,000	6.0
Office supplies	100	0.1
Professional services	1,500	1.0
Equipment depreciation	4,500	3.0
Property tax	250	0.2
Security	1,000	0.7
Total expenses	**74,355**	**49.6%**
Net income	**$ 8,145**	**5.4%**

Figure 11-3. *Operating Expenses by Major Cost Category, Fast Food, Inc.*

Cost Category	**Dollar Amount**	**% Total**
Materials	$ 67,500	47.6
Service labor	43,549	30.7
Technology costs	7,002	4.9
Occupancy costs	21,054	14.8
Other service overhead costs	2,750	2.0
Total operating expenses	**$141,855**	**100.0%**

Step 3. Determine the Direct Costs

Linda can clearly identify the total service labor used during each shift. The head count, labor costs per shift, and the number of orders served are shown in Figure 11-4. She has divided labor costs into frontline labor—all employees who are responsible for preparing or serving customer orders—and support labor—the shift supervisor. The employee salaries, the payroll taxes, and fringe benefits are considered direct costs because they can be specifically identified to each shift. As she reviews her cost detail, she finds that all other costs should be classified as indirect.

Step 4. Identify the Indirect Costs

Linda does not have an automated inventory control system or a costed list of the ingredients used to prepare the different menu

Figure 11-4. *Head Count and Labor Costs by Shift, Fast Food, Inc.*

Employees	Day	Evening	Total
Head count			
Customer service	5	3	8
Food preparation	2	1	3
Supervisor	1	1	2
Total employees	8	5	13
Salaries			
Frontline labor	$18,746	$10,712	$29,458
Support labor	3,600	3,600	7,200
Total salaries	$22,346	$14,312	$36,658
Plus payroll taxes and			
fringe benefits @18.8%[a]	4,201	2,690	6,891
Total labor costs	$26,547	$17,002	$43,549
Number of orders			
served per shift	27,000	15,000	42,000

[a]The percentage of payroll taxes and fringe benefits to apply to salaries is calculated based on the data in Figure 11-2 as follows:

Salaries, hourly	$29,458	
Salaries, supervisory	7,200	
Total base salaries	**$36,658**	
Payroll taxes and fringe benefits	$ 6,891	($4,692 + $2,199)
% of base salaries	**18.8%**	($6,891 ÷ $36,658)

items. Materials costs are determined by taking a physical inventory at month-end and calculating the materials usage.[5] Because she has no mechanism for identifying the materials consumed during each shift, these costs are classified as indirect. Occupancy and other costs are also classified as indirect because they are related to the use of building and the administrative support costs that cannot be identified with a particular shift.

Step 5. Assign the Indirect Costs

Materials costs are directly related to the sales per shift. Because she cannot determine the actual materials costs incurred during each shift, Linda decides to use number of orders per shift as the allocation basis for these costs. The cost allocation rate for materials is calculated as follows:

Materials costs per order $= \dfrac{\text{Total material costs}}{\text{Total number of orders}} = \dfrac{\$67,500}{42,000} = \$1.6071$

The total materials costs allocated to each shift would be:

> **Cost per shift** = Cost per order × number of orders
> Day shift   = $1.6071 × 27,000 = $43,392
> Evening shift = $1.6071 × 15,000 = $24,107 (the rounding differ-
>   ence equals $1)

Her other indirect costs are technology costs, occupancy, and other. She combines these costs into one category: occupancy and other costs. Because these costs are fixed, Linda decides to assign these costs based on a 50/50 split. Figure 11-5 shows the assignment of indirect costs to each shift.

Step 6. Calculate the Total Service Costs

Total costs are obtained by adding the direct and indirect costs of each shift. Costs per order are calculated by dividing the total costs per major cost category by the number of orders served during each shift. Figure 11-6 shows the total costs and the cost per order per shift by major cost category. Average costs per order totaled $3.16 for the day shift and $3.77 for the evening shift.
What can Linda do with this information?

Figure 11-5. *Assignment of Indirect Costs, Fast Food, Inc.*

Materials cost	
Total materials costs	$67,500
Total number of orders	42,000
Materials cost per order	**$1.6071**
Materials cost per shift	
Day shift ($1.6071 × 27,000)	$43,392
Evening shift ($1.6071 × 15,000)[a]	$24,108
Occupancy and other costs	
Technology costs	$ 7,002
Occupancy	21,054
Other service overhead costs	2,750
Total occupancy and other costs	$30,806
Occupancy and other costs per shift	**$15,403**
($30,806 × 50%)	

[a]There is a rounding difference of $1 that was added to the cost of this shift.

Figure 11-6. *Cost per Shift, Fast Food, Inc.*

Total costs	Day	Evening	Total	
Service labor	$26,547	$17,002	$ 43,549	See Figure 11-4
Materials cost	43,392	24,108	67,500	See Figure 11-5
Occupancy and other costs	15,403	15,403	30,806	See Figure 11-5
Total costs	$85,342	$56,513	$141,855	
Cost per order				
Service labor	$0.98	$1.13	$1.04	
Materials cost	1.61	1.61	1.61	
Occupancy and other costs	0.57	1.03	0.73	
Total costs	$3.16	$3.77	$3.38	

Since the labor cost per order in the evening shift is significantly higher than the day shift, Linda decides to examine the labor costs more closely. Average labor costs per order totaled $0.98 for the day shift and $1.13 for the evening shift. She is concerned that the evening shift employees are less productive and therefore more costly than the day shift. She establishes a productivity measure for each shift by calculating the average number of orders served per frontline employee. She also decides to calculate the frontline labor costs per order. The results are shown in Figure 11-7.

The day shift employees are slightly more productive than the evening shift (3,857 versus 3,750 orders per employee), but this difference accounts for only $0.03 ($0.82 versus $0.85 per order) of the total labor cost differential of $0.15 per order ($0.98 versus $1.13). She concludes that the volume of orders served in the evening shift is not enough to recover the cost of the supervisor, creating a labor

Figure 11-7. *Frontline Labor Analysis, Fast Food, Inc.*

Number of Employees	Day	Evening	Total
Frontline labor	7	4	11
Support labor	1	1	2
Total employees	8	5	13
Frontline labor costs			
Salaries	$18,746	$10,712	$29,458
Plus payroll taxes and fringe benefits[a]	3,524	2,014	5,538
Total labor costs	**$22,270**	**$12,726**	**$34,996**
Number of orders served per shift	27,000	15,000	42,000
Average labor cost per order[b]	$0.82	$0.85	$0.83
Average orders per employee[c]	3,857	3,750	3,818

[a]Payroll taxes and fringe benefits are calculated at 18.8 percent of base salary. See Figure 11-4.
[b]Average labor cost per order = Total labor costs ÷ number of orders.
[c]Average number of orders per employee = Number of orders ÷ number of employees.

cost differential per order of $0.12 between the day shift and the evening shift.

What are her options? Cost analysis does not provide answers but highlights areas of opportunity. Some hard questions need to be asked. Why is the number of orders served during the evening shift lower than during the day shift? Can more volume be generated for this shift through improved customer service or special promotional programs? Should she eliminate the evening shift supervisor? One option she could consider is to appoint a group leader from the direct labor crew and eliminate the evening shift supervisor. But although this option would lower labor costs, it also entails some financial and operational risks. Does she have a skilled individual during the evening shift who can handle supervisory responsibilities? Will the elimination of the evening shift supervisor require a more direct involvement on her part? Will this change affect quality or customer service? Linda may choose to keep the evening shift supervisor because the lower costs do not compensate for the financial and operational risks involved with this decision.

Linda also wants to examine occupancy and other costs. She feels that her method of cost assignment (50/50 split) may have unfairly penalized the cost of the second shift. She recalculates total service costs by assigning occupancy and other costs based on an average cost of $0.73 per order ($30,806 total occupancy and other costs ÷ 42,000 orders), as shown in Figure 11-8. The average cost per order changes dramatically, increasing from $3.16 to $3.32 in the day shift and decreasing from $3.77 to $3.47 in the evening shift. Which cost assignment method should she use?

The first method, the 50/50 split, assumes that the day shift and the evening shift generate the same level of indirect costs. Under this assignment method, these costs are fixed and can be evenly distributed between the two shifts. Volume, as measured by the number of orders served, again surfaces as an issue. The evening shift consumes the same level of indirect resources as the day shift but processes a little more than half the volume. Therefore, occupancy and other costs per order are almost double that of the day shift.

The second method of cost assignment based on an average cost per order assumes that all orders consume indirect resources at the same rate of $0.73 per order. This method distorts the total and per unit cost of each shift because it assigns a disproportionate amount of fixed costs to the day shift operations. Therefore, when this method is used, the day shift subsidizes the occupancy and other

Figure 11-8. *Costs per Shift, Fast Food, Inc.*

Total costs	Day	Evening	Total	
Service labor	$26,547	$17,002	$ 43,549	See Figure 11-5
Materials cost	43,392	24,108	67,500	See Figure 11-5
Occupancy and				
other costs[a]	19,804	11,002	30,806	
Total costs	$89,743	$52,112	$141,855	
Cost per order[b]				
Service labor	$0.98	$1.13	$1.04	
Materials cost	1.61	1.61	1.61	
Occupancy and				
other costs	0.73	0.73	0.73	
Total costs	$3.32	$3.47	$3.38	

[a]Average cost per order = $30,806 ÷ 42,000 = $0.7335.
Day shift costs   = $0.7335 × 27,000 orders = $19,804.
Evening shift costs   = $0.7335 × 15,000 orders = $11,002.
[b]Rounded to the nearest cent.

costs of the evening shift, resulting in distorted cost information for management decision making.

As the example shows, the cost assignment method can have a significant impact on the calculated total and unit costs of the desired cost object. The cost analyst should choose the method that more accurately reflects the nature of the underlying business processes. In this example, I recommend the 50/50 split method because it clearly reflects the underutilization of resources in the second shift. This cost allocation method flags volume and capacity utilization as key business issues for this organization.

The calculation of the service costs is merely a number-crunching exercise. The real value-added information is provided by the detailed analysis behind the cost calculation and a thorough examination of the business issues it raises. The analysis highlights areas of opportunity that are often buried in an organization's income statement.

Service Costing in a Job Order Environment

Fast-food outlets resemble service factories. They produce large quantities of like products in a continuous manner. Let us apply the service-costing procedure to a different type of service environment, a service job shop.

Juan Rivera owns an auto repair shop that has five employees. Juan has a job order–costing system that tracks the costs of each repair order separately. Juan uses the six-step costing procedures to calculate his cost per customer repair order, as follows:

Step 1. *Identify the item to be costed.* In a service shop, the cost object is usually the customer order or the repair job.

Step 2. *Classify costs by major cost categories.* The major costs of the auto repair shop can be classified into service labor, parts, occupancy costs, and miscellaneous expenses. Juan combines all indirect costs into a category called general overhead.

Step 3. *Determine the direct costs.* The direct costs of a customer order are labor and materials. Service labor is the time the mechanic spends in performing a general inspection of the vehicle and performing the necessary repairs. Materials are the service parts used in the repair process.

Step 4. *Identify the indirect costs.* Occupancy costs, professional services, insurance, and administrative costs are considered indirect costs. They cannot be traced to a particular type of service or customer order.

Step 5. *Assign the indirect costs.* In the auto repair business, labor time determines the total time that the unit will spend in the shop. Juan feels that it is an appropriate basis for assigning indirect costs to an order. A unit that requires significant labor hours also consumes more indirect resources, such as space, utilities, and management attention. Therefore, the indirect costs should be assigned as a function of labor hours.

Step 6. *Calculate the total service costs.* The sum of all direct and indirect costs equals the total service costs of a repair order.

Figure 11-9 shows the cost data for Job 122, an oil and filter change. Based on this data, the cost of Job 122 is $21.60, as shown in Figure 11-10. Suppose Juan billed his customer $29.95 for this service. His net profit for this job would be $8.35 ($29.95 − $21.60), a 27.8 percent profit margin ($8.35 ÷ $29.95). Why is this cost information important for Juan's business?

Juan can use the cost data to identify his most profitable services and types of customers. He can analyze his cost structure in a detailed or summary manner and make the necessary changes in his operations to lower costs. A monthly profit and loss statement will

Figure 11-9. *Basic Cost Data for Job 122, Auto Repair Shop.*

Direct Costs

Frontline labor

Base wage rate per hour (auto technician)	$20
Estimated payroll taxes and fringe benefits	25%
Total labor costs per hour ($20+ [$20 × 0.25])	$25.00
Labor hours required for oil and filter change (20 minutes)	.33 hour

Materials	Unit of Measure	Cost per Unit of Measure
Oil filter	Each	$4.95
Oil	Quart	1.00

Indirect Costs

Estimated general overhead costs per month	$10,000
Total labor hours billed per month (150 hours/month × 5 employees)	750 hours
Cost allocation rate per labor hour ($10,000 ÷ 750 hours)	$13.33

Figure 11-10. *Detailed Cost Calculations for Job 122, Auto Repair Shop.*

Cost Category	Cost
Service labor ($25.00 per hour × .33 hour)	$ 8.25
Materials:	
Oil filter	$ 4.95
Oil (4 quarts @ 1.00 each)	4.00
	$ 8.95
Occupancy and other costs ($13.33 per hour × .33 hour)	4.40
Total costs for Job 122	**$21.60**

not provide Juan with this information. He needs a cost information system that ties the costs to the services that his business provides.

Capacity and Service Organizations

The understanding of capacity and its impact on costs is an important issue for service organizations. Because of the intangible nature of the product and the lack of clear input-output relationships, capacity is difficult to define. Capacity is the upper limit or constraint on the level of service that the business can provide. Practical capacity should measure the maximum service level that can be provided with the current level of resources without compromising quality or customer service.

Because we rarely think of service businesses as being capacity constrained (in contrast to manufacturing facilities), the definition of capacity is often vague. However, historical data can assist a manager in estimating the practical capacity of her organization.

Let us return to the example of Fast Food, Inc. How many orders can Fast Food, Inc. serve per shift? What limits the number of orders that can be served: facilities, people, equipment, suppliers, or some other factor? How can the owner, Linda Banks, increase capacity? Does she have excess capacity?

Linda can identify some possible excess capacity in her evening shift. As shown in Figure 11-7, the day shift employees are serving an additional 107 orders per employee per quarter (3,857 orders versus 3,750 orders). Therefore, the evening shift could probably serve at least 428 more orders per quarter (107 orders × 4 employees) without straining the organization. We do not know how much excess capacity Linda has in her organization since the maximum number of orders that can be served with the current level of resources has not been determined.

Managers in service factories have a clearer notion of capacity than their counterparts in other types of service organizations. In some service factories, industrial engineering techniques have greatly improved employee productivity, scheduling, and capacity utilization. However, capacity utilization is an issue for all service organizations. Excess capacity results in higher costs that may make an organization uncompetitive in the marketplace. A capacity shortfall results in lost sales or missed opportunities. Managers should attempt to quantify the impact of capacity utilization in their costing exercises whenever possible.

Chapter Summary

Service costing has received serious attention from the accounting profession only in recent years. Most cost management literature is focused on manufacturing industries, where the cost-accounting principles were developed and practiced. In the past, the primary focus was on product costing for inventory valuation purposes. This focus has no relevance for service industries, which do not manufacture or inventory a product.

The degree of labor intensity and the extent of customer contact make service industries a complex and challenging environment for costing purposes. Although manufacturing cost techniques can be used in most service organizations, their application must be tailored to meet the needs of service managers. A lump sum of overhead may not be particularly relevant to a telecommunications manager who wants to understand the profitability of long-distance services.

The diversity of service organizations implies that each situation will present unique challenges. Different organizations have different needs for cost information. For some companies, a monthly income statement is adequate to manage the business on a regular basis. Other organizations may require detailed service costs, which are integrated into their performance measurement system. As opposed to product costs, which are used to value inventory, service costs are calculated with the sole purpose of assisting management decision making. Therefore, service costs should reflect the nature of the underlying processes and highlight areas for cost improvement or business opportunities.

Notes

1. An on-line search under the subject of cost accounting was performed in the Baker Library at Harvard University and the Green Library at Stanford University. This search produced some references of cost-accounting practices in specific service industries, such as banks, hospitality, railroads, universities and colleges, health care, and hospitals. However, there was no general reference on costing practices in a service environment. Moreover, a subject search of the Harvard Business School Publishing Division found 91 case studies under the topic of cost accounting. Of these case studies, only 19 percent (17 cases) related to service industries, and only 13 percent (12 cases) specifically addressed service costing. Of these 12 cases, 9 were authored or coauthored by Robert Kaplan of Harvard University. Clearly this is an area where more research is necessary (and would be welcome by industry practitioners).
2. See William J. Stevenson, *Production/Operations Management* (Homewood, Ill.: Richard D. Irwin, 1990), pp. 20–22.
3. Ibid.; also see Roger W. Schmenner, *Service Operations Management* (Englewood Cliffs, N.J.: Prentice Hall, 1995), pp. 7–9.
4. Very few cost-accounting textbooks discuss in detail how to cost a service. See Charles T. Horngren, George Foster, and Srikant M. Datar, *Cost*

Accounting: A Managerial Emphasis (Englewood Cliffs, N.J.: Prentice Hall, 1997), pp. 96–97, for a discussion of job costing in service organizations. This approach can be applied to any service-costing situation once the cost object has been properly identified.

5. This method of inventory accounting is called the periodic inventory method. In this method, the cost of goods sold is calculated by the following formula: Beginning inventory + purchases − ending inventory = cost of goods sold. Ending inventory levels are determined by a physical inventory count at month-end. This method is in contrast to the perpetual inventory method that records each inventory transaction as it is received or sold. The periodic inventory method is traditionally used by companies that sell low-value, high-volume items that are too difficult and expensive to track individually. However, although this method is less expensive to administer, it provides little information on the potential sources of scrap, waste, or theft, which may be draining the organization.

Chapter 12

Cost Allocations

C ost allocations are the subject of endless discussions in many organizations. Managers often view them as arbitrary, unfair, and excessive in relation to the services received. At times, the cost allocations are revised so that a more acceptable figure can be presented to the next level of management. Previous chapters have discussed how to allocate indirect costs to a product or service based on resource consumption or cause-effect. Now we examine the cost allocation topic in more depth, looking at the purpose, the process, and the allocation bases that are commonly used to distribute costs.

A **cost allocation** is the process of identifying and tracing indirect or common costs to a **cost object**, a product, service, activity, or segment of the organization for which a separate cost measurement is desired. The **allocation base** provides a mechanism to link a cost or group of common costs with the cost object. This cost or group of common costs is known as a **cost pool**. A cost pool can be an individual cost category (telephone expense, electricity costs), a department (information systems, quality control), a work center (assembly), or a group of common costs that are added together for allocation purposes (administration expenses).

Why Allocate?

Companies generally allocate costs for specific reasons. For example:[1]

- *To make decisions regarding the allocation of resources.* Costs provide an estimated measure of the resources that the organization uses in providing a product or service. By understanding their costs, managers can make trade-off decisions to use their resources more effectively. Should a facility be shut down or relocated? Should legal services be decentralized? These are some examples of decisions for which cost allocations may be used.

- *To provide motivation to managers and employees.* Management may use cost allocations to encourage (or discourage) specific behaviors. The following example illustrates this point. One of my clients had a problem with absenteeism at company training seminars. To discourage this behavior, the human resources department started charging department managers $500 per employee for each unjustified absence. While absenteeism did drop significantly, this policy had an unexpected consequence. Managers would have their employees sign the attendance sheet at the start of the training session and then pull them out as needed during the day. Cost allocations for motivational purposes can have unintended consequences that should be evaluated prior to their implementation.

- *To satisfy legal and management reporting requirements.* Generally accepted accounting principles (GAAP) require that inventories be recorded at full manufacturing cost. Indirect manufacturing costs must be allocated among the items produced to comply with this requirement. Some companies also allocate their centralized support services (e.g., legal, human resources, information systems, R&D) to the operating divisions or the strategic business units for legal and tax reporting purposes. Sometimes the cost allocation is purely for internal reporting purposes to ensure that the operating divisions can fund the cost of centralized support services.

- *To cost products or services for contract purposes.* Contracts are often negotiated using a cost-sharing, cost-reimbursement, or cost-plus formula. Cost allocations allow a company to recover the direct cost of the contract and a fair portion of the indirect costs that are necessary to manage the business. Defense contracts are an example of an area where costs are used to establish a fair price for the product.

Cost allocation practices can have serious consequences for an organization. In 1990 and 1991, federal investigators accused Stanford University of wrongly billing the federal government an estimated $200 million in the 1980s under various federal research contracts.[2] At issue was the indirect-cost recovery rule whereby a university can charge the government for the portion of its overhead costs that supports government research, such as utilities, maintenance and equipment depreciation. Although the university was exonerated of any wrongdoing, Stanford spent more than $25 million on outside accounting firms and consultants to provide independent verification of its work and to assist it in responding to the government claims.[3]

The purpose of the cost allocation will determine how the cost will be allocated and the level of precision required. For example, allocations that affect cost reimbursements and government reporting may require a higher degree of accuracy and documentation than those that are used to influence employee behavior. The finance department should periodically review cost allocations with management to ensure that these allocations are currently serving a business need. The annual planning cycle is an excellent time to perform this review. In my experience, organizations establish allocation procedures and use these procedures year after year without questioning whether there is still a valid business reason to perform this allocation. Allocations should serve a purpose. Management should eliminate allocations with no identifiable purpose within the organization.

The Cost Allocation Process

There are six principal steps in the cost allocation process (they are outlined in Figure 12-1).

Step 1. *Determine the cost object.* The cost object is the item for which the costs will be calculated. A cost object can be almost anything in the organization: a product, a service, an activity, a project,

Figure 12-1. *Cost Allocation Process.*

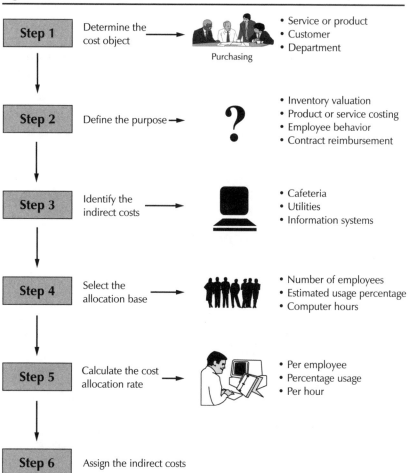

or a department. In Figure 12-1, the cost object is the company's purchasing department.

Step 2. *Define the purpose.* Management should define the purpose of the cost allocation before choosing a particular assignment method. The purpose of the cost allocation may determine the complexity and the level of precision required of the allocation methodology. In the example in Figure 12-1, the purpose of the cost allocation is to provide more cost control over shared resources by assigning each user department its fair share of the costs.

Step 3. *Identify the indirect costs.* In this step, the cost analyst or manager identifies the common costs that are related but cannot be directly traced to the cost object. Indirect costs usually include facilities maintenance, depreciation, utilities, information systems, administration expense, and customer service, among many others. In our example, there are three indirect cost pools: cafeteria, utilities, and information systems.

Step 4. *Select the allocation base.* Once the indirect costs have been identified, the cost analyst or manager must select an allocation base to link the costs to the cost object. These costs should be linked on some reasonable basis. In Figure 12-1, the allocation bases for each pool of indirect costs are the number of employees (cafeteria), the estimated usage percentage (utilities), and the number of computer hours (information systems).

Step 5. *Calculate the cost allocation rate.* The cost allocation rate determines how the costs will be assigned to the cost object. It can be expressed in terms of a percentage (e.g., as a percentage of sales or percentage of usage) or as an absolute dollar value (cost per machine hours, cost per order). In Figure 12-1, the cost allocation rate is expressed in terms of a cost per employee, an estimated usage percentage, and a cost per computer hour.

Let us calculate the cost allocation rate for an information systems department. The information systems manager evaluates two alternatives: (1) allocate costs based on a fixed percentage for each user department or (2) set a fixed billing rate for the actual computer hours used each period. This usage percentage could be calculated based on historical data (actual computer hours used by department ÷ total available computer hours), or it could be an estimated figure based on experience that is negotiated with the users during the annual budgeting cycle. In this example, the purchasing manager and the information systems manager agree that the annual usage will be approximately 10 percent of total available computer time.

Another alternative is to calculate a fixed cost rate that will allow him to recuperate his costs at year-end. This cost rate will be used to bill out the costs of his department based on the actual usage. Suppose that the department incurs annual operating costs of $400,000. It operates 24 hours per day, 5 days a week, 52 weeks per year. The fixed cost rate would be $64 per computer hour, calculated as follows:

$$\text{Cost per computer hour} = \frac{\text{Total costs}}{\text{Total available computer hours}}$$

$$= \frac{\$400,000}{(24 \text{ hours} \times 5 \text{ days} \times 52 \text{ weeks})}$$

$$= \$64 \text{ per hour}$$

This rate would be used to assign the costs of the information systems department to the purchasing department as explained in Step 6.

Step 6. *Assign the indirect costs.* The indirect costs are assigned to the cost object by multiplying the cost allocation rate by the amount of the resource consumed. If we use the estimated usage percentage, the purchasing department would be assigned $40,000 of information systems costs annually (10% × $400,000). If we use the fixed cost rate and assume an annual usage of 1,000 computer hours, the department would be assigned $64,000 of the costs of the information systems department for that year (1,000 hours × $64/hour).

You can now see the importance of defining the purpose of the cost allocation before selecting a particular allocation methodology. The manager or cost analyst should choose the method that best achieves the stated purpose of the cost allocation. In the example, both allocation methods are acceptable. However, in Step 2, we defined improved cost control as the primary purpose of the cost allocation. A cost allocation based on an estimated usage percentage would not give the purchasing manager enough information about the consumption of the information systems resources to be able to control this cost effectively. An allocation method based on actual usage would be better suited for these purposes.

Selecting the Allocation Base

Most cost allocation controversies that I have witnessed center on how the cost is allocated. Managers do not question the need to allocate the cost. However, they do take issue with the manner in which the allocation is performed. Many times, the allocation base is the focal point of these discussions. The following criteria can assist you in choosing the proper allocation base.[4]

Cause-and-Effect Relationship

The cause-and-effect criterion establishes a logical relationship between the cost object and the incurrence of the indirect costs. Costs are allocated based on the demand for services placed by the user departments. For example, a facilities manager may estimate the kilowatt-hours per area for each user department and use this figure to allocate electricity costs. There is a direct relationship between the resource consumption (electricity) and the costs charged to the cost object.

The cause-and-effect criterion also gives managers a tangible basis to control indirect costs, which could result in overall savings for the organization. For example, suppose an information systems department bills its users based on computer time and provides its users with detailed information on computer usage and cost. A manager could use this information to explore ways to reduce her department's demand for computer time (e.g., logging off the system when not in use, reviewing how jobs are scheduled and run) and thereby releasing information systems resources for the company.

The use of the cause-and-effect relationship often relates the cost allocation to a physical measure that can be monitored and controlled. It is intuitive to operating managers and therefore minimizes hours of fruitless discussions on this subject.

Benefits Received

Costs may be allocated based on the perceived benefits obtained by the user groups. This criterion relates a physical measure of size or volume, such as the number of employees, to the benefits received from the use of shared resources. There is no attempt to associate common costs with the actual demand for services. Consider an organization that embarks on a company-wide training program. The cost of the program is assigned to each division based on head count. The rationale behind this approach is that divisions with more employees receive more benefits from the training program and therefore should absorb a greater portion of its costs.

Fairness

Costs may be assigned based on equity or fairness. The government often uses this criterion in determining indirect costs that are chargeable to government contracts. Fairness is difficult to define; therefore, I advise avoiding the use of this criterion to minimize cost allocation controversies.

Ability to Bear

Costs are allocated based on the cost object's ability to bear these costs. It assumes that a more profitable product, service, or business unit can absorb more costs. Consider the plant manager who is submitting his product costs to corporate headquarters. Product X is a low-volume product that consumes a high level of resources and is marginally profitable. Product Y is a high-volume product that is very profitable. The use of a cause-effect criterion would result in Product X showing a loss, which could have undesirable consequences for the plant (e.g., the product gets transferred to another manufacturing facility). Therefore, the plant manager may opt to assign indirect costs to Products X and Y based on the ability-to-bear criterion. This allocation base results in an "acceptable" level of profit for both products.

The ability-to-bear principle may subsidize poor performers such as Product X and should be used with caution. I discourage its use in product or service costing situations if management desires a realistic cost assessment. At a more macrolevel, such as distributing the cost of centralized functions worldwide, the use of this criterion may be quite appropriate.

* * *

The criteria used to select an allocation base should be consistent with the purpose of the cost allocation and the level of accuracy desired by the management team. Common cost pools and suggested allocation bases are shown in Figure 12-2.

A Practical Example of Cost Allocation

Gadgets Electronics, Inc. is a producer of electronic computer games for children. The finance department currently assigns the costs of

Figure 12-2. *Common Cost Pools and Allocation Bases.*

Cost Pool	Possible Allocation Bases
• General production overhead	• Labor hours, machine hours, units
• Electricity	• Kilowatt-hours
• Water	• Cubic meters
• Building costs	• Square footage
• Quality control or incoming inspection	• Test hours, number of tests
• Customer service or tele-marketing	• Number of clients assisted, number of calls handled
• Maintenance	• Specific charges per work order
• Information systems	• Computer time, number of jobs scheduled, number of service requests
• Shipping or receiving	• Number of orders received or shipped, number of items handled
• Accounting	• Number of transactions processed
• Human resources	• Head count
• Purchasing	• Number of purchase orders, number of line items
• Internal audit	• Audit hours
• Cafeteria	• Head count

the quality control (QC) area based on an estimated usage percentage provided by the department manager each month. This percentage is an estimate of the inspection time consumed in each production area. The production managers have complained to the controller that the allocation of QC costs is too high and out of their control. How can this allocation process align more closely to the operations?

Step 1. *Determine the cost object.* In this example, the cost objects are the areas that require services from the QC department: the insertion and final assembly work centers.

Step 2. *Define the purpose.* The purpose of the cost allocation is to provide more cost control over the QC resources by assigning each user its fair share of the operating costs of the department based on its demand for services.

Step 3. *Identify the indirect costs.* In this example, only the costs of the QC department will be allocated. In practice, there are many indirect costs, such as facilities, training, and others that may be assigned to user departments, products, services, or customers.

Step 4. *Select the allocation base.* The purpose of the cost allocation requires the selection of an allocation base that establishes a cause-effect relationship between the QC costs and the demand for services placed by the users. At Gadgets Electronics the QC department performs tests on the output of the insertion and final assembly areas to ensure that these products meet the company's quality specifications. Therefore, one possible allocation base is the total number of tests performed in each area for a specific time period. Another could be the total amount of test hours required by each area. Which allocation base is more appropriate?

Let us suppose that Gadgets Electronics manufactures two products, A and B. In discussions with the QC manager, the cost analyst determines that each product goes through a series of standard tests in each area, one test per unit produced. Each test, however, requires a different number of test hours depending on the product (see Figure 12-3). An allocation based on the number of tests assumes that all tests consume an equal amount of QC resources. However, the test times shown in Figure 12-3 demonstrate that each test consumes a different amount of QC resources depending on the product. Therefore, test hours is a more appropriate allocation base for these costs because they are directly related to how this resource is consumed in each production area.

Step 5. *Calculate the cost allocation rate.* Figure 12-3 shows the calculation of the cost allocation rate per test hour. Using the production volume for the prior three months, the cost analyst calculates the total test time required per product in each area (time per test × number of units) and determines the cost per test hour ($70,000 ÷ 1,150 hours = $60.87 per test hour).

Step 6. *Assign the indirect costs.* The cost per test hour is used to assign QC costs to the user departments, as shown in Figure 12-4. Moreover, the cost analyst can also identify the QC costs to each individual product. Although product cost accuracy was not the primary purpose of the cost allocation, in this situation, it is an added benefit of changing the allocation methodology.

How can a production manager use this information to reduce costs? The allocation method establishes a relationship between the

Figure 12-3. *Calculation of Cost per Quality Control Test Hour.*

Units Produced	[1]	Product A 7,500		Product B 5,000		
Department	Time/ Test	Total Time	Time/ Test	Total Time	Total
	[2]	[1] × [2]				
Insertion						
Test 1	0.01	75	0.06	300	375
Test 2	0.02	150	0.03	150	300
Subtotal time	0.03	225	0.09	450	675
Assembly						
Test 3	0.05	375	0.02	100	475
Total time	0.08	600	0.11	550 [3]	1,150
Department costs					[4]	$70,000
Cost per test hour				[4] ÷ [3]	$ 60.87

Figure 12-4. *Assignment of Quality Control Costs.*

Cost per test hour	[1]	$61				
	Product A Total Time	Dollars	Product B Total Time	Dollars	Total Dollars
	[2]	[1] × [2]			
Insertion	225	$13,696	450	$27,391	$41,087
Assembly	375	22,826	100	6,087	28,913
Total	600	$36,522	550	$33,478	$70,000
Units produced		7,500		5,000	
QC cost per unit		$ 4.87		$ 6.70	

usage of the shared resource and its corresponding costs. It provides detailed cost information that can highlight improvement opportunities for both the users and the service provider. In the example, a manufacturing manager can use the cost data to raise some interesting questions. Are all tests necessary to ensure that the product conforms to engineering specifications? Are any tests redundant? Can testing procedures be changed to reduce the amount of time required by each product? The cost allocation method has achieved the purpose stated in Step 2: to provide more cost control over QC resources that are shared among various user areas.

Allocation of Support Department Costs

Support departments provide services to operating departments such as production, telemarketing, or regional offices. An **operating department** is where the production occurs or the service is provided. Traditional allocation methods assign the cost of support departments to operating departments before developing overhead or cost allocation rates for these areas. There are three basic methods for allocating support department costs: the direct method, the step-down method, and the reciprocal method.

The **direct method** allocates the cost of each service directly to the operating departments. There are no intermediate allocations to other support departments that may also receive services. Figure 12-5 shows an example of the direct method. In this example, the company is a distribution center that has two support departments, facilities and the cafeteria, and two operating departments, order processing and the warehouse. Management assigns the cafeteria costs based on head count and the facilities costs based on square footage. Although the cafeteria and facilities departments also provide services to each other, these reciprocal services are ignored for cost allocation purposes. The costs of the support departments are charged directly to the operating departments.

The direct method is straightforward and simple. It is appropriate when management wishes to assign support department costs with minimal complexity and is not concerned with linking the support department costs to the demand for services. The direct method does not reflect the actual resource consumption by the user departments because services to other support departments are ignored for allocation purposes. Therefore, it provides management with lim-

Figure 12-5. *The Direct Method.*

	Support Departments		Operating Departments	
	Facilities	**Cafeteria**	**Order Processing**	**Warehouse**
Department costs	$50,000	$25,000	$30,000	$40,000
Square footage	21,000	2,000	4,000	15,000
Head count	6	4	20	15
Cost allocations				
Facilities[a]	($50,000)	—	$10,526	$39,474
Cafeteria[b]	—	($25,000)	14,286	10,714
Total allocated costs	$ —	$ —	$24,812	$50,188

[a]Order processing = [4,000 ÷ (15,000 + 4,000)] × $50,000 = $10,526.
  Warehouse   = [15,000 ÷ (15,000 + 4,000)] × $50,000 = $39,474.

[b]Order processing = [20 ÷ (20 + 15)] × $25,000 = $14,286.
  Warehouse   = [15 ÷ (20 + 15)] × $25,000 = $10,714.

ited information to identify process improvements and cost reduction opportunities.

The **step-down method** considers the services performed by one support department for another. This method requires a hierarchy of allocation levels; once a support department's costs have been allocated, it cannot receive any additional charges from other support departments. The method begins with the department that renders services to the largest number of users and continues in a step-down fashion, ending with the departments that provide the least amount of services. Another alternative is to start the sequence with the department that has the highest costs and end with the department that has the lowest costs.

Figure 12-6 shows the results of the method using the data provided in the prior example. The step-down sequence starts with the facilities department because it has the highest cost and services the largest number of users. Because the method considers intermediate services, it is a more accurate representation of the demands placed by the user departments.

The **reciprocal method** takes into account mutual services rendered among support departments. It allows the incorporation of in-

Figure 12-6. *Step-Down Method.*

	Support Departments		Operating Departments	
	Facilities	**Cafeteria**	**Order Processing**	**Warehouse**
Department costs	$ 50,000	$25,000	$30,000	$40,000
Square footage	21,000	2,000	4,000	15,000
Head count	6	4	20	15
Cost allocations				
Facilities[a]	$(50,000)	$ 4,762	$ 9,524	$35,714
Cafeteria[b]	—	(29,762)	17,007	12,755
Total allocated costs	$ —	$ —	$26,531	$48,469

[a]Cafeteria   = 2,000/21,000 × $50,000 = $4,762.
Order processing = 4,000/21,000 × $50,000 = $9,524.
Warehouse   = 15,000/21,000 × $50,000 = $35,714.

[b]Order processing = 20/(20 + 15) × $29,762 = $17,007.
Warehouse   = 15/(20 + 15) × $29,762 = $12,755.

terdepartmental services into the cost allocation model. The method requires the use of simultaneous algebraic equations and can be quite complex. There are two types of complexities: the mathematical and the modeling. The mathematical complexity involves the difficulty in performing the calculations of the model. A computer can typically handle this complexity. The modeling complexity, however, involves the understanding of the simultaneous equations and their meanings by someone in the organization. Managers must decide in choosing the reciprocal method whether the added complexity of the reciprocal method is compensated by the value of the information obtained from this process. If not, a simpler method, such as the direct or step-down method, should be chosen. In my experience, the reciprocal method is not commonly used.[5]

Practical Considerations in Cost Allocation

There are several points to consider when establishing the cost allocations for your company:

- What is the purpose of allocating costs in the organization? Is the current allocation scheme fulfilling this purpose? If not, why?
- Are cost allocations arbitrary or tied to usage? Are users complaining that their cost allocations are unfair or inaccurate?
- Are cost allocations motivating the desired behavior in your organization? Do they support the organization's strategic objectives?
- Do users understand how costs are allocated to their departments, products, or services?
- Are the users receiving information that details the charges allocated to their areas? Can they act on this information to lower costs?

These questions will determine if your cost allocation system is working or if a reevaluation is in order. At a minimum, you should review your cost allocation system (what is allocated and how it is allocated) annually.

Trends in Cost Allocation Practices

One of the major trends in cost allocation practices is an increase in the percentage of indirect costs that can be classified as direct cost. Advances in computer technology have allowed companies to trace costs more precisely to their cost objects. For example, companies can install usage meters to measure electricity or water consumption in production and administration areas. Photocopiers are also equipped with usage meters that trace usage directly to individual employees, departments, or jobs.

A second trend is that the continuous improvement and reengineering movement have encouraged accountants to reconsider how they are allocating costs. Managers and their accountants are questioning the how and why of cost allocations. The emphasis is on providing value-added information and the simplification of accounting practices.

Finally, the rise of activity-based accounting, discussed in Chapter 14, has significantly influenced cost allocation practices. Companies are creating more indirect cost pools and using a diverse set of allocation bases, as shown in Figure 12-2. For example, a former client had a bottling facility with six production lines. Each production line had different machinery, required different crew sizes, and could run only certain products. In the past, the overhead costs for all lines were charged to all products. When we redesigned the cost system, we identified the labor and overhead associated with each line and assigned these costs only to products that were manufactured on that line. Therefore, the product cost was a more accurate reflection of the resources consumed in the manufacturing process.

Chapter Summary

Cost allocations should be simple and understandable to the users of financial information. The purpose of the allocation should be clear, and the allocation process should be consistent with its stated purpose. Moreover, the key managers in the organization should agree on the allocation model and mechanics. This consensus-building process is important. If managers understand and agree on the allocation methodology, they can focus on the business issues rather than argue about how the numbers were calculated. Cost allocations can have a significant impact on organizational behavior. Companies should ensure that the cost allocation system is consistent with the strategic direction of the organization and that it motivates the appropriate employee behavior in support of these objectives.

Notes

1. See Charles T. Horngren, George Foster, and Srikant M. Datar, *Cost Accounting: A Managerial Emphasis* (Upper Saddle River, N.J.: Prentice Hall, 1997), pp. 473–474, and Harold Bierman, Jr., Thomas R. Dyckman, and Ronald W. Hilton, *Cost Accounting: Concepts and Managerial Applications* (Boston: PWS-Kent Publishing Company, 1990), pp. 502–503.
2. Rich Jaroslovsky, "Called to Account," *Stanford Magazine* (June 1991): 18–29.
3. See Gerhard Casper, "Statement of the Resolution of Outstanding Disputes Between Stanford and the Government on Indirect Cost Issues," October 18, 1994, available on the Stanford Web Site, www.stanford.edu.
4. See Horngren, Foster, and Datar, *Cost Accounting*, pp. 475–477, and Jae K. Shim and Joel G. Siegel, *Modern Cost Management and Analysis* (Hauppauge, N.Y.: Barron's Educational Series, 1991), pp. 68–69.
5. For a good overview of this method, see Horngren, Foster, and Datar, *Cost Accounting*, pp. 486–489.

Chapter 13

Standard Cost and Variance Analysis

*"Tonight we will attempt to answer three
metaphysical questions: 1. How did the universe come to be?
2. What is the meaning of life? and 3. What the hell are standard costs all about?"*

S tandard costs are widely used by manufacturing organizations. In a survey of management accounting practices conducted in the early 1990s, 67 percent of the respondents used standard cost systems.[1] Moreover, 87 percent of the respondents employed the same cost system for internal and external reporting.[2]

This chapter examines standard cost systems in a real-world setting. It covers the advantages and disadvantages of standard cost systems, explains the standard-setting process, and shows how to perform variance analysis. The discussion focuses on manufacturing entities, the primary users of standard cost systems. Nevertheless, it also contains a section on standard costs in the service sector that explains how service organizations can use these costs.

What Are Standard Costs?

Standard costs are predetermined costs that are usually expressed on a per unit basis.[3] They constitute a carefully formulated estimate of what future costs should be, based on a desired level of productivity and process efficiency, and a set of assumptions about the operating environment. The set of factors that can affect standard costs was discussed in Chapter 10 (see Figures 10-5 and 10-6).

Standard costs generally consist of three major elements: labor, materials, and overhead. How to calculate each cost element and perform a cost rollup was discussed in Chapter 10. These procedures do not change under a standard cost system. However, in a standard cost system, the management team establishes the standards of performance up-front, such as the amount of labor hours required, the expected materials usage, the process yield, and normal scrap levels. These physical standards are priced and then added together to calculate the standard cost of the product or service. Once the standard cost has been established, it is typically not changed until the next standard-setting cycle.

Standard Costs as a Management Control System

Management control is the process by which managers influence other members of the organization to implement the organizational strategies. Figure 13-1 depicts the functions of a typical management control system.[4] The organization makes plans, implements these plans, and then has a mechanism to monitor the actual results against the plan. A standard cost system is part of the management control process. Other management control systems are budgets, performance evaluations, and quality control. A control system operates through a repetition of five sequential steps:[5]

Step 1. *Establish standards of performance.* Standards of performance apply to many aspects of the organization, such as cost, quality, and customer service. Cost standards typically incorporate more than one standard since they reflect expected levels of manufacturing performance, such as process yields, product quality, and overhead spending levels.

Step 2. *Measure actual performance.* The organization measures the actual results of the process. Manual or automated data collection systems are required to gather information about the process. In a standard cost system, the information collected usually includes labor hours, machine hours, and materials usage. This information is generally collected on the production floor.

Step 3. *Analyze performance and compare it with the standards.* Once the actual results have been measured, these are compared against the standard to identify significant deviations in the expected performance. A **standard cost variance** is the difference between the actual cost and the standard cost of a product or service. Managers and their accountants identify and analyze variances on a regular basis. This process is called **variance analysis**. Variances often signal problems that may require investigation and possible action.

Step 4. *Construct and implement an action plan.* This step is a critical aspect of any management control system. In a standard cost system, the variance analysis will highlight potential problem areas. Then management must identify the source of the problem and develop plans to correct or improve the situation. The effectiveness of a standard cost system depends on management's ability to act on the information provided.

Step 5. *Review and revise standards.* Modern organizations are in a constant state of change. This dynamic business environment requires that cost standards be updated periodically to reflect these changes. Typically cost standards are updated at least once a year during the standard-setting process. However, if the variances are significant, the cost standards should be revised during interim periods.

Advantages and Disadvantages of Standard Costs

Standard costs have multiple uses. They provide a mechanism to *control costs* by monitoring actual versus planned results. They are a basis for isolating unanticipated product costs at various points in

Figure 13-1. *The Management Control System.*

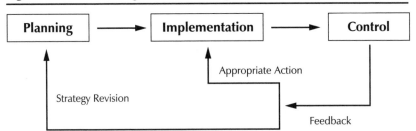

Source: Adapted from Accounting Texts and Cases (8th edition), Robert N. Anthony and James S. Reece, McGraw-Hill Companies, 1989. Used with permission.

the manufacturing process and highlighting areas that require attention.

Standard costs are also used to *establish budgets*. Physical standards of labor and materials assist the organization in planning the materials and capacity requirements of the firm. They are used to develop budgeted unit costs that later become the standard costs for the next fiscal year.

Standard costs can provide a simple means to *value inventory*. Once standard costs are established, the total inventory value can be easily calculated by multiplying the units in inventory at the end of an accounting period by their respective standard costs. Inventory valuation using standard costs is not accepted by generally accepted accounting principles (GAAP). Companies that use standard cost systems must adjust their inventory at reasonable intervals using one of the recognized valuation methods.[6]

Another use of standard costs is the determination of product *profitability*. By comparing the expected selling price to the standard cost, you can understand the product's contribution to the bottom line. This information can assist managers in deciding their product mix and directing sales and marketing strategies.

Standard costs are used to *motivate employees*. They provide an incentive to achieve a tangible goal. This use of standard cost may not be as prevalent as in the past. Manufacturing managers have physical standards that they use to control and monitor performance on the floor. The standard cost system often provides information that is too late and too summarized to be useful to production personnel.

Finally, standard costs are said to *reduce the paperwork* involved in recording inventory transactions. This statement is less true today than it was 20 or 25 years ago. Current inventory management systems can record inventory transactions at actual cost with no incremental paperwork or record-keeping. However, standard costs provide more direct traceability between the physical movement of inventory and the values reported in the general ledger. For example, suppose a cost analyst wanted to verify the cost of sales figure reported in the monthly income statement. He could multiply the standard cost per unit times the number of units sold to obtain the standard cost of sales for the period. Under an actual cost system, he would have to obtain the cost of each inventory transaction at the time it was recorded in the general ledger and then sum all these transactions to calculate the cost of sales. A standard cost system makes it easier to reconcile and report inventory flows because the cost does not vary from period to period.

Standard cost systems have three major drawbacks. One is the lack of flexibility. In most organizations, standard costs are prepared once a year.[7] Once set, they are rarely changed. This accounting practice is in direct conflict with current management thinking that emphasizes flexible processes and adaptability to the environment.

The second major drawback is the *complexity* of standard cost systems. Generally these systems are not user friendly. They are designed by accountants and for accountants without considering the needs of manufacturing personnel. Moreover, variance analysis often adds a layer of complexity to the record-keeping process that makes it difficult to understand and analyze cost behavior. Accountants spend a substantial amount of time and effort analyzing cost variances instead of helping line managers identify problems and opportunities in a more timely manner.

The third drawback is that *standard costs do not necessarily reflect the actual costs incurred.* If cost variances are significant, the actual cost may be higher or lower than the standard. Cost variances, however, are commonly reported as an aggregate number and are rarely used to calculate the actual manufacturing cost per unit on a regular basis. Standard costs, which management uses as the basis of many business decisions during the year, may or may not reflect the actual manufacturing costs of the product.

Standard cost systems can be a valuable tool if they are properly designed and administered by the management team in coordination with the finance department. It is particularly appropriate for organizations that operate in a stable environment and have not implemented sophisticated computer applications to help run the business. Management control should take place on the production floor or on the service frontline, not in the finance department. Cost analysts should spend less time analyzing cost variances and more time helping managers understand their cost structure and how their decisions affect product or service costs.

The Standard-Setting Process

Standard setting usually occurs once a year during the budget preparation process. Accountants generally coordinate the process and are responsible for issuing the guidelines, setting due dates, assigning responsibilities, and communicating management expectations. Figure 13-2 summarizes the steps in setting standards and who is responsible for each step. The steps are in sequential order, although some may be done in parallel with others. Some areas have joint responsibility for a task—for example, the review of the bill of materials and the routing file. This joint responsibility encourages consensus building among areas and ensures the accuracy of the information provided. In some companies that I have visited, the engineering group reviews the labor standards and the bill of materials, with little input from production personnel. This process results in labor standards that are perceived as too tight by the production employees and bills of materials that do not accurately reflect what is happening on the production floor.

Once the responsible parties have submitted all the information, the cost analyst prices the physical standards and performs the cost rollup. She then reviews the information for reasonableness and highlights inconsistencies, problems, or opportunities to management. The mechanics of this calculation were discussed in detail in Chapter 10.

How to Set Standards

Physical standards of performance are the basis of standard costs. Management defines the specifications for the quantities of labor, material, and other services that should be consumed in the manufacture of a product or the delivery of a service. These physical standards are priced to obtain the standard cost.

Figure 13-2. *The Standard-Setting Process.*

Task	Responsibility
1. Issue calendar, management guidelines, key assumptions, and identify tasks and responsibilities	Accounting
2. Determine new product transfers and process or product design changes	Engineering
3. Review and update bill of materials structures	Engineering/production
4. Review and update labor standards and routing file	Engineering/production
5. Obtain sales or production forecasts	Production planning
6. Issue salary guidelines	Human resources
7. Review historical cost data, pending contract negotiations, expected cost increases	Purchasing/materials management/ accounting
8. Set raw materials standards	Purchasing/materials management
9. Budget overhead spending levels	Production and support departments
10. Calculate overhead rates	Accounting
11. Perform cost rollup	Accounting
12. Review and analyze costs	All
13. Finalize cost standards	Accounting/all

Materials Quantity Standards

Material quantity standards are based on the standard bill of materials (BOM), which is developed from the product specifications. These standards identify the type of material required and the amount that should be used to manufacture the product. There are three methods that can be used to set materials quantity standards:[8]

■ *Engineering studies.* These studies identify the best type of material for the purpose and the proper quantity to use. They focus on finding those materials that will provide the best combination of quantity, production methods, quality, functionality, and cost. Many companies rely on engineering studies to set their materials quantity standards.

- *Analysis of past experience.* This method considers the materials consumption patterns for the same or similar products in prior periods. The standards are based on historical data that may include an undetermined amount of waste and excess usage. This shortcoming may be minimized by an arbitrary reduction in the quantity of materials allowed to compensate for known excess usage. In contrast to the use of engineering studies, this method does not focus on finding the best materials available that meet manufacturing criteria. However, it is a less costly method and may be quite satisfactory depending on the company's business needs.

- *Test runs under controlled conditions.* In this method, standards are defined by running tests under conditions that can be standardized and controlled. It avoids one of the principal drawbacks of the past experience method in that external causes of variations can be isolated and eliminated during the test runs.

The physical quantity standards are converted to cost standards by multiplying the standard quantity by the standard materials price per unit. Materials price standards should represent the expected cost of materials for the time period covered by the standard-setting cycle.

Labor Standards

Labor standards have been used extensively to improve productivity and reduce costs. These standards are established by determining the time required to complete an operation when working under standard conditions. In setting labor standards, it is important not only to time the operation but also to take into account other factors that may influence the effectiveness with which an employee performs a task—for example, the facilities layout, the condition of the equipment, the quality of the materials, and employee training.

There are two methods that can be used to set labor standards. The first method relies on the use of experts, who determine what the standard should be and how it should be set. These experts can be company employees or outside consultants. The second method relies on a variety of industrial engineering techniques such as time and motion studies, work sampling, work activity analysis, and detailed flowcharting.[9]

Labor performance standards are converted to cost standards by multiplying the standard labor time by the standard labor rate, which represents the expected cost of direct labor employees over the standards period. It is largely determined by external factors such as labor regulations or minimum wage laws. However, a manager usually has discretion over the mix of employees used in an operation and in this manner can affect the standard labor rate for that particular operation.

Overhead Standards

The technique for setting overhead standards differs from labor and materials because the overhead category covers a variety of costs. Some of these costs are fixed, such as building depreciation, and others vary with the level of activity, such as electricity. The first step is to develop a budget for the indirect costs that will be charged to the product or service. This budget is usually developed by a cost center. The total indirect costs for each cost center are divided by a measure of activity that is then used to assign the overhead costs to the product or service. The finance department typically determines the overhead assignment methodology and calculates the standard overhead rate. Generally a manufacturing facility has multiple overhead rates. Chapter 10 discussed how to calculate the overhead rate and how to use this rate to assign indirect costs to a product (see Figures 10-8 and 10-9). Traditional standard cost systems have used direct labor hours, machine hours, or unit volume to assign overhead costs to products or services.

How Tight Should the Cost Standards Be?

This question is often debated back and forth by operations managers. There is a wide range of possibilities depending on the performance expectations of management and their assessment of how the standards may affect employee behavior. **Theoretical standards** are the costs that can be achieved under the best possible conditions; it is extremely unlikely that they will occur. Theoretical standards can create motivational problems because managers and their employees will be judged against a goal that they perceive is unattainable. **Practical or currently attainable standards** are those that are achievable within a specific set of performance parameters. These costs allow for inefficiencies, such as scrap and yield losses, that occur as a normal part of the production process. Management can set practical standards in two ways. One way is to set reasonable standards that employees consider achievable. These standards may incorporate inefficiencies that management has identified in advance, such as new employees, a new product introduction, or a change in suppliers. Another way is to set ambitious standards that are tighter than reasonable standards but looser than perfection. Only a very efficient operation would achieve these standards.

The relative tightness or looseness of a cost standard is negotiated during the standard-setting process and is determined by the line managers. Although accountants may advise and influence the process, the final decision rests with the line management, not the finance group. Consensus building is important. If the standard is viewed as unrealistic or imposed from above, it will undermine the effectiveness of the system as a management control tool.

Variance Analysis

Variance analysis examines the differences between actual and standard costs to determine their underlying causes and identify opportunities for cost improvement. The variance calculation is generally done by a computer application. However, cost analysts should understand how the calculation is performed and should be able to duplicate the calculation if asked. Although most computer applications that I have worked with use the general formulas I outline in this chapter, some companies have adapted these formulas to their particular situation. Therefore, the variance calculation formula for your company may vary somewhat from the formulas presented here.

Cost analysts need a solid understanding of the manufacturing processes and a good relationship with production personnel to analyze variances effectively. Cost variances should contain no surprises. They should merely highlight the financial results of a situation or decision that management already knows.

This section reviews the calculation of labor, material, and overhead variances and discusses the possible sources of these variances. All calculations are based on the data furnished in Figure 13-3 for The Computer Company.

Materials Variances

A **materials variance** is the difference between the actual materials costs and the standard materials costs for the actual volume of units

Figure 13-3. *Standard and Actual Cost Data, The Computer Company.*

Standard cost		
Materials	2 units @ $3.50 per unit	$ 7.00
Labor	.20 hours @ $5.50 per hour	1.10
Overhead	1 unit @ $6.00 per unit	6.00
Total standard cost per unit		$14.10
Actual costs incurred		
Materials used	2,000 units	
Materials purchased	4,000 units @ $4.00 per unit	$16,000
Labor	400 hours @ $5.25	$ 2,100
Overhead costs		$ 5,000
Other information		
Budgeted volume		1,000
Actual volume produced		1,200

purchased, or produced. It is broken down into a price variance and an efficiency or usage variance. A **materials price variance** is the difference between the actual and the standard unit price multiplied by the actual quantity of materials purchased or used. The formula is as follows:

Materials price = (Actual unit price − standard unit price) ×
variance   actual quantity purchased or used.

The materials price variance can be computed at the time of purchase (a materials purchase price variance) or at the time the materials are issued to the production floor. The materials purchase price variance for The Computer Company is calculated as follows:

Materials   = (Actual price standard − price) × actual quantity
purchase   purchased
price variance = ($4.00 − $3.50) × 4,000 units
                  = $2,000 Unfavorable

If the price variance were calculated at the time of usage, the calculation would be:

Materials price variance = (Actual price − standard price) × actual quantity used
= ($4.00 − $3.50) × 2,000 units
= $1,000 Unfavorable

The materials price variance is unfavorable because the actual unit price of $4.00 is greater than the standard of $3.50. Companies generally compute the materials price variance at the time of purchase. Most computer applications provide reports that detail the materials price variances for the components purchased or used during the month.

A **materials efficiency variance** is the difference between the actual quantity of materials used and the standard quantity that should have been used for the actual output achieved, multiplied by the standard unit price. The standard quantity per unit of output is found in the bill of materials. In the example, the standard quantity allowed to make 1 unit of finished product is 2 units of raw materials. This quantity is multiplied by the 1,200 units produced to obtain the total expected materials usage for the period. The materials efficiency variance is calculated as follows:

Materials efficiency variance = (Actual quantity − standard quantity) × standard price
= (2,000 − [2 units × 1,200 units]) × $3.50 =
(2,000 − 2,400) × $3.50
= $1,400 Favorable

In this example, the variance of $1,400 is favorable because the actual quantity used, 2,000 units, was less than the standard quantity of 2,400 units required to produce 1,200 units of the end product.

Labor Variances

Labor variances show the difference between the actual labor costs incurred and the expected labor costs for the actual output achieved. Labor variances are also divided into a **labor price variance** (also known as labor rate variance) and a **labor efficiency variance**. The labor price variance is caused by paying more or less than the standard rate. In the example shown in Figure 14-3, this variance is calculated as follows:

Labor price = (Actual price − standard price) × actual hours
variance   worked
            = ($5.25 − $5.50) × 400 hours
            = $100 favorable

The price variance of $100 is favorable because the actual amount paid, $2,100, was less than the expected amount of $2,200 based on the standard wage rate ($2,200 = $5.50 × 400 labor hours).

The labor efficiency variance measures the savings or the additional costs incurred because the hours worked were different than the standard allowed. The standard hours allowed for 1,200 units was 240 hours (.20 unit × 1,200 units). The labor efficiency variance is calculated as follows:

Labor   = (Actual hours − standard hours) × standard rate
efficiency = (400 − [.20 per unit × 1,200 units]) × $5.50
variance = (400 − 240) × $5.50
            = $880 Unfavorable

The variance of $880 is unfavorable because the actual hours used exceeded the standard allowed for 1,200 units by 100 hours.

Overhead Variances

An **overhead variance** is the difference between the actual overhead costs incurred and the total overhead costs charged to the products or services for the period. Theoretically, variances are calculated separately for variable and fixed overhead. There are two variable overhead variances (a spending variance and an efficiency variance) and two fixed overhead variances (the budget variance and the volume variance). This type of analysis is known as a **four-way variance analysis** and in my experience is not widely used. Generally companies compute only two variances: the spending variance and the volume variance. The **spending variance** isolates how much of the total overhead variance was due to spending more or less money than what was called for in the budget. The **volume variance** shows what portion of the variance resulted from the failure to operate at the budgeted activity level. The overhead variances for The Computer Company are shown in Figure 13-4.

In this example, the spending variance of $1,000 is favorable because the actual overhead costs incurred of $5,000 were less than the budgeted amount of $6,000. The volume variance of $1,200 is

Figure 13-4. *Overhead Variance Calculations, The Computer Company.*

Actual Costs Incurred $5,000	Budgeted Costs $6,000 ($6.00 × 1,000 units)	Total Standard Overhead Costs $7,200 ($6.00 × 1,200 units)

Spending $1,000 Favorable	Volume $1,200 Favorable

Total Overhead Variance $2,200 Favorable

Spending variance = (Actual costs − budgeted costs)
= ($5,000 − $6,000)
= $1,000 Favorable

Volume variance = (Budgeted costs − standard costs)
= ($6,000 − $7,200)
= $1,200 Favorable

Total overhead variance = $1,000 + $1,200
= $2,200 Favorable

also favorable because the company operated at higher activity levels (1,200 units) than was originally budgeted (1,000 units).

Sources of Variances

Variance analysis can highlight opportunities for cost reduction and continuous improvement if the causal factors are identified and acted on. The many factors that can generate a cost variance fall into four major categories:

- *Inefficient operations.* The operations did not perform as expected due to machine breakdowns, labor absenteeism, power blackouts, water shortages, or other difficulties.

- *Inaccurate standards.* The standard cost was incorrect due to an error in the bill of materials, an incorrect routing, an erroneous labor standard, or an error in forecasting material prices or labor rates.

- *Incorrect actual costs.* The costs were not properly recorded in the general ledger. This mistake is more common than you might think—for example, an accountant charges utilities to the wrong department; an accounting clerk keys in the wrong data into the accounts payable system; a production manager puts the wrong account number on a purchase order. An error in the recording of actual costs will most likely result in a cost variance.

- *An implementation breakdown.* This variance occurs because the operations did not happened as planned, such as a delayed installation of new machine, a parts shortage, or a canceled product.

The cost analyst should assist the responsible manager in identifying significant variances and their causes. Variances should be examined individually and as a whole. An unfavorable variance in one area can be offset by a favorable variance in another.

Let us return to The Computer Company. The favorable labor variance and the favorable materials efficiency variance of $100 and $1,400, respectively, offset the $1,000 unfavorable materials price variance. One possible explanation for this situation is that although the company purchased a more expensive component, it was smaller and easier to handle. As a result, the production employees were able to work at a faster pace with less materials losses than with the original part.

The variance analysis is the heart of a standard cost system. It provides a systematic mechanism to compare actual versus expected performance and pinpoint potential problem areas. Because standard costs contain numerous assumptions about the internal and external environment, managers and accountants should expect cost variances to occur within normal limits. They show the financial consequences of actions that initially appear as nonfinancial measures, such as material losses or process yields.

Variance analysis can provide useful information to management. Unfortunately, I have seen managers dismiss variance reports because they are too late, too summarized, or not relevant to the current operating environment. A good cost analyst can compensate for these deficiencies by tailoring variance information to meet the needs of the operations personnel.

Standard Costs in the Service Sector

Standard cost systems are primarily found in the manufacturing sector. However, service organizations also use standards for planning and control purposes. Examples of service organizations that use standards include banks, fast food chains, hospitals, and insurance companies. In a service setting, the standard cost is the expected cost of a unit of service. Its cost elements vary depending on the type of service organization.

Formal standard cost systems are more likely to be found in service factories or service shops whose operations resemble manufacturing entities. These operations can be controlled in many of the same ways that one controls a manufacturing firm. Service standards can be clearly established, and a control mechanism can be put in place to compare the actual and the expected levels of performance. As one moves up the service continuum, from service factory to professional service organizations, the use of standards to control quality and cost becomes more difficult.

Standard costs also can be very useful to service organizations for planning purposes. Knowing how much it should cost to provide a service can be of great assistance to managers in their decision-making process. They can use this information to outsource services, negotiate contracts, or make decisions on the nature of their service offerings. Moreover, materials quantity standards and labor time standards can be used to plan inventory levels, schedule labor, determine service capacity, and estimate total costs.

The Future of Standard Cost Systems

Despite the prevalence of standard cost systems in manufacturing enterprises, these systems have serious limitations for organizations that operate in a dynamic business environment. Standard costs were designed for another time and era when cost accounting systems were used to control the production floor. Computer technology has shifted the control process to operations personnel, where it rightfully belongs. Management information systems can provide performance results on a real-time basis. Managers do not have to wait until the end of the week or month to obtain feedback on their operations. As a control tool, standard cost systems may have outlived their usefulness. Unfortunately accounting professionals are reluctant to let go of a practice that has worked for decades. Even the newer concepts such as activity-based accounting are often implemented within a standard cost framework.

Standard cost systems can also steer managers in the wrong direction. In companies that use standard cost systems, managers often lose sight of the actual manufacturing cost of a product. Standard cost systems focus on identifying and explaining cost variances. They often do not report actual cost information per unit. When the cost variances are significant, the standard cost is not an accurate representation of the actual production costs incurred for a given product. If the sales and marketing functions of an organization rely on standard cost information to determine product profitability and make pricing decisions, important business decisions could be based on faulty information. Some companies that use standard cost systems calculate actual costs on a regular basis. At one of my former employers, we reported actual cost every quarter for all major products. Significant deviations to the standards were analyzed and explained in this report. Management used this report primarily for planning and measurement.

In the future, I envision more companies moving toward actual cost systems. Standard cost variance analysis will no longer be required because inventory transactions will be recorded at actual cost. This change will free up significant resources in the finance department and will allow cost analysts to function more as business partners within the organization. The accounting focus will shift from variance analysis to understanding the underlying cost structure of a product or process, highlighting significant cost trends, identifying cost reduction opportunities, and educating operations personnel on the financial impact of their day-to-day decisions. The analyst's role will become proactive instead of reactive. Companies will still need physical standards to estimate their unit costs for planning purposes. These expected unit costs, based on the most recent information on prices and usage requirements, will be used to compare actual cost figures for management decision making. Standards for control purposes will be less important as variances to physical standards are tracked in real time on the production floor or the frontline operations.

Chapter Summary

Standard cost systems are widely used in manufacturing organizations. They can also be found, though to a lesser degree, in service factories and service shops. Standard costs are budgeted unit costs that are established to motivate a desired performance level. They can serve a variety of purposes in an organization but are used primarily for planning and control.

Standard costs consist of three major elements: labor, materials, and overhead. Operations personnel usually establish labor or materials quantity standards, which are converted to cost standards by multiplying these by a standard price or rate. Variance analysis compares the actual cost against the standard cost to identify problem areas and possible cost reduction opportunities.

Standard cost systems may have limited usefulness for companies that operate in a dynamic business environment. Because standard costs are set for a given time period—usually six months or a year—they may not reflect the actual or even the expected cost based on the most recent price and usage information. Moreover, finance departments spend a significant amount of resources analyzing and explaining standard cost variances that provide little value added to the organization. Although physical standards are important to monitor the actual results of the operations, deviations from standards are best controlled at the source, on the production floor, or in the frontline operation. Although standard costs systems may not be replaced in the near future, I envision more organizations moving toward actual costs systems as computer technology continues to evolve and integrated business applications become more widely used.

Notes

1. Jeffrey R. Cohen and Laurence Paquette, "Management Accounting Practices: Perception of Controllers," *Journal of Cost Management* (Fall 1991).
2. These findings confirm my own research in the manufacturing industry. Lianabel Oliver, "The Current State of Cost Accounting Practices in Modern Manufacturing Firms" (unpublished manuscript, 1991).
3. See Charles T. Horngren and George Foster, *Cost Accounting: A Managerial Emphasis* (Englewood Cliffs, N.J.: Prentice Hall, 1991), p. 222.
4. Robert N. Antony and James S. Reece, *Accounting Text and Cases* (Homewood, Ill.: Richard D. Irwin, 1989), p. 8.
5. See Irvin N. Gleim and Dale L. Flesher, *CMA Review*, 6th ed. (Gainesville, Fla.: Gleim Publications, 1994), 1:530–539, for an overview of the controlling process.
6. For valuation purposes, inventory costs may be determined by specific identification: first-in, first-out (FIFO); last-in, last-out (LIFO); and average costs. It is beyond the scope of this book to explain the different inventory valuation methods for financial statement reporting. See Belverd E. Needles, Jr., Henry R. Anderson, and James C. Caldwell, *Principles of Accounting* (Boston: Houghton Mifflin, 1990), pp. 429–436.
7. Cohen and Paquette, "Management Accounting Practices."

8. For more information, see *Standard Costs and Variance Analysis* (Montvale, N.J.: Institute of Management Accountants, 1974), pp. 26–51.
9. In **motion studies**, the actions of individual workers are broken down into its constituent parts and these parts are studied to determine where improvements can be made. **Time studies** use stopwatches and videotaping to time the elements of a job to determine where improvement opportunities exist and how the job can be redesigned. **Work sampling** is used to set standards for jobs that have a high variety built into them. In this method, an analyst observes what the workers are doing at random points in time, thereby providing the analyst with insight into the percentage of time spent doing a variety of tasks. **Work activity analysis** lists in chronological order the work performed, noting the task, the time spent on it, and the number of items completed. **Detailed flowcharting** shows a precise diagram of the job and examines this diagram for improvement and standard setting. See Roger W. Schmenner, *Service Operations Management* (Englewood Cliffs, N.J.: Prentice Hall, 1995), Chap. 6.

Chapter 14

Activity-Based Costing

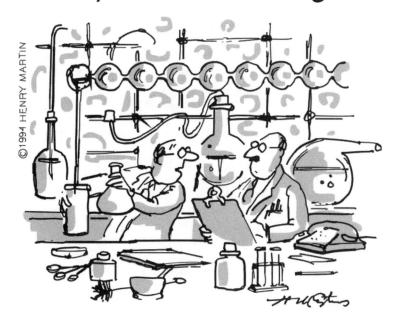

©1994 HENRY MARTIN

"Quick! Get Alfie on the phone!
I just discovered what it's all about!"

A ctivity-based costing (ABC) is a cost management approach
that identifies the processes involved in supplying a product
or service and the resources that these processes consume. It
uses this information to assign costs, eliminate waste, and improve
processes. ABC is a powerful tool to understand the components of
a company's costs and their underlying causes. By focusing on the

causal factors or cost drivers, ABC can help identify opportunities for cost reduction.

Activity-based management (ABM) is a discipline that focuses on the management of activities to improve continuously the value that customers receive. It draws on ABC as a major source of information. ABM complements a continuous improvement philosophy by highlighting waste and opportunities for cost reduction. This chapter presents the basic concepts of ABM systems. It also explains how to perform an activity analysis and determine the total cost of an activity.[1]

Activity-Based Information

Activity-based information focuses on the activities that an organization performs to manufacture a product or provide a service. Cost drivers affect activities. **Cost drivers** are factors that affect the resources required by an activity and therefore cause costs to be incurred by the organization. Examples of cost drivers are product or process design, customer specifications, corporate requirements, and government regulations.[2]

Activity-based information systems have two major views: a cost assignment view and a process view.[3] These are shown in Figure 14-1. Activities are at the center of both views. ABC is the *cost assignment* view. It answers the question: How much does the product or service cost? ABC assumes that activities consume resources and cause costs. Products or services do not *cause* costs; they *incur* costs by the activities that they require. ABC traces costs to products or services through activities. It provides a better costing method by establishing a more direct link between the product and the resources that it consumes.

ABM is the *process view*. It analyzes activities and determines how well these activities are being executed. It manages activity information to improve processes continuously and provide value to the customer. ABM answers the questions: How well are we doing? Are we doing things right? ABM draws on ABC as a major source of information. It seeks to identify opportunities by understanding the factors that drive cost. ABM includes activity analysis, cost driver analysis, and performance analysis.

When Is ABC Appropriate?

ABC is recommended when one or more of the following situations occur:

Figure 14-1. *Activity-Based Information.*

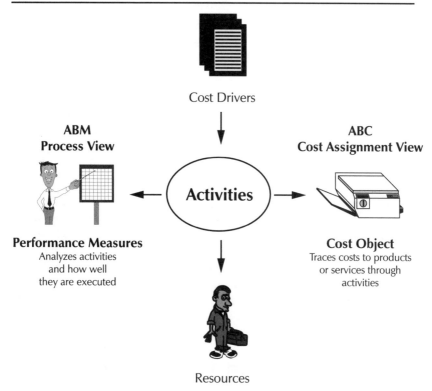

Source: Adapted from *Common Cents: The ABC Performance Breakthrough,* Peter B. B. Turney (Portland, Ore.: Cost Technology, Inc.).

- *The products are diverse.* Different products place different demands on the organization's resources. ABC assigns costs based on the pattern of resource consumption by the product. Therefore, it results in more accurate product costs.

- *Overhead costs are relatively high.* If an organization's overhead costs are high, ABC can provide insight into the activities that cause these costs. It can identify the nature of the activities such as value added, nonvalue added, primary or secondary and tie these to their cost. This information can be used to support cost reduction efforts.

- *Production volumes vary significantly.* Many companies that have embarked on ABC projects have found that high-volume products subsidize low-volume ones. Low-volume products typically consume a significant amount of resources that are unrelated to volume (e.g., engineering support). This situation is not visible in a traditional costing system that allocates overhead based on volume (labor hours or machine hours).

■ *Operating managers do not believe their product costs.* A cost system should be reevaluated if the operating managers do not believe that it provides meaningful costs. Sometimes operational managers design parallel costing systems that are used for decision-making purposes. ABC ties costs to the underlying production processes, making it easier for operational managers to understand and use cost information.

■ *Managers want a better understanding of their cost structure.* Sometimes managers want to understand their costs from a business perspective, not a financial perspective. Traditional financial reports will not provide this view. ABC/ABM allows managers to link their costs to the key activities performed by the organization. This linkage provides valuable information on resource consumption and can be used to evaluate the effectiveness of an activity in relation to the amount of resources deployed.

Advantages of Activity-Based Information

Activity-based information has several advantages over the traditional cost allocation systems:

■ *More accurate cost and performance goals.* A cost is considered accurate when it reflects the underlying business process. Activity-based accounting identifies all traceable activities and determines how much of the activity's output is dedicated to the product or service. The costing process is more accurate because it is based on how much each product or service requires of an activity. Activity costs can also be used to benchmark performance for a particular process.

■ *Identification of cost improvement opportunities.* Activity information can highlight waste and opportunities for cost reduction. It allows a company to quantify the cost of nonvalue-added activities.

- *Identification of cost drivers.* Activity information looks for the source of the cost. It answers the question, what causes costs to occur in this activity? By identifying the causal factors, managers can gain a better understanding of the organization's cost structure and how it can be changed to improve their competitive position.

- *Use of a common language.* Because managers participate in the system design and implementation, a common language evolves between operations and accounting that everyone can use and understand. Robert Kaplan describes the experience of one company: "The managers said that the activity-based cost information provided a much better language for everybody to use in their everyday discussion. Everybody was now talking from the same page. Before, there was tremendous conflict."[4]

- *Improved management information.* Activity information provides a link among activities, resource consumption, and costs. It identifies what an organization does, how it does it, and how much it costs. Management can evaluate if these activities support corporate objectives or if the resources should be deployed elsewhere.

What Is an Activity?

An **activity** is a description of the work that gets done in an organization. It is the combination of people, technology, materials, processes, and environment that produces a product or service.[5] An activity view of an organization can be quite different from the traditional functional view. Figure 14-2 shows a functional view for a human resources department. Figure 14-3 shows the activity view for the same organization.

An activity is not necessarily an existing function, department, or cost center. Some activities may cross departmental or functional boundaries (e.g., expediting an order). The materials procurement process in Figure 14-4 is an example of an activity that crosses organizational boundaries.

An Implementation Approach

There are many ways to implement an activity-based accounting system. Each organization must determine the right approach given its informational needs, the available resources, and the company cul-

Figure 14-2. *Functional View of a Human Resources Department.*

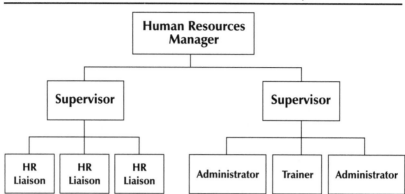

Figure 14-3. *Activity View of a Human Resources Department.*

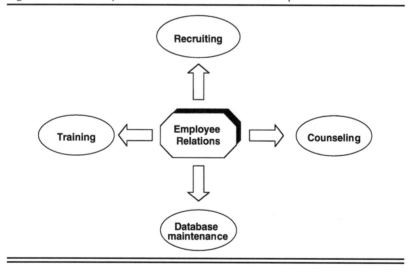

Figure 14-4. *The Materials Procurement Process.*

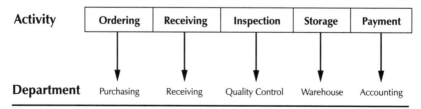

ture. The following steps, summarized in Figure 14-5, may be used to approach an ABC implementation.

Figure 14-5. *Summary of the ABC Approach.*

1. Identify the purpose.
2. Perform an activity analysis.
3. Trace resources to activities.
4. Select the appropriate activity measure.
5. Calculate the activity cost.
6. Trace activity costs based on usage.
7. Establish performance measures.

1. *Identify the purpose.* What is the purpose of the system? What are we trying to improve or fix? How does it further the organizational objectives? ABC can be used for different purposes. It is important to identify the specific purposes for which the model will be used. The project team should design a model that satisfies these objectives.

2. *Perform an activity analysis.* The project team analyzes all the significant activities of the organization and classifies these activities according to the characteristics of the data. For example, *value added* and *nonvalue added* are terms commonly used to describe activities.

3. *Trace resources to activities.* Each organizational unit has an assigned set of resources. Some resources are unique to a particular activity; others are used in multiple activities. The challenge in this step is to identify the resources involved in performing each activity.

4. *Select the appropriate activity measure.* All activities have inputs, which trigger transactions, and outputs, which are the products of an activity. These input-output measures must be identified and collected for each activity. These measures will be used as a basis for cost assignment.

5. *Calculate the activity cost.* Once the resources are identified, these resources must be costed. This step involves restating costs into an activity view.

6. *Trace activity costs based on usage.* This step ties the cost directly to the consumption of the activity by the product or service.

The input or output measures determined in item 4 will be the basis of the cost assignment.

7. *Establish performance measures.* What are the organization's long-term and short-term goals? What is important for the organization? A company operating in a continuous improvement environment typically focuses on cost, quality, and customer service. An ABM system should provide information to measure performance in these key areas. This step ensures that the performance measures support company objectives and moves the organization in the direction that management desires. These measures can be financial and nonfinancial indicators, such as the number of back orders, defect per million, processing time per application, or number of minutes per call.

*   *   *

There is no one right way to implement an activity-based information system. Key elements for a successful implementation are top management support and cross-functional involvement in the system design and implementation. Implementation issues are beyond the scope of this book. Additional information on this topic can be found in the ABC references included in the bibliography. We will discuss activity analysis, activity cost, and cost assignment in more detail.

Activity Analysis

Activity analysis examines the major activities of the organization and categorizes them in a meaningful manner. **Activities** describe what gets done in an organization. All activities have inputs and outputs. In production departments, inputs and outputs are fairly easy to identify. Inputs are materials, labor, and overhead (e.g., electricity, supplies). The output is the intermediate or finished product. Figure 14-6 shows some possible inputs and the output for the capsule manufacturing operations of a pharmaceutical company. For service organizations or departments, this identification process may be more difficult. Figure 14-7 shows possible inputs and output measures for support activities.

Seven main steps are recommended to perform an activity analysis. These steps are summarized in Figure 14-8.[6]

Step 1. Determine the Scope

The scope should clarify the extent of the activity analysis. Will it cover the entire organization, a division, a new product transfer, or

Figure 14-6. *Input-Output of a Manufacturing Operation.*

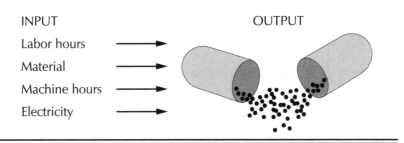

ACTIVITY
Capsule Manufacturing

INPUT   OUTPUT

Labor hours

Material

Machine hours

Electricity

Figure 14-7. *Possible Input-Output Measures for Support Activities.*

Activity	Input	Output
Pay employees	Time cards	Checks
Receive material	Material received; packing slip	Receiving report
Prepare engineering change order	Phone call; memo	Engineering change order
Maintain facilities	Request for services	Work order completed

Figure 14-8. *Steps to Perform an Activity Analysis.*

1. Determine the scope.
2. Identify the areas for analysis.
3. Define activities.
4. Gather the data.
5. Organize the data.
6. Classify activities.
7. Finalize and document.

a single product line? A clear definition will ensure that the analysis is applied to high-priority areas for the organization. In addition, it will limit the range of activities to be analyzed, allowing data to be collected more efficiently.

Step 2. Identify the Areas for Analysis

Once the scope has been established, it is important to identify the areas of the organization that will be included in the analysis. The organizational units can be a production line, a work center, a department, or a business process. This identification will drive the extent of the data-gathering process. The materials procurement process shown in Figure 14-4 involves various departments in an organization. An organizational chart or process flow analysis can provide the starting point for the analysis.

Step 3. Define Activities

Because individuals can have different definitions for similar activities, the project team should establish an activity dictionary before the start of the data collection process. The **activity dictionary** should define all of the significant activities performed in the organization and, if possible, detail the tasks that form part of these activities. The development of an activity dictionary will ensure that consistent definitions of activities are used throughout the organization and will facilitate the data collection process. The activity dictionary can be prepared on a macro- (big picture) or micro- (detailed) level. The activity dictionary should be modified as the data is collected and reviewed. Figure 14-9 shows an example of an activity dictionary.

Step 4. Gather the Data

Once the project team has agreed on a preliminary set of definitions, it can start the data-gathering process using a variety of techniques to obtain an accurate assessment of the business process.

Review of Historical Records

A review of historical information is the logical starting point for any activity analysis. It will help the team move faster up the

Figure 14-9. *Example of an Activity Dictionary.*

Production planning. Review the sales forecast provided by the marketing organization, develop the actual and forecasted production plan, prepare revised production schedules based on changes to the sales forecast.

Receiving—raw materials. Sign delivery receipt. Visually inspect and, if required, count materials. Process materials receipt transaction.

Incoming inspection—raw materials. Inspect and validate the quality of all raw materials entering the plants. Perform sample tests to ensure materials conform to user requirements. Work with supplier and purchasing to handle nonconforming materials.

Administration. All activities relating to the administration of an area or department. These activities include the budgeting, performance evaluations, supervision, and meeting time related to administrative functions. Secretarial support will be classified under administration.

learning curve and provide an overview of the organization and the different activities performed within it. The review should include financial statements, performance reports, organizational charts, job descriptions (if available), computer records, diaries and logs, flowcharts, prior studies, and any other pertinent records.

Interviews

After reviewing the historical data, team members should request an interview with an expert in the area—perhaps the department manager, the supervisor, or an individual who has considerable knowledge of the area. The team should prepare a list of standard questions to focus the interview on key information and to speed up the interview process. During the interview process, the interviewer should verify the information obtained from organizational charts and job descriptions. In today's dynamic environment, these documents do not always reflect the current organizational structure or what employees actually do. More than one interview may be required to obtain the necessary data.

Questionnaires

A less time-consuming alternative is the use of a questionnaire. Like the interview, a questionnaire requires preparation based on the review of historical data. The use of a questionnaire has three major advantages. First, it consumes less time for both parties (the administrator and the receiver). Second, the receiver of the questionnaire can fill out the document at her convenience. Third, it allows the collection of large amounts of information in a fairly efficient manner. The major disadvantage of a questionnaire is the lack of interaction between the administrator of the questionnaire and the receiver. There is no opportunity to clarify questions or obtain feedback. I recommend the use of personal interviews unless the number of interviewees is very large.

Observation

Another excellent technique is observation. The team members should go to the area and observe how people work. Are the observations consistent with the data gathered so far? Are there inconsistencies? The project team should use multiple data-gathering techniques to ensure that the information obtained provides an accurate picture of the organization as it currently exists. This process may result in a modification of the initial activity dictionary. Once the data-gathering process is completed, the team must organize the data to obtain a manageable set of activities.

Step 5. Organize the Data

Individuals who are unfamiliar with activity-based information often believe their biggest obstacle in the system design and implementation will be the identification of the activities within the company. In fact, the opposite is true. The most common problem facing project teams is not identifying activities but summarizing them in a reasonable manner.

Activities can be defined at a broad macrolevel, or at a detailed microlevel. The level of definition should match the purpose of the system. For costing purposes, macrolevel activities should be used; for process improvement efforts, a detailed breakdown of activities is required. Referring to the example in Figure 14-4, procurement is a macrolevel activity; ordering, receiving, inspection, storage, and payment are microlevel activities. Microactivities should have a common purpose and can be described by a single activity measure. (Activity measures are explained later in this chapter.) When combining microactivities into macro ones, care should be taken to avoid combining dissimilar activities. If this occurs, cost distortions are inevitable.

The use of activity information for performance improvement requires the use of microlevel activities and the breakdown of these activities into detailed tasks. It also requires the identification of performance indicators to measure activity efficiency and effectiveness. Key areas of measurement are cost, customer service, quality, and flexibility. Ultimately the level of detail will depend on the team's willingness to trade off simplicity versus complexity and precision versus the cost of measurement. A detailed breakdown of activities will entail more complexity and higher costs of measurement. The team must find an acceptable balance that will satisfy the objectives of the model without distorting the organization's cost structure.

Step 6. Classify Activities

Once activities have been identified, they should be classified according to the nature of the activity. This classification focuses the organization on those activities with the largest tactical or strategic benefits:

- *Repetitive or one time.* Activity-based information should focus on repetitive activities, not special projects or one-time programs.

- *Primary or secondary.* Primary activities are directly related to the mission of the department or function; secondary activities support the primary activity. In an accounting department, paying bills is a primary activity; supervision is a secondary activity. A rule of thumb is that 80 percent of the resources should be devoted to performing primary activities.

- *Required or optional.* Optional activities are performed at the discretion of the manager; required activities are those that must be performed by the department or function. For example, filing tax returns is a required activity for the accounting department; attending training sessions is an optional activity.

- *Degree of control.* Activities can be classified by the degree of control the organization can exert over its performance. Is the activity required by corporate policy or government agencies? Is it performed at the discretion of local management? Many factors determine an activity's performance. Internal factors (company procedures) can be influenced more successfully than external factors such as weather or regulatory requirements.

- *Value added or nonvalue added.* Value-added activities are those activities that customers perceive add value to the products or services they purchase or satisfy an organizational need. Nonvalue-added activities do not contribute to customer value or satisfy an organizational need.[7] These activities can be redesigned, reduced, or eliminated without reducing the quantity, responsiveness, or quality of the product or service. This attribute is used to identify opportunities for cost reduction and the elimination of waste.

- *Cost of quality.* Activities can provide information on the cost of quality by assigning them into four major categories: prevention, appraisal, internal failure, and external failure.[8]

- *Leverage in the marketplace.* The organization should focus on activities that provide a competitive advantage in the marketplace, such as product design, product quality, customer service, and distribution.

Step 7. Finalize and Document

The final step is to document the activity analysis. Good documentation ensures continuity as project members are added to or replaced on the team. It also facilitates the review and validation of the system by both internal and external auditors. The documentation should be well-organized and support the conclusions that the project team arrives at.

How to Calculate the Activity Cost

The **activity cost** identifies the way a company uses its resources by activity to achieve the established business objectives. It calculates the total cost of all resources assigned to perform an activity and expresses this cost in terms of an activity measure. The determination of the activity cost requires the identification of all the resources consumed by an activity and their cost. An activity can have direct costs or indirect costs. Direct costs are incurred entirely as a result of a specific activity. For example, maintenance supplies are directly related to an activity called maintenance, and payroll checks are a direct cost of an activity called payroll. Indirect costs are incurred by more than one activity. These costs must be traced to the specific activities based on the usage of the resource (people, machines, supplies). The **activity measure** is a quantitative measurement of the activity levels. It can be based on inputs (e.g., payroll time cards), outputs (e.g., payroll checks), or physical attributes (e.g., square footage). The activity measure is the factor that best explains variations in the cost of an activity.

The activity cost is expressed as a function of the activity measure—for example, a cost per machine hour or cost per purchase order. The activity measure is used to assign the costs of an activity to the product or service based on the frequency or the intensity of use of an activity by the cost object.

The activity cost provides a more accurate mechanism for assigning overhead costs to products. It relates costs to physical measures such as space, time, materials, and usage that managers can directly associate with the operations. This linkage makes it easier for managers to understand and use the cost information to manage the business. The cost per activity can also be used as a productivity measure. It can serve as a tool to benchmark the performance of an activity against other functions or divisions.

The calculation of the activity cost involves six major steps. Figure 14-10 summarizes the steps to calculate the cost of an activity.[9] This cost will be used to assign the cost of the activity to the cost object based on its consumption of the activity measure.

Figure 14-10. *How to Calculate the Activity Cost.*

1. Select the cost basis.
2. Trace resources to activities.
3. Determine the activity measure.
4. Assign secondary activities.
5. Calculate the activity cost.
6. Determine the activity performance measurement.

Step 1. Select the Cost Basis

An ABC system can be based on historical, standard, budgeted, or estimated costs. ABC experts prefer the use of historical costs to derive the initial cost model. This method ensures that the model reflects the actual cost structure of the company. Budgeted and standard costs may reflect a desired set of operating conditions or strategies that are not realized during the year. The use of historical costs, however, is not appropriate if the company is experiencing significant changes in its business processes. In these situations, cost estimates based on the new operating environment would provide a better basis for developing the ABC model.

Step 2. Trace Resources to Activities

In general, companies rely on the information in the general ledger to obtain the necessary financial data to cost activities. The budget may also be a source of financial data. Information on the consumption of resources by activities may be found in interview data, log books, and computer records.

Resources categories in the general ledger that are related should be grouped to facilitate the cost assignment to activities. Some suggested categories are:

- *Labor*—for example, salaries, fringe benefits, overtime, training, cafeteria, and other similar expenses
- *Materials*—for example, purchase price variance, scrap, and manufacturing variances
- *Equipment*—for example, all equipment and technology-related costs such as depreciation, maintenance and repair, and operating supplies
- *Facilities*—for example, water, electricity, rent, and maintenance

Labor often constitutes between 70 and 80 percent of departmental spending. Appendix G examines in more detail how to trace labor costs to activities.

Step 3. Determine the Activity Measure

The activity measure is a quantitative measurement that best explains variations in the cost of an activity and will be the basis used to assign the cost of the activity to a product or service. The choice of the activity measure determines the accuracy of the cost assignment. The activity measure should reflect the cost behavior pattern of the activity.

Step 4. Assign Secondary Activities

Secondary activities such as supervision and training should be assigned to the primary activities of a department or process. The assignment can be based on specific data (e.g., supplies consumed in machine maintenance) or some other reasonable basis (e.g., estimates of time spent). Secondary activities should be traced whenever possible and allocated only as a last resort.

Step 5. Calculate the Activity Cost

The final step in determining the activity cost is simple arithmetic. It divides the total cost of the activity by the total activity measure to obtain a cost per unit of consumption. The formula is as follows:

$$\frac{\textbf{Activity cost}}{\textbf{per usage}} = \frac{\text{Traceable resources + secondary activities}}{\text{Activity measure quantity}}$$

The cost per unit of usage can also be used as a productivity measure because it shows the amount of input required per unit of output.

Step 6. Determine the Activity Performance Measurement

Activities can be measured in financial and nonfinancial terms. Activity accounting not only considers cost, but other nonfinancial performance measures that provide added information about the activity. Activity performance measures focus on the factors that are critical for success in a continuous improvement environment, such as cost, time, quality, and flexibility. These measures should also be consistent with the company's stated objectives.

* * *

Because the choice of the activity measure will determine the accuracy of the cost assignment, some additional considerations must be discussed before explaining the final stage of cost assignment to the product or service.

Activity Measures and Cost Behavior Patterns

The activity measure should reflect the cost behavior of the activity. Traditional systems distinguish two patterns of cost behavior: fixed and variable. These categories, however, are not sufficient to characterize the cost behavior of activities. ABC recognizes four cost behavior patterns, which are shown in Figure 14-11.[10]

Unit-level activities are performed each time a unit is produced such as drilling a hole, processing an order, or testing a product. The cost of these activities is directly proportional to volume. Conventional cost systems assume all overhead activities in the enterprise are unit-level activities, assigning costs based on measures such as direct labor hours or machine hours.

Batch-level activities consume resources each time a batch or **workorder** is produced, such as cleaning equipment, setting up machines, or pulling components from the warehouse. Activity measures should relate the resource consumption to the number of batches produced.

Product-sustaining activities are necessary to maintain each different type of product or product line, such as documenting products specifications, developing promotional campaigns, or preparing an engineering change order. In these activities, the number and complexity of the products determine cost variability.

Facility-sustaining activities support the organization's general business process, such as building maintenance, security, and janitorial services. These costs are insensitive to unit or batch variability and ultimately must be recovered through volume. Some ABC theorists argue that these costs should not be included in an ABC model because they do not have a direct cause-and-effect relationship with

Figure 14-11. *Cost Behavior Patterns.*

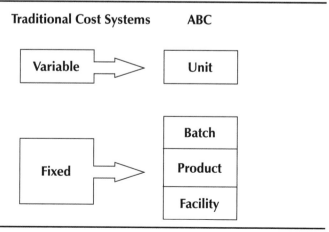

the products or the processes. Most companies continue assigning these costs to products or services on some reasonable basis (e.g., square footage).

The cost behavior pattern of an activity will largely determine the choice of an activity measure. A batch-level activity such as machine setup should not be assigned using a unit volume measure such as machine hours or labor hours. This latter activity measure does not reflect that manner in which the batch-level activity consumes resources and therefore will result in inaccurate costs.

Activity Measures and Cost Drivers

The term *cost driver* is often used to describe the assignment basis that will be used to trace costs to products or services. In fact, much of the literature on ABC uses the term *cost driver* for what is in fact an activity measure.[11]

Cost drivers are structural causes of the cost of an activity and differ in the extent to which they can be controlled by the company. One or more cost drivers can determine the cost of a particular activity. Typical cost drivers in a manufacturing or service facility are product design, process design, information technology, company policies or procedures, government regulations, and customer requirements. An activity measure is a quantitative factor that describes a particular business process and may explain variations in costs. Common activity measures are the number of purchase orders, number of transactions, machine hours, labor hours, and test hours. An activity measure is a way to characterize an activity and provides a systematic mechanism for assigning the cost of an activity to a product or service. The difference between a cost driver and an activity measure is best illustrated in the following example:

Activity	Taking an order
Activity measure	Number of sales orders processed
Cost driver	Policies and procedures, process design, data processing application

An activity measure does not *cause* costs. It is a way to measure the volume of an activity (e.g., number of tests) or the intensity of its use (e.g., test hours) and use this information for cost assignment and performance measurement.

Activity Measure Considerations

Several considerations are important when choosing the activity measure for cost assignment purposes. One is resource consumption or how the activity consumes resources. The activity measure should reflect the manner in which the resource is consumed by the products. A simple example will illustrate this point.

Suppose a company manufactures two products, Product A and Product B. The data is provided in Figure 14-12. If costs are assigned based on the number of tests, each product will be assigned the same level of cost even though Product B consumes significantly more of this activity than Product A. Thus, test hours would be a more appropriate measure to trace the cost of this activity to the product.

Another consideration is the relative cost of the activity. How significant is the cost of this activity when compared to total product costs? If the cost is not significant, activities may be grouped into broader categories. Less precise activity measures may also be used. Activities that have high costs should have more precise activity measures to reflect their usage accurately.

Activity Measure Characteristics

As the basis for assigning costs in an ABC system, activity measures constitute an important element of system design. The choice of the

Figure 14-12. *Activity Measure Considerations.*

Cost of testing activity	$100,000
Total number of tests	10,000
Total number of test hours	20,000
Cost per test[a]	10
Cost per test hour[b]	$ 5

	Product A	**Product B**
Number of tests required	1	1
Test hours required	1	3
Cost assigned based on number of tests[c]	$10	$10
Cost assigned based on test hours[d]	$ 5	$15

[a]Cost per test = $100,000 ÷ 20,000 tests = $10.00 per test.
[b]Cost per test hour = $100,000 ÷ 20,000 test hours = $5.00 per test hour.
[c]Product A and B = 1 test × $10.00 per test.
[d]Product A = 1 test hour × $5.00 per hour; Product B = 3 test hours × $5.00 per hour.

appropriate activity measure should be guided by the following factors:

- *Activity measures should be simple.* Preferably they should be measures that the organization already understands and uses.

- *Activity measures should be easy to measure and access.* System designers should avoid choosing activity measures for which there is no data or the data is not readily accessible. Most manufacturers have a wealth of data in their current information systems. System designers should leverage the existing information base.

- *Activity measures should be directly related to the business.* Since ABC creates a common language between finance and operations, it is important that the activity measures are related to the business functions and processes. Activity measures should be meaningful to nonfinancial users.

- *Activity measures should encourage improved performance.* They should provide information that can be used to achieve organizational objectives. Activity measures should motivate behavior that is consistent with the direction of the organizational unit and the corporate directives.

- *Activity measures require consensus.* If the managers do not agree with the choice of activity measures for their area, they will not believe in the numbers generated by the system. Several interviews may be required before the activity measures are agreed on.

Cost Assignment Using ABC

ABC assigns costs to products or services based on the activities that they require. So far, we have assigned resources to activities and determined the activity cost. We will now use this information to trace overhead costs to the product or service.

Figure 10-7 shows the traditional cost allocation model. In this model, resources are traced to departments; these costs are then allocated to the product using unit-level allocation bases such as direct labor hours or machine hours. This methodology assumes that products cause cost. Each time a unit is produced, costs are incurred. This assumption is not valid when activities are performed in batches or by product. Conventional cost systems assign costs directly to units regardless of the cost behavior pattern of the activity. Hence, they distort the true cost of the product or service.

Figure 14-13 shows the ABC approach.[12] ABC uses the activity measure to assign overhead costs to products. The appropriate activity measure is identified when computing the unit activity cost. ABC establishes a cause-and-effect relationship between the activity and the allocation basis used to assign costs to the product.

An ABC system requires information about the activity usage of the product or service being costed. Some companies define a bill of activities, which is analogous to the bill of materials. It contains all the activities that are required to manufacture a product or provide a service, the activity measures, and the quantities or levels of activity usage. The quantity multiplied by the cost per activity will equal the total cost of the activity that is traceable to the product. The use of a bill of activities allows a mix of different cost behavior patterns (unit, batch, product) in the computation of the product cost. Figure 14-14 illustrates the use of a bill of activities in calculating overhead costs for a product.

Users of ABC information must be cautious in how they interpret the information derived from the system. ABC calculates the total overhead costs of the product based on activities and then divides this number by the production volume to obtain a unit cost. However, the cost components of this unit cost do not all vary according to the volume. Assigning expenses to individual units may

Figure 14-13. *The ABC Approach.*

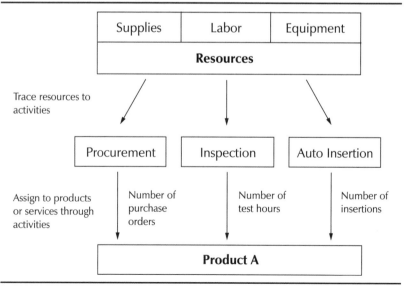

Figure 14-14. *Example of a Bill of Activities.*

Product Number: A143
Annual Volume: 2,000 units

Activity	Activity Measure	Activity Usage	Cost per Activity	Total Cost
Unit level				
Final assembly	Labor hours	1,000	$ 10	$10,000
Inspection	Test hours	250	25	6,250
Batch level				
Procurement	Purchase orders	60	50	3,000
Shipping	Orders shipped	100	20	2,000
Product level				
Engineering	Change orders	20	$200	4,000
Total cost				**$25,250**
Unit cost				**$ 12.63**

Source: Adapted from *Common Cents: The ABC Performance Breakthrough,* Peter B. B. Turney (Portland, Ore.: Cost Technology, Inc.).

convey the wrong message to persons who are unfamiliar with ABC methodology.

Let us return to Figure 14-14. If we reduce the number of purchase orders for Product A143 from 60 to 30, the activity cost of procurement will drop from $3,000 to $1,500. However, this cost reduction will occur only if the resources associated with the additional 30 orders are eliminated or reassigned to other areas. If this resource reduction does not occur, we have generated excess capacity that will be charged to the current products unless specific actions are taken to isolate this cost.[13]

The Evolution of ABC Systems

Early ABC systems were designed to correct the deficiencies of traditional costing methods. They were not meant to substitute current cost accounting practices in the general ledger but to provide an alternative costing method for strategic decision making.[14] This approach was strongly criticized by accounting practitioners who argued that one cost system should satisfy both needs. Since this time, many companies have redesigned their cost system using an ABC framework. Some companies have integrated the ABC approach into their standard cost system.

The results have been mixed. Whereas articles in professional journals praise the virtues of an ABC/ABM system, ABC critics have argued that it is too costly and too complex.[15] ABC systems can also have unexpected consequences. There is anecdotal evidence of one well-known manufacturing subsidiary that reverted from an ABC system to a more traditional cost allocation method for financial reporting purposes. The ABC implementation generated a great deal of political infighting and resulted in products being transferred out to a lower-cost facility. This lower-cost facility was not using an ABC system to cost their products.

Despite its critics, ABC systems can provide more meaningful cost information. Each organization should determine how best to implement ABC concepts in the context of its needs and operating environment. ABC systems do not have to be integrated into the company's financial reporting system. There can be one system for general ledger and financial reporting purposes and another for product or service cost calculation. However, the cost calculation, if based on historical data, should be reconciled to the general ledger to ensure the accuracy and reliability of the numbers.[16]

Chapter Summary

Activity-based accounting is a management information system that identifies the activities performed in an organization and analyzes their cost and performance. It has two major components: activity-based costing (ABC) and activity-based management (ABM). ABC is the cost assignment view. It assumes that products and services require activities that place demands on the resources of the organization, generating costs. ABC traces costs to product or services through activities.

ABM takes the process view. It analyzes activities and determines how well these are being executed in light of the organization's long-term objectives. ABM uses the information derived from the ABC system to identify cost improvement opportunities and waste reduction. By identifying the causal factors or cost drivers, ABM can focus on the management of key activities to improve the value received by customers and lower its costs.

Activity-based accounting supports and complements other management philosophies, such as continuous improvement and total quality management. It is a management tool for understanding the relationship among resource spending, consumption, and cost. However, the system must be accompanied by management action to produce effective results. The following quotations from Robert Kaplan and Robin Cooper, both renowned ABC experts, illustrate this point:

> [Kaplan] ABC is not just getting the numbers. For an ABC program to be successful, organizations have to get people to buy into the actions, and that takes time. Then they have to implement the actions, and that takes time. Then they have to take the next stage of action, either to use the excess capacity that has been created or to manage the excess capacity out of the system.

> [Cooper] It is important to realize that ABC triggers actions but by itself does not cause saving to occur. If the ABC system is well designed it adds to managerial intuition, enabling people to put energy where previously they may not have put it.[17]

Activity-based information can highlight opportunities for action. However, management must act on the information to obtain the true benefits of an ABC implementation.

Notes

1. This chapter integrates the published literature on ABC systems from multiple sources. It also draws on my own experience in the design and development of product costing systems. The reader is referred to the bibliography for additional references on ABC systems.
2. Michael Porter, *Competitive Advantage* (New York: Free Press, 1985), defines a cost driver as follows: "Cost drivers are the structural determinants of the cost of an activity, and differ in the extent to which a firm controls them. Cost drivers determine the behavior of costs within an activity, reflecting any linkages or interrelationships that affect it" (p. 63). Porter goes on to identify 10 major cost drivers: economies of scale, learning, the pattern of capacity utilization, linkages, interrelationships, integration, timing, discretionary policies, location, and institutional factors. These are explained in detail in chapter 3 of his book.
3. These views are summarized in the ABC Cross, which was developed

by Peter B. B. Turney and Norman Raffish. It is discussed at length in Turney's book, *Common Cents: The Performance Breakthrough* (Hillsboro, Ore.: Cost Technology, 1992). Figure 14-1 is an adapted version of the ABC Cross.

4. Alfred M. King, "The Current Status of Activity-Based Costing: An Interview with Robin Cooper and Robert S. Kaplan," *Management Accounting* (September 1991): 23.

5. James A. Brimson, *Activity Accounting: An Activity-Based Costing Approach* (New York: Wiley, 1991), p. 203.

6. Ibid., pp. 78–97.

7. The classification of value-added and nonvalue-added activities has been the subject of great debate in the accounting and operations literature. Different writers and academicians present slightly different definitions depending on their point of reference. Some writers argue that only activities that add value to the customer should be considered as value added. This definition leaves some essential activities such as human resources, accounting, and other service areas in limbo. This chapter uses the definition developed by Computer Aided Manufacturing-International, Inc. (CAM-I), an organization at the forefront of cost management practices. See Norm Raffish and Peter B. B. Turney, eds., "Glossary of Activity-Based Management," *Journal of Cost Management* (Fall 1991): 57–63.

8. For more information on cost of quality, see Philip B. Crosby, *Quality Is Free,* referenced in the bibliography.

9. See Brimson, *Activity Accounting,* pp. 122–152.

10. This concept was first discussed by Robin Cooper, "Cost Classification in Unit-Based and Activity-Based Manufacturing Cost Systems," *Journal of Cost Management* (Fall 1990): 4–13. A more recent publication on ABC published by the Institute of Management Accountants, *An ABC Manager's Primer*, expands this hierarchical model of cost variability to include technology sustaining and customer sustaining activities.

11. In "The Two Stage Procedure in Costing Accounting—Part Two," *Journal of Cost Management* (Fall 1987), Robin Cooper introduces the term *cost driver* in the context of the two-stage cost allocation model: "The second stage of this process traces costs from the cost pools to the products by using a measure of the quantity of resources consumed by each product. This measure is frequently called an allocation basis; however, this column uses the term cost driver to convey the idea of the products driving the consumption of cost as opposed to that of allocating costs because they exist and must be assigned to the products" (p. 41).

12. Ibid.

13. Although I strongly discourage this practice, many companies include the cost of excess capacity in the current costs of their products. This practice overstates the product or service costs and may lead managers to make the wrong decisions regarding their product or service mix. This issue was discussed in detail in Chapter 11.

14. Robin Cooper and Robert S. Kaplan, "Measure Costs Right: Make the Right Decisions," *Harvard Business Review* (September–October 1988): 96–105.

15. See William L. Ferrara, "The New Cost/Management Accounting—More

Questions Than Answers," *Management Accounting* (October 1990): 48–52, and H. Thomas Johnson, "It's Time to Stop Overselling Activity-Based Costing," *Management Accounting* (September 1992): 26–35. The common pitfall of ABM and some possible solutions are discussed in "Implementing Activity-Based Management: Avoiding the Pitfalls," in *Statements on Management Accounting,* Statement No. 4CC (Montvale, N.J.: Institute of Management Accountants, 1998).

16. See Robert S. Kaplan, "The Four-Stage Model of Cost Systems Design," *Management Accounting* (February 1990): 22–27. In this article, Kaplan discussed the four stages of development of cost systems. Stage 1 systems are characterized by poor data quality. Stage 2 systems focus on external reporting but are inadequate for managerial purposes. Stage 3 systems retain the existing financial reporting system but start to develop managerially relevant operational control and ABC costs. Stage 4 systems provide cost systems that are integrated to the operational control system. Since that article was written, integrated cost systems (Stage 4) have become a reality. Enterprise resource planning systems provide the possibility of integrating operational learning and control systems to strategic cost systems (Stage 4 systems). In his latest article, however, Kaplan warns of the potential dangers of integrated cost systems. See "The Promise—and Peril—of Integrated Cost Systems," *Harvard Business Review* (July–August 1998): 109–119. "Integrated costs systems have the potential to deliver distorted information every single day. . . . Managers should not be seduced by the availability of real-time information into using their ABC systems for real-time operational control." He argues that operational control systems and ABC systems should talk to each other, exchanging valuable information that allow managers to think prospectively about strategic costs and profitability.

17. King, "Current Status," p. 23.

Chapter 15

Cost Analysis
for Management
Decision Making

*At the time of the first walk on the moon, a reporter asked one
of the astronauts if he had been nervous when he was strapped
into his seat before going into space.*

*"Well," the astronaut said, "of course I was. Who wouldn't
be? There I was, sitting on top of 9,999 parts and bits—each of
which had been made by the lowest bidder!"*

Managers must constantly choose among alternative courses of action and make decisions regarding the allocation of scarce resources. What products should we make? What price should we bid on a contract? Should we accept a special order? Who is our most profitable customer?

So far, we have discussed costing principles and systems using a full cost approach. Full costs are the total resources that the organization consumes in providing a product or service. However, in the short run, many organizational costs are fixed; they do not change in total with changes in volume or activity levels. Although an organization must recover all its costs in the long run to be financially viable, for short-term, nonroutine decisions, a manager may choose not to consider these costs in her decision-making process.

The contribution margin approach and relevant cost analysis provide managers with valuable decision-making tools for certain business situations. They can help managers choose among competing alternatives as well as evaluate the performance of a specific department or an organizational unit. This chapter discusses how to apply relevant cost concepts and the contribution margin approach to address specific business situations. It explains how to calculate the contribution margin and how to use this number in a break-even analysis. It defines and explains other contribution margin concepts such as margin of safety, target income sales volume, and the contribution margin income statement. Finally, it presents specific examples of how managers can use contribution margin and relevant cost analysis in their decision-making processes.

Contribution Margin

Contribution margin analysis shows the relationship between fixed and variable costs in relation to sales. It provides business professionals with additional information on cost behavior that may not be visible using a full cost approach. The **contribution margin** (CM) is the difference between sales and the variable costs of the product or service. It is the money left over after recovering the variable costs that will be used to cover fixed costs and generate a profit. The CM can be calculated in total, per unit, or as a percentage of sales depending on the information available and the purpose of the costing exercise.

Let us return to the Meneer Company, discussed in Chapter 9, to demonstrate some fundamental concepts of CM analysis. Figure

15-1 shows the detailed price and cost information for the Meneer Company's products. The cost information originally presented in Figure 9-1 has been separated into its variable and fixed components.

We can calculate the CM per unit by applying the following formula to the information presented in Figure 15-1:

CM per unit = Sales price per unit − variable costs per unit.

Therefore, the CM per unit for Products J, K, and L is, respectively, $7, $8, and $9, as shown in Figure 15-2. We can also calculate the CM ratio for each product as follows:

CM ratio = (CM ÷ sales) × 100.

Figure 15-2 also shows this calculation. The **contribution margin ratio** tells us on a percentage basis how much money this product contributed to recover the company's fixed costs. It can sometimes give more meaningful information than the gross margin percentage, which is based on full cost. The following example shows how this information can be used for management decision making.

Suppose the management of Meneer Company receives an addi-

Figure 15-1. *Price and Cost Data, Meneer Company.*

Product	Sales Volume	Sales Mix	Sales Price	Variable Costs	Fixed Costs	Full Cost
J	1,000	50.0%	$10	$3	$2	$5
K	750	37.5	10	2	5	7
L	250	12.5	10	1	2	3
Total	2,000	100.0				

Figure 15-2. *Calculations for the Contribution Margin, Meneer Company.*

Product	Sales Price (1)	Variable Costs (2)	CM per Unit[a] (3)	CM Ratio[b] (4)
J	$10	$3	$7	70%
K	10	2	8	80
L	10	1	9	90

[a]CM = Sales price − variable costs = (1) − (2).
[b]CM ratio = CM ÷ Sales = [(3) ÷ (1)] × 100.

tional order of 250 units for Product K. Since the company has limited capacity, it can produce these additional 250 units only by producing less of another product. Should it accept this order? Figure 15-3 shows the CM and the gross margin ratios for Products J, K, and L. If management analyzes this special order on a gross margin basis, it would reject the order because Product K has a gross margin of 30 percent versus Product J's or L's gross margin of 50 percent and 70 percent, respectively. However, if management analyzes this order based on the CM ratio, it may choose to accept the order since Product K has a CM ratio of 80 percent versus Product J, which has a CM ratio of 70 percent. All other things being equal, the company would be better off by producing 250 additional units of Product K because it contributes $250 more to the recovery of fixed costs and profits.[2]

The CM calculation requires a clear separation of fixed and variable costs. As we discussed in Chapter 2, this separation is difficult and often arbitrary. A simple approach is to classify semivariable costs as either fixed or variable. Although this approach may create some inaccuracy, its significance will depend on the magnitude of the semivariable portion in relation to the total costs.

CM Income Statement

Sometimes it is neither feasible nor practical to analyze CM per unit. For example, the owner of a retail candy store or the manager of a

Figure 15-3. *Comparison of Contribution Margin and Gross Margin, Meneer Company.*

Product	Sales Price (1)	Variable Costs (2)	CM per Unit[a] (3)	CM Ratio[b] (4)	Full Cost[c] (5)	Gross Margin[d] (6)	Gross Margin %[e] (7)
J	$10	$3	$7	70%	$5	$5	50
K	10	2	8	80	7	3	30
L	10	1	9	90	3	7	70

[a]CM = Sales price − variable costs = (1) − (2).
[b]CM ratio = (CM ÷ sales price) × 100 = [(3) − (1)] × 100.
[c]Full cost = Variable costs + fixed costs. See Figure 15.1.
[d]Gross margin = Sales price − full costs = (1) − (5).
[e]Gross margin % = (Gross margin ÷ sales price) × 100 = [(6) ÷ (1)] × 100.

Figure 15-4. *Sample Format for a CM Statement.*

Sales	$XXX,XXX
Less variable costs	XX,XXX
= Contribution margin	**XX,XXX**
Less fixed costs	XX,XXX
= Operating income	$ X,XXX

large department store may find it impossible to calculate the CM on a product-by-product basis. In addition, a manager may wish to evaluate the profitability of an entire product family versus an individual product. In these situations, the manager can request a CM income statement to analyze the cost behavior of his particular area of interest. This statement shows the contribution to income by an organizational unit such as a sales office, a product line, a department, or an activity. The format of the statement is as shown in Figure 15-4.

In this type of statement, variable costs are subtracted from sales to obtain the CM for the organizational unit. Variable costs include not only manufacturing or merchandising costs but any variable selling and administrative expenses such as sales commissions. Figure 15-5 shows a CM income statement for the Meneer Company.[3] The total CM of $15,250 is equal to the total sales of $20,000, less the variable cost of sales of $4,750. The CM ratio represents the average CM percentage for the current composition of sales or the sales mix. It is important to note that any change in the sales volume or sales price of any product will affect the total CM and the average CM ratio.

The CM income statement can help a business professional decide whether to drop or continue a product line, analyze alternatives arising from production or sales, and evaluate organizational performance. The remaining sections of this chapter explain how to use this information, combined with relevant cost analysis, as a tool for management decision making.

Breakeven Analysis

Breakeven (BE) analysis, also known as cost-volume-profit analysis, examines the interrelationships of changes in costs, volume, and

Figure 15-5. *Contribution Margin Statement, Meneer Company.*

Sales	$20,000
Variable cost of sales	4,750
CM	**$15,250**
CM ratio	76%
Fixed manufacturing costs	6,250
Less fixed selling expenses	2,000
Less fixed administrative expenses	3,000
Total fixed expenses	11,250
Net income	**$ 4,000**

profits. It helps answer questions on how changes in price, volume, or costs affect profitability. BE analysis is based on the calculation of the **breakeven point**, the volume level where the total revenues and the total expenses are equal. At this level, there is no profit or loss. The BE point can be expressed in units or dollars and is calculated as follows:

BE point in units   = Fixed costs ÷ unit CM
BE point in dollars = Fixed costs ÷ CM ratio

Let us start with a simple example to illustrate the BE calculation.

Advanced Diagnostics Imaging is a start-up company with one product. Figure 15-6 shows the budgeted income statement for the year. The BE point in units would be calculated as follows:

$$\text{BE in units} = \frac{\text{Fixed costs}}{\text{Unit CM}} = \frac{\$58,000}{\$12.00} = 4{,}833 \text{ units}$$

$$\text{BE in dollars} = \frac{\text{Fixed costs}}{\text{CM Ratio}} = \frac{\$58,000}{.60} = \$96{,}667$$

The BE point is 4,833 units and $96,667 in sales dollars. In other words, Advanced Diagnostics Imaging must sell at least 4,833 units or $96,667 before it can start to generate a profit. In general, a high BE point represents a greater operating risk since the company must generate a high sales volume to recover its costs.

Figure 15-6. *Budgeted Income Statement, Advanced Diagnostics Imaging.*

Advanced Diagnostics Imaging, Inc.
for the Year Ended December 31, 2XXX

	Total	Per Unit
Sales (5,000 units)	$100,000	$20.00
Variable cost of sales	40,000	8.00
CM	**60,000**	**12.00**
CM ratio	60.0%	60.0%
Fixed manufacturing costs	40,000	8.00
Selling and administrative expenses	18,000	3.60
Total fixed operating expenses	**58,000**	**11.60**
Operating income	**$ 2,000**	**$ 0.40**
% of sales	2.0%	2.0%

Margin of Safety

A business professional can also use BE analysis to explore how a change in price, volume, or costs can affect the BE level. A tool for this type of sensitivity analysis is the **margin of safety**, the difference between the actual or projected sales and the BE point. It answers the question of how far sales can drop before the company stops generating a profit. For Advanced Diagnostics Imaging, the margin of safety is 177 units, or $3,333, calculated as follows:

Margin of safety = Sales volume in units − BE point in units
in units = 5,000 units − 4,833 units
  = 177 units

Margin of safety = Sales volume − breakeven point in dollars
in dollars = $100,000 − $96,667
  = $3,333

A manager can perform a sensitivity analysis by calculating the BE point and the margin of safety at different prices, volumes, or cost levels. This analysis will provide an understanding of how a change in the assumptions affects the results of the BE model.

Target Income Volume

BE analysis can also be used to determine the sales required to attain a desired level of income, called the **target income**. It can be established on a before-tax or after-tax basis.[4] Let us suppose that Advanced Diagnostics Imaging wanted to generate a pretax operating income of $20,000. How many units must it sell to achieve this result? We would use the following formula to calculate this number:

$$\textbf{Target income volume} = \frac{\text{Fixed costs} + \text{target income}}{\text{Unit CM}}$$

$$= \frac{\$58,000 + \$20,000}{\$12.00} = 6,500 \text{ units}$$

$$\textbf{Target income dollars} = \frac{\text{Fixed costs} + \text{target income}}{\text{CM Ratio}}$$

$$= \frac{\$58,000 + \$20,000}{0.60} = \$130,000$$

Therefore, Advanced Diagnostics Imaging would have to sell 6,500 units or $130,000 to achieve its desired income level of $20,000. Figure 15-7 is a pro forma income statement that illustrates this result.

As sales exceed the BE point, the CM per dollar or per unit flows directly to the bottom line or operating income. Once the BE point has been reached, fixed costs have been recovered. Therefore, the excess of sales over variable costs will be directly reflected as an

Figure 15-7. *Target Income, Advanced Diagnostics Imaging.*

	Total	Per Unit
Sales (6,500 units)	$130,000	$20.00
Variable cost of sales	52,000	8.00
CM	**78,000**	**12.00**
CM ratio	60.0%	60%
Fixed manufacturing costs	40,000	6.15
Selling and administrative expenses	18,000	2.77
Operating income	**$ 20,000**	**$ 3.08**
% of sales	15.4%	15.4%

increase in operating or net income. In the Advanced Diagnostics Imaging example in Figure 15-7, the 1,667 units that are sold beyond the BE point generate the $20,000 in operating income (1,667 units × $12 CM = $20,000 rounded).

The Effect of the Sales Mix

In a company that has multiple products, the relative combination of products that constitutes sales, or the **sales mix**, will affect the BE point. BE analysis is based on an average CM per unit for a given sales mix. Therefore, it assumes that the projected sales mix will remain constant over the period covered by the analysis. The formula for calculating BE in a multiple-product company is as follows:

BE points in units   = Fixed costs ÷ average CM per unit

BE point in dollars = Fixed costs ÷ average CM ratio

After the BE point is calculated in total units, the percentage that each product represents of the sales mix must be applied to this figure to obtain the number of units that must be sold of each product to achieve the BE level. Let us return to the Meneer Company to show an example of BE analysis in a multiple-product setting.

Figure 15-8 shows the BE calculation for the Meneer Company in total units. Fixed costs are $11,250 (see Figure 15-5). The average CM of $7.63 and the average CM ratio of 76 percent are used to calculate the BE point in units and dollars, respectively. The BE point is 1,474 units and $14,803 in sales dollars. The percentage of the sales mix would then be applied to this total figure to determine how many specific units of Products J, K, and L must be sold to obtain this BE level, shown in Figure 15-9.

Assumptions Underlying BE Analysis

Volume, price, and costs are only three factors of many others that affect the cost relationship, such as production efficiency, government intervention, and technology. BE analysis, like any other cost model, is based on a set of assumptions that should be understood and considered in interpreting the results. These assumptions are listed in Figure 15-10.

In practice, some of these assumptions are usually violated to some degree. BE analysis does not have to adhere rigidly to the un-

Figure 15-8. *Multiple Product Breakeven Analysis, Meneer Company.*

Product	Sales Volume	Total Sales Dollars	Sales Mix	Sales Price	Variable Costs	CM per Unit	Total CM
J	1,000	$10,000	50.0%	$10	$3	$7	$ 7,000
K	750	7,500	37.5	10	2	8	6,000
L	250	2,500	12.5	10	1	9	2,250
Total	2,000	$20,000	100.0%				$15,250

Average CM per unit	$ 7.63
= Total CM ÷ sales volume	
= $15,250 ÷ 2,000	
Average CM ratio	76%
= (Total CM ÷ sales dollars) × 100	
= ($15,250 ÷ $20,000) × 100	
Fixed costs	$11,250
BE point in units	1,474
= $11,250 ÷ $7.63	
BE point in dollars	$14,803
= $11,250 ÷ .76	

Figure 15-9. *Breakeven Units and Dollars by Product, Meneer Company.*

Total BE units	1,474
Total BE dollars	$14,803

Product	% Sales Mix	BE Units[a]	BE Dollars[b]
J	50.0	737	7,401
K	37.5	553	5,551
L	12.5	184	1,850
Total	100.0	1,474	14,803

[a]**BE units** = % sales mix × total BE units.
[b]**BE dollars** = % sales mix × BE dollars or unit sales price × BE units; minor differences due to rounding.

derlying assumptions. For example, inventory levels usually change over time, and variable costs do not vary directly and proportionately with changes in volume. The real benefit in preparing a BE analysis is understanding at a macrolevel how cost behavior patterns change with volume and what this information says about the business.

Figure 15-10. *Key Assumptions Underlying Break-even Analysis.*

1. All costs have been accurately identified and can be properly classified as fixed or variable.
2. The unit sales prices and the unit variable costs remain unchanged across a specific range of activity known as the relevant range.
3. Volume is the only factor that affects costs. Total variable costs will change directly and proportionately with changes in volume, whereas fixed costs will remain relatively unchanged.
4. If more than one product is considered in the analysis, the sales mix, or composition of sales, remains constant.
5. The sales volume and the production volume are equal. Beginning and ending inventory remain unchanged.

In summary, BE analysis is a useful tool for planning and decision-making purposes. Figure 15-11 highlights the key points discussed throughout this section. The next section discusses how you can use BE concepts and CM analysis to evaluate different types of business situations and guide decision making.

Figure 15-11. *Summary of Breakeven Analysis as a Management Decision-Making Tool.*

- The BE model and the CM statement can be used to evaluate alternative planning and decision scenarios.
- A change in unit selling price or the unit variable cost will change the CM, the CM margin ratio, and the BE point.
- As sales exceed the BE point, the CM for these units flows directly to the bottom line because all fixed costs have been recovered.
- Companies with a high BE point represent a greater operating risk than companies with lower ones, all other things being equal.
- A large margin of safety decreases operating risk for a company since it could withstand a large decrease in sales without incurring any losses.
- In a multiproduct company, management should emphasize high-margin products to maximize profitability, assuming the consumption of fixed resources does not vary significantly from product to product.

Applying Contribution Margin and Relevant Cost Analysis to Business Situations

Cost analysis is often a critical element of the decision-making process. Although each situation is different, the cost concepts discussed in Chapter 2 and the costing guidelines provided in Chapter 9 should help you to identify the relevant cost data for each type of situation. Any type of cost analysis for decision-making purposes always looks at a minimum of two alternatives: the decision at hand versus the "do-nothing" alternative. *Only those costs or revenues that are different among competing alternatives should be considered in the cost analysis.* Costs or revenues that are the same for all alternatives have no impact on the end result and should be ignored. They add complexity (but no value) to the cost analysis. Sunk costs, because they have already been incurred and cannot be changed by any future action, are also not relevant in the evaluation process. The next section shows how to combine relevant cost and CM analysis to assist in management decision making.

Product Line Profitability

Business owners and managers often face the decision of adding or dropping a product line. These individuals often rely on gross margin and operating income data to evaluate product line profitability. However, the use of this information could lead to an erroneous decision. The following example illustrates this point.

Tropical Delights, Inc. is a food-processing manufacturer with three major product lines: Guava, Pineapple, and Mango. The Mango product line has shown consistent losses for the past 12 months. Figure 15-12 shows the performance results for the prior quarter by product line. The management of Tropical Delights is extremely disappointed with the performance results of the Mango line and is considering dropping this product line and focusing its efforts on the Guava and Pineapple lines.

The controller of Tropical Delights is not convinced that this action is a financially sound decision. She reformats the income statement in Figure 15-12 to a CM format. The results are shown in Figure 15-13. Based on this information, the Mango product line covers its variable costs and contributes $0.50 of every dollar sold to recover fixed costs. The decision to drop the Mango product line will depend on whether the fixed costs that are charged to this product

Figure 15-12. *Income Statement by Product Line, Tropical Delights.*

Tropical Delights, Inc.
For the Three Months Ended December 31, 2XXX

	Guava	**Pineapple**	**Mango**
Sales	$465,750	$920,016	$291,929
Cost of sales	308,000	617,500	293,165
Gross margin	**$157,750**	**$302,516**	**$ (1,236)**
Gross margin ratio	33.9%	32.9%	−0.4%
Selling and administrative expenses	$101,500	$131,806	$ 28,567
Net income	**$ 56,250**	**$170,710**	**$ (29,803)**
% of sales	12.1	18.6	−10.2

line could be reduced or eliminated as a result of this decision. If the fixed costs can be totally eliminated, then the company could increase its profitability by $29,803 by dropping this product line.

Now let us suppose that the fixed manufacturing, selling, and administrative costs for the facility will not be significantly reduced by eliminating the product line Mango. The company would be worse off by dropping Mango because the fixed manufacturing costs of $147,201 and the fixed selling and administrative costs of $28,567 would have to be absorbed by the remaining two product lines. Therefore, this decision would reduce company profitability by $175,768, the amount of fixed costs charged to the Mango product line.

If management decides to keep the Mango product line, additional cost analysis would be required to determine a course of action. Does the cost methodology accurately reflect the manufacturing process? Can the manufacturing cycle time or direct labor hours be reduced? Can the sales price be increased, and how would this increase improve the CM and the gross margin for the product line? The CM analysis provides the starting point for further cost analysis before deciding on the specific actions required to improve the profitability of this product line.

Capacity Utilization

CM analysis can also be used to determine the best use of the available capacity to maximize profitability. In general, an emphasis on

Figure 15-13. *Contribution Margin Income Statement, Tropical Delights.*

Tropical Delights, Inc.
For the Three Months Ended December 31, 2XXX

	Guava	Pineapple	Mango
Sales	$465,750	$920,016	$291,929
Variable cost of sales	184,800	401,050	145,965
Contribution margin	**$280,950**	**$518,966**	**$145,965**
Contribution margin	60.3%	56.4%	50.0%
Fixed manufacturing costs	$123,200	$216,450	$147,201
Total manufacturing costs	308,000	617,500	293,165
Gross margin	**$157,750**	**$302,516**	**$ (1,236)**
Gross margin ratio	33.9%	32.9%	−0.4%
Selling and administrative expenses	$101,500	$131,806	$ 28,567
Net income	**$ 56,250**	**$170,710**	**$ (29,803)**
% of sales	12.1	18.6	−10.2

high-margin products will increase the company's net income. However, a product with a high unit CM may put excessive demands on a scarce resource that limits the production or sale of another product that places less demand. Therefore, when capacity is constrained, management should focus on obtaining the highest CM per unit of the constraining factor versus per unit of output. The constraining factor is the resource that limits the production or sale of a particular product. Typical constraints in a manufacturing or service organization are labor hours, machine hours, and space. The following example illustrates this situation.

Plasticor, Inc. is a small industrial pipes manufacturer with 21 production lines. It operates three eight-hour shifts, five days a week. The process is heavily automated and machine dependent; the operating costs of each line are relatively fixed. Since machine time is the constraining factor in the manufacturing process, management should produce the products with the highest CM per machine hour and emphasize these products in its marketing and sales strategies. The use of the CM per unit and the CM ratio could lead managers to choose a less than desirable product mix because it does not consider the demands of each particular product on machine time.

Suppose the company manufactures four products in Line 1. Pricing, cost, and CM information is shown in Figure 15-14. This figure also shows the production rate per machine hour for each product measured in feet per hour, the industry standard. If management used the CM per foot to determine the production plan, then it would maximize the production of Product D, since it has the highest CM per unit of measure. On the other hand, if management uses the CM ratio, it would choose Products A and B over Products C and D, because these products have the highest CM ratio. Neither the CM per foot nor the CM ratio captures the demand these products make on the constraining factor.

The total CM per machine hour is a measure that considers both the CM per unit and the demand of the product on the constraining factor, which is machine time. This number is calculated by multiplying the CM per foot times the production rate per hour. In the example, if we calculate the total CM per machine hour, we discover that the company would be better off to maximize the production of Product B, followed by Products D, C, and A.

This information is very useful to both sales managers and production managers. Sales managers could use this information to identify the high-margin products that could be marketed aggressively. Production planners could use this information to develop a production plan that not only satisfies customer demands but also maximizes profits through the best use of the available manufacturing capacity.

In my experience, many companies use gross margin to evaluate the optimal sales mix and production plan. The use of gross margin versus CM for cost analysis will depend on the specifics of the situation at hand. However, in general, if the fixed costs are relatively constant regardless of which product is manufactured, then the CM approach is more appropriate to determine the optimal use of capacity.

Figure 15-14. *Contribution Margin Analysis, Plasticor, Inc.*

Product	Sales Price	Variable Costs	CM per Foot	CM Ratio	Production Rate (feet/hour)	Total CM per Hour
A—2-inch pipe	$0.70	$0.20	$0.50	71%	500	$250.00
B—4-inch pipe	2.00	0.75	1.25	63	250	312.50
C—6-inch pipe	3.50	1.75	1.75	50	150	262.50
D—8-inch pipe	6.75	3.50	3.25	48	90	292.50

Special Orders

Sometimes companies receive special orders that are priced significantly lower than the normal selling price of the product. Their decision to accept or reject this type of order is typically based on the
projected profitability of the order expressed in terms of gross margin. However, as we have seen, the gross margin calculation typically includes fixed costs that will not change regardless of whether
the order is accepted. Therefore, if a company has excess capacity, it
may be better off accepting a special order at a reduced sales price
and receive some incremental revenue than to receive nothing at all.
Let us return to Plasticor, Inc.

Suppose Plasticor receives a special order for 10,000 feet of
Product D at a selling price of $5.50 per foot. Should the company
accept this order? If management bases its decision on the recovery
of full manufacturing costs (see Figure 15-15), then it should reject
the order. At a selling price of $5.50 per foot, the order would gener-
ate a loss of $5,000:

Sales price per foot	$5.50	
Less full manufacturing costs	6.00	
Gross margin per foot	($0.50)	
Number of feet to be sold	10,000	
Total profit (loss) per order	**($5,000)**	($0.50 × 10,000 feet)

However, suppose Plasticor has excess capacity on the production line that manufactures Product D. Its fixed costs would remain
unchanged regardless of whether it accepts the order. Therefore, the
fixed costs are not relevant to this decision and should be excluded

Figure 15-15. *Cost Data for Special Order Analysis, Plasticor, Inc.*

Product	Sales Price	Variable Costs	Fixed Costs	Total Manufacturing Costs	CM per Foot	Gross Margin per Foot
A—2-inch pipe	$0.70	$0.20	$0.30	$0.50	$0.50	$0.20
B—4-inch pipe	2.00	0.75	1.00	1.75	1.25	0.25
C—6-inch pipe	3.50	1.75	1.10	2.85	1.75	0.65
D—8-inch pipe	6.75	3.50	2.50	6.00	3.25	0.50

from the analysis. On a CM basis, Plasticor receives $1.50 of incremental revenue for every unit sold, as follows:

Sales price per foot	$5.50
Less variable costs	3.50
CM per foot	**$1.50**
Number of feet to be sold	10,000
Incremental revenue per order	**$15,000** ($1.50 × 10,000 feet)

Therefore, the company would be better off accepting this order, even at a lower-than-normal selling price, because the incremental revenue will cover its variable costs and contribute to the recovery of its fixed costs. Since the total fixed costs remain unchanged, this incremental revenue of $15,000 translates into increased profitability.

The assumption in the prior example was that the acceptance of the special order would not increase fixed costs. Now suppose that Plasticor had to pay additional freight charges of $16,000 to expedite the material required for this order. In this situation, Plasticor should reject the special order because the incremental revenue is insufficient to cover the incremental costs of the order, as follows:

Sales price per foot	$5.50
Less variable costs	3.50
Contribution margin per foot	**$1.50**
Number of feet to be sold	10,000
Subtotal CM per order	$15,000
Less additional freight charges	(16,000)
Incremental revenue (loss) on the order	**($1,000)**

The analysis of special orders should consider all incremental or relevant costs—not only the CM per unit or per order, but also all other incremental or relevant costs that will be incurred as a direct result of accepting this order, such as additional equipment, shipping, insurance, and overtime.

CM analysis is a short-term decision-making tool that is appropriate when a company has excess capacity, is in a distress situation, or is in a competitive bidding situation. This approach is not appropriate for long-range planning or ongoing business decisions. In the long run, a company must recover all its costs to be profitable.

The airline industry provides an example in the service sector that makes extensive use of CM analysis for pricing purposes. Since the costs of operating an aircraft are primarily fixed, the companies use CM pricing to fill empty seats. Once a plane takes off, any unfilled seat becomes a cost that will never be recovered. By using CM pricing, the airlines can generate incremental revenue on these otherwise empty seats to recover the fixed costs of operating the aircraft.

Contract Bids

CM and relevant cost analysis can also be used to determine contract bids. An example from the service sector illustrates this situation.

Lu Wei runs a training and consulting firm specializing in accounting processes. The state government has asked him to submit a bid to provide training seminars for its employees in the area of business controls. Lu evaluates his costs for this project based on the costs per seminar, as shown in Figure 15-16. Variable costs are estimated at $1,180 per seminar, for a total of $59,000. In addition, he will have to hire additional administrative support to handle the seminar logistics, the preparation of training materials, and other duties. Total costs for this project are estimated at $75,000, or $75 per participant. He would also like a 25 percent margin over and above his total costs. Since the majority of his costs do not fluctuate with the level of participants, he would be best off to submit a total bid amount versus a bid per participant. Therefore, he should submit a total bid of $100,000 for this project. A bid of $100 per participant could result in decreased profitability since a large portion of his costs are related to the number of seminars, not the number of participants per seminar. These costs will remain relatively unchanged whether there is one person per seminar or 20.

Suppose the state government asked Lu to submit his bid on a per participant basis. How could he use CM information to help him prepare the bid proposal? In the example in Figure 15-16, he based his analysis on the variable costs per seminar, not the variable costs per participant. On a per participant basis, the majority of his costs are fixed, as shown in Figure 15-17. Therefore, he must negotiate a minimum number of participants in order to recover his fixed costs and obtain the desired gross profit level on this contract.

Figure 15-16. *Contract Bid Determination Based on Costs per Seminar.*

Key business assumptions
Number of participants: 20 per seminar
Number of seminars: 50

Variable costs per seminar
- Labor
  Seminar hours   = 8 contact hours × $50 per hour $400
  Preparation hours = 8 hours @ $50 per hour   400
- Training materials = $15/participant × 20 participants   300
- Equipment rental   = $65 per seminar   65
- Travel costs   = $15 per seminar   15
Variable costs per seminar   **$1,180**

Total variable costs ($1,180 × 50 seminars)   **$59,000**

Incremental fixed costs
- Additional administrative support $15,000
- Office supplies and materials   1,000
Total fixed costs   **$16,000**

Total contract costs $75,000
Total number of participants   1,000
Cost per participant   **$75.00**

Bid price per participant   **$100.00**
[Desired profit = 25% gross margin = $75/(1 − .25)]

Total bid price per contract   **$100,000**

Due to competitive pressures, Lu estimates that the maximum bid price per participant cannot exceed $100 for each seminar. More-over, he desires a gross profit level of $15,000, which is 25 percent over and above his fixed costs ($60,000 × 25%). The BE and the target income volume analyses are shown in Figure 15-18. Lu would need the government to guarantee a minimum number of 706 partici-pants to break even on this contract and 882 participants to obtain the desired profit level of $15,000. The difference between these two figures, 176 participants, is the margin of safety—the number of par-ticipants by which the contract could be reduced and still be profit-able for the company. If the government is not willing to guarantee a fixed number of participants, then Lu should seriously consider not

Figure 15-17. *Contract Bid Determination Based on Costs per Participant.*

Number of seminars:	50		

Variable costs per participant
Training materials = $15/participant

Fixed costs—Seminars
- Labor
  - Seminar hours = 8 contact hours × $50 per hour $400
  - Preparation hours = 8 hours @ $50 per hour   400
- Equipment rental = $65 per seminar   65
- Travel costs = $15 per seminar   15

Subtotal fixed costs—seminars   **$880** × 50 **$44,000**

Other fixed costs
- Additional administrative support $15,000
- Office supplies and materials   1,000

Subtotal other fixed costs   **$16,000**

Total fixed costs   **$60,000**

submitting a bid for this project, since most of his costs are fixed and do not vary with the number of participants per seminar.

Managers can use CM and relevant cost analysis to evaluate many different situations. As in any other costing analysis, the purpose of the exercise will determine the appropriate costing methodology that should be used to perform the financial analysis. Keep in mind that the financial analysis of a possible course of action is only one of several important elements that should be considered in the decision-making process. For example, product quality, customer service, employee morale, and community relations are sometimes difficult to quantify in financial terms, but they can have a significant impact on the success of the proposed action or plan. These factors should be explicitly considered as risks or opportunities during the evaluation of alternatives.

Chapter Summary

This chapter has provided examples of how relevant costs and CM analysis can assist business professionals in the decision-making process. CM analysis, however, is not the same as relevant cost anal-

Figure 15-18. *Breakeven and Target Income Volume Analysis for Contract
            Bid Determination.*

Number of seminars:	50

Bid price	$100
Variable costs	15
CM per participant	**$ 85**

BE analysis	= Fixed costs ÷ CM per participant
	= $60,000 ÷ $85
	= 706 participants
Target income volume	= (Fixed costs + desired profit) ÷ CM per participant
	= ($60,000 + $15,000) ÷ $85
	= 882 participants
Margin of safety	= 882 − 706
	= 176 participants

ysis. Relevant cost analysis focuses on a specific business situation.
It identifies the incremental revenue and costs that will be incurred
as the result of choosing one alternative versus another. It then uses
this information to make a decision after evaluating all other nonfinancial considerations. CM analysis can be performed at any time to
gain a better understanding of the cost structure of the business.
Some companies, for example, use a CM income statement to evaluate the financial performance of the organization or its subunits. CM
analysis and relevant costs, however, can complement each other in
evaluating a specific business situation.

Notes

1. Reprinted from *How to Be the Life of the Podium* by Sylvia Simmons.
   Reprinted by permission of AMACOM, a division of American Management Association International, New York, NY. All rights reserved. http://
   amanet.org.
2. The $250 is calculated as follows: CM Product J = 250 × $7 = $1,750;
   CM Product K = 250 × $8 = $2,000. The incremental CM by producing
   250 units of Product K versus Product J is $250 ($2,000 − $1,750 =
   $250).
3. This CM statement is based on the numbers in Figure 15-1. Although I
   used the unit cost data in this particular example to allow you to follow

the computations, I could have prepared this statement based on the total dollars reported in the sales, cost of sales, and operating expense accounts in the general ledger for this company. You do not need unit cost information to prepare a CM income statement. The detailed computations for each line item on this statement are as follows:

Sales	$= (1{,}000 \times \$10) + (750 \times \$10) + (250 \times \$10)$
	$= \$10{,}000 + \$7{,}500 + \$2{,}500 = \$20{,}000$
Variable cost of sales	$= (1{,}000 \times \$3) + (750 \times \$2) + (250 \times \$1)$
	$= \$3{,}000 + \$1{,}500 + \$250 = \$4{,}750$
CM	$= \$20{,}000 - \$4{,}750 = \$15{,}250$
CM ratio	$= \$15{,}250 \div \$20{,}000 = 76\%$
Fixed manufacturing	$= (1{,}000 \times \$2) + (750 \times \$5) + (250 \times \$2)$
costs	$= \$2{,}000 + \$3{,}750 + \$500 = \$6{,}250$
Fixed selling and	$=$ For this example, we assume $3,000 in selling
administrative	expenses and $2,000 in administrative ex-
expenses	penses.
Net income	$= \$9{,}000 - \$3{,}000 - \$2{,}000 = \$4{,}000$

3. If the target income is established on an after-tax basis, the BE formula is modified to consider the tax rate as follows:

Target income volume
$$= \frac{\text{Fixed costs} + [\text{target after-tax income}/(1 - \text{tax rate})]}{\text{unit CM}}$$

Target income dollars
$$= \frac{\text{Fixed costs} + [\text{target after-tax income}/(1 - \text{tax rate})]}{\text{CM ratio}}$$

Part IV

Conclusion

Chapter 16

How to Apply Cost Management Tools to Your Organization

Two explorers in the jungle come across a ferocious lion. One explorer takes off his boots and puts on running shoes. The other one, a bit puzzled by this action, tells him, "You are wasting your time my friend. You cannot outrun the lion." The other one looked at him squarely in the eye and responded, "You are wrong, my friend; I just need to outrun you."

F inancial information can provide you with a valuable tool for understanding how well your organization is performing. Every decision a manager makes has financial implications for the company. It is important that managers learn to use financial information to manage their operations effectively and achieve the strategic goals of the organization.

Throughout the book I have emphasized some key themes. The first theme is the importance of strategic planning for the long-run viability of your company. Strategic planning defines who you are, where you are going, and how you are going to get there. All elements of the organization should be consistent with the company's long-term direction. These elements include the organizational structure, the business processes, the capital investments, and the management information systems. When these critical elements are not aligned with long-term goals, the organization wastes precious resources in actions that are disjointed and do not further its strategic objectives.

The second theme relates to the preparation of cost information. Cost information should reflect the company's underlying business processes. The activity-based costing (ABC) revolution began because operating managers did not believe the cost information generated by their accounting systems. This situation led practitioners and academicians to look for alternative costing methods that would reflect the true cost structure of the organization. ABC, however, is only one alternative for the redesign of a cost information system. Traditional cost-accounting concepts, if properly applied, can accurately reflect product or service costs and provide good cost information for management decision making. It is not the traditional accounting concepts that have failed in the past, but the way accountants have applied these concepts in their organizations. We have continued to use systems design dating from the 1950s and 1960s in an increasingly automated and rapidly changing business environment.

Cost systems are dynamic; they should evolve as the organization grows and matures. Users of cost information should periodically reexamine their cost preparation methods to ensure that these continue to reflect the business of the organization. Recently one of my clients requested a revision of the product cost model for its manufacturing facility. We had designed the cost model when the company was much smaller, the information systems nonexistent, and detailed information of the production processes unavailable. The model was adequate for the stage of development of the company at that time. However, four years later, we continued to use the same cost model even though the company had doubled in size, implemented a computerized information system, and obtained more knowledge on the demands of the manufacturing process on the resources of the company. The existing cost model was moving the organization in a direction that would not sustain long-run profitability. The moral of this story is that as the organization grows and evolves, the cost model should be revised to reflect the changes in the business.

The third theme centers on the importance of understanding the key assumptions and the preparation methods used to generate financial information. Financial information is not black and white. It is based on assumptions, estimates, and preparation methods that affect the results and, ultimately, how the numbers are interpreted. Financial information can be prepared in many different ways and presented in many different formats. Although the technical details behind a financial calculation can get fairly complicated, users should not lose sight of the big picture. What are the important factors affecting the decision? How are these factors incorporated into the financial analysis? What are the key assumptions? What is the risk, and how is it reflected in the numbers? If managers insist that their financial experts tell them the assumptions behind the numbers, they will be much clearer about what the numbers are really telling them and whether they agree or disagree with the results.

The fourth theme revolves around the notion of simplicity. Financial personnel often devise complex cost models, allocation schemes, or reports that provide relatively little value to their users. ABC systems, for example, have been criticized for the complexity of their design and the difficulty in maintaining the information updated over time. Financial analysts and users should strive for simplicity in the design and development of cost information systems. They should evaluate whether the added complexity of a cost model, allocation scheme, or report is justified by the value of the information provided. They should strive to make accounting information user friendly, presenting it in a simple and nontechnical format.

Finally, the business needs, not the systems applications, should determine how cost information is prepared and reported. Most financial system applications have a costing module that calculates product or service costs according to some specific parameters, such as labor hours or machine hours. However, many of these applications are inflexible and can handle only a traditional cost system design. Cost analysts must ensure that the business drives the cost model and not the limitations of the computer system applications.

An anecdote from my consulting experience illustrates this point. One of my clients uses a well-known integrated systems application. The design of this system assumes that setup costs will always vary as a function of labor hours. However, in this company, some products have both labor setup hours and machine setup hours that are independent of each other. Because the systems application does not provide for machine setup hours in its design, we had to "fool" the system so that it would calculate setup costs correctly. We did not let the limitations of the computer system drive our cost model. Instead, we worked around these limitations so that the cost model drove the systems application.

This book has attempted to provide you with a greater understanding of how financial information is prepared and reported and a number of cost management tools that can assist you in the decision-making process. Financial information can reveal many sources of hidden opportunities. As you expand your financial knowledge, you can tap into this wealth of information to uncover new horizons and boost your company's profitability.

Appendix A: The Basic Financial Statements

F inancial statements are the primary mechanisms for communicating information on the company's financial performance for a specific period of time. The preparation and analysis of financial statement information on a regular basis can help business managers to detect problems, opportunities, or trends and revise their business strategies accordingly.

Financial statements are not perfect representations of the real world. They will not tell you the age of the current CEO, measure the level of customer service, or alert you to a declining market share. They are an accountant's best efforts to portray the business in financial terms and are limited to information that can be quantified in monetary terms.

There are four major financial statements that are used to communicate the results of the business:

- Balance sheet (or statement of financial position)
- Income statement (or statement of profit and loss)
- Statement of stockholders' equity (or statement of capital)
- Statement of cash flows

The **balance sheet** shows the financial position of the business as of a specific date (e.g., as of December 31, XXXX). It presents all the economic resources of the company and all the claims (either external such as creditors or internal such as stockholders) against these resources.

The **income statement** is a summary of the revenues and expenses incurred by the business over a period of time. Many people (including managers) consider it the most important financial statement because its primary purpose is to measure whether the company has earned an acceptable income level.

The **statement of stockholders' equity** shows the changes in the capital invested and retained in the company over a period of time. Stockholders' equity is the sum of the capital invested plus the cumulative net income earned over the life of the organization.

The **statement of cash flows** shows the cash produced by operating activities, as well as the cash inflows and outflows from financing and investing activities that took place during the period. The statement of cash flows compensates for a major deficiency in the income statement: the inability to account for changes in cash.

Financial statements can be prepared for internal or external use. External users include stockholders, government agencies, investors, suppliers, and banks. Internal users are management, employees, and directors.

Financial statements for external use must adhere to a set of standard practices known as generally accepted accounting principles (GAAP). **Generally accepted accounting principles** are the standard accounting concepts, rules, and procedures that govern accepted accounting practices at a particular time. They arise from a broad agreement of accounting practitioners in academia, government, and industry and evolve with changes in business conditions. Many organizations directly or indirectly influence GAAP, such as the Financial Accounting Standards Board (FASB), the American Institute of Certified Public Accountants (AICPA), and the Securities and Exchange Commission (SEC). Financial statements for internal use can be tailored toward the specific needs of the organization and do not have to conform to GAAP.

Most organizations prepare a balance sheet and an income statement on a regular basis and use these reports to measure financial performance. The statement of capital and the statement of cash flows are generally prepared on an annual basis to comply with the external reporting requirements and the information needs of external users. Therefore, the discussion in this appendix focuses on the balance sheet and income statement because these are the primary tools that internal decision makers use.

The Balance Sheet

The balance sheet is like a photograph; it captures a picture of the financial condition of your company at a fixed point in time. It shows the economic resources and the claims against those resources as of a particular date. The balance sheet consists of three principal elements: assets, liabilities, and stockholders' equity.

Assets are the company's economic resources. Anything of value that is owned or legally due the business is classified as an asset. There are various subcategories of assets:

- **Current assets** are cash or other assets that can reasonably be expected to be realized in cash, sold, or consumed during the next year or during the normal operating cycle of the business (if longer than a year). Examples are cash, accounts receivable, marketable securities, and inventory.

- **Investments** are generally long term in nature, not used in the normal operation of business, and not expected to be converted to cash within the next year. Examples include securities held for long-term investment and land held for future use.

- **Property, plant, and equipment** (or **fixed assets**) are resources that are used in the continuing operation of the business and are not intended for resale. Regardless of their market value, fixed assets are always listed as cost less an allowance for accumulated depreciation. The only exception is land. Land does not depreciate nor appreciate over time for accounting purposes.

Depreciation is a systematic mechanism to spread the cost of an asset over the number of periods that it is expected to benefit. **Accumulated depreciation** reflects the amount of the asset's total cost that has been charged against income. On the balance sheet, accumulated depreciation is deducted from the original cost of the asset to arrive at the net property, plant, and equipment amount. The purpose of showing the accumulated depreciation is to give the user an idea of the relative age of the assets in question.

- **Intangible assets** have no physical substance but have a value based on rights or privileges that belong to the owners. Examples include patents, copyrights, and goodwill.

- **Other assets** is a category some companies use to describe assets that do not fit any of the other categories. It may also be used to group all assets that the company owns that are not current assets or property, plant, and equipment.

Liabilities are divided into two categories: current liabilities and long-term or noncurrent liabilities:

■ **Current liabilities** are obligations due within one year or the normal operating cycle of the business, whichever is longer. These liabilities are generally paid with current assets or other short-term liabilities. Examples include accounts payable, notes payable, and wages payable.

■ **Noncurrent or long-term liabilities** are debts of the business that are due beyond one year or the normal operating cycle of the company. Examples of noncurrent liabilities are bonds payable and long-term debt.

■ **Net worth** represents the owners' claims against the assets of the organization once all liabilities have been paid. It is the difference between assets and liabilities. *Net worth, stockholders' equity, owner's equity,* and *capital* are terms that are used interchangeably. Because most assets are recorded at cost rather than market value, stockholders' equity is not a measure of the true net worth of the corporation. Owners' equity includes the capital invested in the organization plus the accumulated earnings that have been reinvested in the business. These accumulated earnings are known in accounting circles as **retained earnings**.

As the name of the statement indicates, the balance sheet must always balance. Figure A-1 shows the basic accounting equation. The two sides of the equation must always be equal. Figure A-2 shows a sample balance sheet for a small, closely held corporation.

Figure A-1. *The Basic Accounting Equation.*

Assets = Liabilities + net worth

The economic resources of the company must be equal to the claims against those resources from either external sources such as creditors or the owners of the business.

Income Statement

The **income statement** shows the total actions of a business over a period of time, whether it is a month, a quarter, or a year. It details the revenue earned and the expenses incurred resulting in a net profit or loss. In contrast to the balance sheet, the income statement is like a video camera: It captures all the actions that occurred during

Figure A-2. Example of a Balance Sheet.

XYZ Company, Inc.
Balance Sheet
As of December 31, XXX1 and XXX0

	XXX1	XXX0
ASSETS		
Current Assets		
Cash	$ 14,000	$ 9,000
Accounts receivable	12,000	5,675
Inventory	8,765	10,765
Subtotal current assets	**34,765**	**25,440**
Property, plant, and equipment	131,300	131,300
Less accumulated depreciation	(20,000)	(18,000)
Net property, plant, and equipment	**111,300**	**113,300**
Other assets	5,000	3,000
Total assets	**$151,065**	**$141,740**
LIABILITIES AND STOCKHOLDERS' **EQUITY**		
Current liabilities		
Accounts payable	$ 5,000	$ 3,180
Payroll taxes withheld	2,000	2,000
Current portion of bank loan	6,500	6,500
Subtotal current liabilities	**13,500**	**11,680**
Bank loan	50,000	53,000
Other liabilities	1,000	2,300
Total liabilities	**64,500**	**66,980**
Stockholders' equity		
Common stock	22,000	22,000
Retained earnings	64,565	52,760
Net worth	**86,565**	**74,760**
Total liabilities and stockholders' **equity**	**$151,065**	**$141,740**

a specific time period. In the heading, the income statement shows the period of time covered by the report, for example, for the 12 months ended December 31, XXXX.

Income statements are prepared on either a cash basis or an accrual basis. **Cash basis accounting** recognizes revenues and expenses on the basis of cash received or cash paid. This type of accounting is used by small businesses and individuals, primarily for tax purposes. Cash basis accounting is subject to manipulation by deferring the timing of cash receipts and cash disbursements and therefore is not recognized by GAAP.

Accrual accounting records the financial effects of transactions and other events when they occur rather than the period when the cash is received or paid. Under this method, revenue is recognized in the period it is earned, not when the cash is received. In the same way, expenses are recognized in the period incurred, not when the cash is paid. This method requires the use of **accruals**, expenses that have been incurred but not yet paid or revenues that have been earned but not yet billed. Most medium-size and large organizations use accrual accounting for the preparation of their financial statements.

The income statement has three major elements: revenues, expenses, and net income. The basic income statement equation is as follows:

$$\text{Revenues} - \text{expenses} = \text{Net income}$$

Revenue is defined as all income flowing into the business as a result of services rendered or goods sold. Examples of revenue are sales of products, services rendered, fees earned, ticket sales, and interest income. **Expenses** are the cost of goods and services consumed in the course of earning revenues. Examples of expenses are wages, utilities, travel, and telephone. **Net income** represents the net increase in owners' equity resulting from the operations of the business. It is the difference between the income flowing into the business and the resources consumed to produce that income. Figure A-3 shows an example of an income statement for Company XYZ, Inc.

Income statements prepared for internal uses are similar to the income statements prepared for external reporting. Both are prepared using the same fundamental accounting principles discussed in this appendix. Both use common accounting terminology to describe the types of business transactions (e.g., sales, cost of sales).

Figure A-3. *Example of an Income Statement.*

Company XYZ, Inc.
Income Statement
For the year ended December 31, XXX1 and XXX0

	XXX1	XXX0
Sales		
Sales	$225,000	$200,000
Cost of goods sold	140,913	126,625
Gross margin	84,087	73,375
Operating expenses		
Wages and salaries	45,996	43,500
Utilities	11,695	10,731
Insurance	3,000	3,000
Office supplies	7,000	6,347
Subtotal operating expenses	67,691	63,578
Operating income	**16,396**	**9,797**
Income taxes paid	4,591	3,126
Net income	**$ 11,805**	**$ 6,671**

However, the format of these reports for internal purposes generally varies with each company and the needs of its internal users.

Absolute monetary figures are relatively meaningless unless they are compared to another figure. For external purposes, GAAP requires the presentation of prior period information for comparative purposes in the financial statements. For internal purposes, financial results are usually compared against the annual budget, the forecast, or prior period results. This comparison provides a frame of reference to evaluate the company's financial performance.

Appendix B: Mission Statement Example, LOS CIDRINES

Mission

LOS CIDRINES is a company that manufactures and sells bread, pastry, and other related products to the wholesale and retail markets. Our mission is to maintain ourselves as leaders in the industry inspired by a high sense of commitment, quality, and customer service. These attributes will allow us to prosper as a business and continue our growth and development.

Corporate Values

The fundamental values to achieve this mission are:

Customer Service. Our client is the reason for our existence and the most important part of our business. We are committed to provide a service of excellence that will always fulfill our customer needs.

Quality. Quality is EVERYTHING: taste, presentation, freshness, excellent service, and impeccable hygiene among others. It is our commitment to do things well and in a consistent manner to meet our customer expectations so we can count on their continued patronage. It requires that our image, the presentation of our products, and our services should always be in excellent condition.

Our People. LOS CIDRINES are its people and the strength of its existence. They represent us to our customer and the community, reinforcing our image and reputation. It will be a requirement for our people to maintain a high level of leadership, professionalism, commitment, punctuality, and assistance. We want our people motivated and proud of the success of their company. We promote teamwork, mutual respect, and consideration for others. These are our people.

Operational Excellence. Operational excellence involves the use of the available resources in a creative, efficient, and effective manner. LOS CIDRINES will promote operational and administrative excellence with an emphasis on cost control.

Suppliers and Distributors. Our suppliers and distributors are our partners. LOS CIDRINES is committed to maintain a mutually beneficial relationship with our suppliers, distributors, and other business associates.

Social Responsibility. LOS CIDRINES believes in thanking the community for their continued patronage through the sponsorship of activities of a recreational, social, and humanitarian nature, directing its efforts toward children.

Profits. Profits are the fuel of our business; they measure how well we are serving our customers and fulfilling their needs. They are necessary to survive and continue our growth.

Appendix C: How to Calculate Total Available Labor Hours

Total available labor hours are often used as a basis to distribute indirect costs for a service department. The indirect costs are divided by the total available hours to obtain a standard cost rate. This rate is used to charge user areas by multiplying the total labor hours consumed by the area or job during the period by the standard cost rate.

In manufacturing, total available direct labor hours are used for capacity planning. The number of direct labor employees needed can be estimated by dividing the total labor hours required according to the production plan by the labor hours available per employee. If the number of employees required by the production plan exceeds the number of employees in a particular area, management must devise alternative strategies to fill the labor gap, such as shifting resources from one area to another, hiring temporary labor, or working overtime.

Total available labor hours are calculated based on the actual hours worked by an employee. This figure is calculated on an annual basis by subtracting the nonproductive time from the total hours paid in a year. Nonproductive time includes vacation, sick leave, holidays, mandated breaks, training, and meetings. The manager or cost analyst should determine the nonproductive time that will be deducted from the annual hours paid. Some of this time will have to be estimated based on experience. For example, a company may pay an employee for five sick days a year, but on average, an employee uses only two days per year. Two, not five, would be the appropriate number to include in the labor hours calculation.

Figure C-1 shows a sample calculation of total labor hours available. In this example, total labor hours available are 85 percent of the total hours paid. This calculation has implications for both service and manufacturing industries. If a service cost allocation is based on the actual hours paid, the cost rate will be understated since an employee works fewer hours than what he actually gets paid for. In manufacturing, labor planning based on actual hours paid will understate the number of employees needed to run a production line. An example illustrates these points.

Suppose a service department incurred costs totaling $125,000 in the prior quarter. This department employs 15 employees who provide direct services to its customers. This department is billed out to its users at a standard cost rate that is calculated based on the actual departmental costs for the prior quarter. The cost rate for the next quarter for this department would be calculated as shown in Figure C-2. If the billing rate had been calculated based on the actual hours paid, the standard labor rate would decrease to $16 per hour (see Figure C-3).

This labor rate, however, will not fully recover the costs of the department because the employees in this department on average will work 442.50 hours per quarter, not 520 hours. Therefore, an estimated $18,600 of departmental costs will not be recovered using this billing rate.[1]

In manufacturing, the total labor hours available affects capacity

Figure C-1. *Sample Calculation of Total Labor Hours Available.*

Total hours in one year (52 weeks × 40 hours/week)	2,080
Holidays (10 days × 8 hours/day)	80
Vacation days (10 days × 8 hours/day)	80
Sick leave (4 days × 8 hours/day)	32
Mandated breaks (.5 hour/day × 236 days)[a]	118
Total available labor hours per year	**1,770**
% of total hours paid	**85%**

[a]Mandated breaks are based on 236 working days. This number is obtained by taking the total number of workdays in the year, 260, and subtracting the days of vacation, sick, and holiday, which in this example totals 24.

Figure C-2. *Sample Calculation of the Standard Cost Rate Based on Hours Available.*

Actual cost prior quarter	$125,000
Total available hours per quarter[a]	6,638
Standard cost rate per hour (rounded to the nearest dollar)	**$19**

[a]Total available hours per quarter is calculated by dividing the annual hours available per year by 4 and multiplying this number by the number of employees in the department. Total available labor hours per quarter = (1,770 ÷ 4) × 15 employees.

Figure C-3. *Sample Calculation of the Standard Cost Rate Based on Hours Paid.*

Actual cost prior quarter	$125,000
Total hours paid per quarter[a]	7,800
Standard cost rate per hour (rounded to the nearest dollar)	**$16**

[a]Total hours paid per quarter = (2,080 ÷ 4) × 15 employees.

planning. Suppose the production plan for the quarter requires 7,000 labor hours. Based on the total labor hours available, the number of employees required is 15.8 (7,000 hours ÷ 442.50 hours/employee). Based on total hours paid, the number of employees required drops to 13.8. If labor planning is based on the total hours paid, there will be insufficient employees to meet production demands unless alternative measures are taken.

Note

1. Unrecovered costs = (actual hours paid − actual hours worked) × standard cost rate (paid hours) × number of employees
   = (520 − 442.50) × $16 × 15 employees
   = $18,600.

Appendix D:
The Austin Division:
A Budgeting Example

Next Year Strategies

Quanta Computer

•Maintain current market share

•Increase net earnings by 10%

•Increase flexibility to respond to customer's needs

•Produce high quality product at lowest possible cost

•Invest in the future

Austin Division

• Reduce costs

• Decrease lead time
• Improve product availability

• Improve quality of products and processes
• Invest in people
• Invest in new technology

Next Year Strategies

Austin Division

•Reduce material costs

•Decrease lead time

•Improve product availability

•Improve quality of products and processes

•Invest in people
 Invest in new technology

Purchasing Dept

•Include purchasing in new product contract negotiations
•Create contract negotiations function
•Evaluate new vendors

•Negotiate more flexible contract terms

•Implement system tracking
•Develop second and local sources

•Increase utilization of system capacities

•Implement EDI
•Increased skills through training

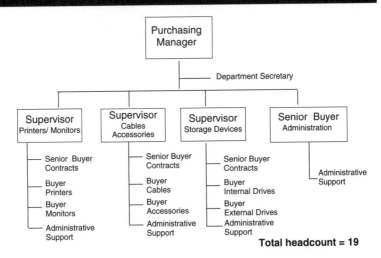

Austin Division
Purchasing Department (Current Year)

Purchasing Manager

— Department Secretary

| Supervisor
Printers/ Monitors | Supervisor
Cables
Accessories | Supervisor
Storage Devices | Senior Buyer
Administration |

— Senior Buyer Contracts
— Buyer Printers
— Buyer Monitors
— Administrative Support

— Senior Buyer Contracts
— Buyer Cables
— Buyer Accessories
— Administrative Support

— Senior Buyer Contracts
— Buyer Internal Drives
— Buyer External Drives
— Administrative Support

— Administrative Support

Total headcount = 19

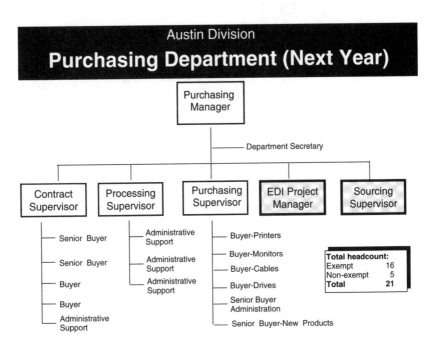

Austin Division
Purchasing Department (Next Year)

Purchasing Manager

— Department Secretary

| Contract Supervisor | Processing Supervisor | Purchasing Supervisor | EDI Project Manager | Sourcing Supervisor |

— Senior Buyer
— Senior Buyer
— Buyer
— Buyer
— Administrative Support

— Administrative Support
— Administrative Support
— Administrative Support

— Buyer-Printers
— Buyer-Monitors
— Buyer-Cables
— Buyer-Drives
— Senior Buyer Administration
— Senior Buyer-New Products

Total headcount:	
Exempt	16
Non-exempt	5
Total	**21**

The Austin Division
Departmental Expense Budget
Purchasing

	CURRENT YEAR			NEXT YEAR		
	Projected	Budget	Projected versus Budget	Proposed Budget	Proposed Budget versus Projected	% increase over Projected
Headcount: Exempt	14	14	0	16	2	14%
Non-exempt	5	4	1	5	0	0%
Total	19	18	1	21	2	11%
Labor						
Salaries (exempt)	$ 583,000	$ 632,000	$ (49,000)	$ 730,000	$ 147,000	25%
Salaries (non-exempt)	77,000	74,000	3,000	92,000	15,000	19%
Overtime	8,000	2,000	6,000	2,000	(6,000)	-75%
Fringe benefits	264,000	282,400	(18,400)	325,200	61,200	23%
Subtotal labor	**932,000**	**990,400**	**(58,400)**	**1,149,200**	**217,200**	**23%**
Operating expenses						
Outside contracted services	5,000	-	5,000	65,000	60,000	1200%
Training	6,750	7,000	(250)	6,000	(750)	-11%
Dues and subscriptions	2,500	3,000	(500)	2,500	-	0%
Employee relations	1,750	1,500	250	1,550	(200)	-11%
Travel	55,000	45,000	10,000	70,000	15,000	27%
Supplies	10,260	9,800	460	10,500	240	2%
Equipment	10,500	7,000	3,500	10,000	(500)	-5%
Depreciation - office equipment	10,500	9,000	1,500	11,400	900	9%
Subtotal operating expenses	**102,260**	**82,300**	**19,960**	**176,950**	**74,690**	**73%**
Allocated costs						
Facilities	228,000	216,000	12,000	252,000	24,000	11%
Cafeteria	11,400	10,800	600	12,600	1,200	11%
Information systems	186,887	186,887	-	229,840	42,953	23%
Subtotal allocated costs	**426,287**	**413,687**	**12,600**	**494,440**	**68,153**	**16%**
Department total	**$ 1,460,547**	**$ 1,486,387**	**$ (25,840)**	**$ 1,820,590**	**$ 360,043**	**25%**

Note: Parenthesis indicate a favorable variance

Capital Budget Summary
Purchasing Department

	Capital	Expense	Total Project Cost
EDI Project			
Software development	$25,000		$25,000
Hardware	25,000		25,000
Consulting		25,000	25,000
Headcount		131,600	131,600
Subtotal EDI project	**50,000**	**156,600**	**206,600**
Computer workstations (new hires)	10,000	-	10,000
Total capital projects	**$60,000**	**$156,600**	**$216,600**

Budget Detail for Major Spending Categories

Labor

Job Title	Total	Annual Salary	Monthly Salary	Total Salaries
Purchasing manager	1	$65,000	$5,417	$65,000
Purchasing supervisor	3	53,000	4,417	159,000
Purchasing supervisor	1	49,000	4,083	49,000
Project manager EDI	1	49,000	4,083	49,000
Senior buyers	4	45,000	3,750	180,000
Buyers	6	38,000	3,167	228,000
Total exempt	**16**		**$24,917**	**$730,000**
Department secretary	1	$20,000	$1,667	$20,000
Administrative support	4	18,000	1,500	72,000
Total non-exempt	**5**		**$3,167**	**$92,000**
Total headcount	**21**		**$28,083**	**$822,000**

Outside Contracted Services

Negotiation training seminars -A 3 month intensive training to enhance buyer negotiation skills	$20,000.00
Vendor evaluation service ($5000 per quarter) -Information services contract to access information on vendors	$20,000.00

EDI project
-Consulting services to assist in developing
  protocol for EDI and facilitate the coordination and
  implementation with vendors
	$25,000.00

Total outside contracted services	**$65,000.00**

Travel Expense Detail

Purpose	Number of	Destination	Total Cost
New Product Introductions			
21" Monitor	2	Europe	$8,000
Hard Drive	2	Korea	12000
Japan	2	Japan	10000
Vendor Relations			
Various vendors	3	Japan	$15,000
Vendor A	2	Taiwan	10000
Vendor B, C, and D	6	USA	6000
Sourcing			
Various vendors	3	Canada	$6,000
Various vendors	3	US	3000
Total travel expense			**$70,000**

Estimated travel expenses per trip for an average 3 to 5-day stay	
Japan	$5,000
Korea	$6,000
Europe	$4,000
Taiwan	$5,000
Canada	$2,000
US	$1,000

Other Information

Other Information
- Supplies calculated at an average of $500 per employee
  ($500 per employee X 21 employees = $10,500)
- Workstations for new employees = $3000 hardware + 2000 software
- Depreciation calculated over 5-year useful life
- Allocated costs are based on budget guidelines and were provided by Accounting.

Appendix E: A Capital Budget Justification Example

Project Description

Electronic data interface (EDI) allows direct electronic interchange of information between two companies. In purchasing, EDI is currently being used by many companies to transmit purchase orders, receive confirmation, receive shipment notifications, and make payments.

The implementation of EDI will be a significant improvement over our current procurement process, which requires shuffling paper back and forth with our suppliers. This paper flow not only delays order placement but limits the information on product availability. Many of our current vendors use EDI to send and receive customer information.

EDI would also facilitate vendor payment through an electronic transfer to the vendor account. This form of payment eliminates the need to write and verify checks, resulting in savings in the accounts payable area.

The EDI software will be developed in-house. The project will require two full-time resources for one year: a full-time project manager to coordinate and monitor the project with our vendors and a programmer analyst to install and test the interface programs. The additional programmer analyst has been included in the information systems department's budget. Consulting services on EDI protocol will also be needed and have been included in the purchasing departmental budget.

Total Project Cost

	Expense	Capital	Total
Project manager	$ 68.6K[1]		$ 68.6K
Program analyst	63.0K		63.0K
Consulting	25.0K		25.0K
Hardware		$25.0K	25.0K
Software		25.0K	25.0K
Total project	**$156.6K**	**$50.0K**	**$206.6K**

Expected Benefits

The implementation of this project will result in the elimination of one administrative support person in purchasing and one-half person in accounts payable. These savings will be reflected in the following year's budget.

The increased availability of information will also result in productivity improvements for the buyers since about 25 percent of their time is spent chasing the paper trail. We expect the elimination of one buyer position, given current volumes, after implementation.

Summary of Expected Benefits

1 administrative support	$25.2K
1 buyer	$53.2K
1/2 accounts payable	$12.6K
Total yearly savings	**$91.0K**

Financial Evaluation

Payback	2.27 years
Net present value	$94.8K
(@ 8% discount, 4 years)	

Risks

- Delays in the software development or implementation plan may increase the costs of the project and defer expected cost savings.

- Additional consulting services may be required due to unexpected technical difficulties.
- No increase in productivity is achieved, so cost savings relating to labor are not realized.

Opportunities

- An increase in productivity may be higher than expected, resulting in greater costing savings.
- Savings may be realized in operating supplies (accounts payable checks, purchase orders, etc.) due to reduced paper flow.

Note

1. Note that the symbol K stands for thousands. Therefore, $68.6K represents $68,600.

Appendix F: Performance Summary Example

OPERATIONS SUMMARY:	Actual	Budget	Variance
Customer Service:			
• Unshipped orders (units)	159,455	-	159,455
• Unshipped orders (in dollars)	$ 478,365	-	478,365
Manufacturing Process:			
• Production (units)	1,566,723	1,750,000	(183,277)
• % completion to schedule	90%	100%	-10.00%
• Days worked in period	100	101	(1)
• Manufacturing efficiency	80.57%	90.00%	-9.43%
• Cost improvement opportunity	$ 300,981	$ -	300,981
Human Resources			
• Headcount	42	45	(3)
• Units produced per employee	37,303	38,889	(1,586)
Financial			
• Average cost per unit	$ 2.18	$ 1.99	$ 0.19
• Work in process inventory	$ 176,256	$ 86,927	$ 89,329

COST SUMMARY:	YTD Actual	YTD Budget	Variance
Direct materials	$ 1,519,721	$ 1,488,387	$ 31,334
Water	141,005	125,338	15,667
Electricity	109,671	78,336	31,335
Subtotal variable costs	$ 1,770,397	$ 1,692,061	$ 78,336
Labor	673,691	735,000	(61,309)
Depreciation	391,681	437,500	(45,819)
Maintenance	156,672	192,500	(35,828)
Insurance	15,667	5,250	10,417
Contracted services	7,834	3,500	4,334
Other	6,267	-	6,267
Subtotal fixed costs	$ 1,251,812	1,373,750	$ (121,938)
Total controllable costs	$ 3,022,209	$ 3,065,811	$ (43,602)
Allocated costs	$ 391,681	$ 411,250	$ (19,569)
Total departamental costs	$ 3,413,890	$ 3,477,061	$ (63,171)

Appendix G: How to Trace Labor Costs to Activities

There are three main methods for tracing labor costs to activities: specific employee, job category, and total labor.[1] The **specific employee method** details the time each employee spends on an activity. It then assigns the individual cost of each employee based on the percentage of time spent on each activity. For salaried employees, the team must decide whether to use the actual hours worked or a standard workweek in assigning costs. This decision could affect the allocated costs if salaried employees are working significant amounts of overtime. The specific employee method is the most accurate mechanism to trace labor costs. However, it is time-consuming and can become unmanageable for departments with a large number of employees. In this situation, the other two methods are more practical and cost-effective.

The **job category method** uses total salaries by job classification or an average salary per position to assign labor costs to activities. The average salary can be calculated based on the actual wages of the employees in the department or based on an average provided by the payroll or human resources department. An example is shown in Figure G-1. Although this method is easier than the specific employee one, it can result in cost distortions if there are significant salary differentials among individuals in the same job category.

The **total labor method** is the easiest method to understand and apply. Total department salaries are assigned to activities based on the total time that employees spend on each activity. These total hours are derived from the interview data. This data is summarized by activity to arrive at a percentage of time spent on each activity for

Figure G-1. *The Job Category Method.*

Job Category: Administrative Assistant

González	$20,000
Pérez	15,000
Rodríguez	13,000
Total salaries for job category	$48,000
Average salary for job category ($48,000 ÷ 3)	$16,000

Activity	% Time	Cost
Accounts payable	50	$24,000
Payroll	25	12,000
Budgeting	10	4,800
Inventory control	15	$ 7,200

the total department. This percentage is then used to assign labor costs. Another alternative is to have the department manager, supervisor, or resident expert assign the estimated percentage of time spent on each activity based on experience. Figure G-2 shows an example of the total labor method.

The total labor method is the least accurate of these three allocation methods. Like the job category method, it will produce cost distortions if there are significant salary differences among the employees in an organization. Moreover, it does not reflect the cost differential of the resources required to perform one activity versus another. For example, financial reporting and budgeting activities are usually performed by well-paid financial analysts; accounts pay-

Figure G-2. *The Total Labor Method.*

Total Department Costs $500,000

Activity	Hours	% Time	Cost
Accounts payable	384	20	$100,000
Payroll	192	10	50,000
Planning	576	30	150,000
Inventory control	384	20	100,000
Financial reporting	192	10	50,000
General ledger	96	5	25,000
Other	96	5	25,000
Total department labor costs	1,920		$500,000

able, on the other hand, are handled by lower-paid personnel. On the plus side, the labor method is easy to use and produces fast results. If the cost distortions are not significant, it is a viable method for tracing labor costs.

Note

1. James A. Brimson, *Activity Accounting: An Activity-Based Costing Approach* (New York: Wiley, 1991), pp. 136–142.

Glossary

Absolute reasonableness test Test that compares the calculated cost figure to a historical cost, standard cost, or prior cost estimate of the same product or service.

Accounting An information system that measures, processes, and communicates financial information about an organization or its subdivisions.

Accounting rate of return See *return on investment method*.

Accounts Major categories used in accounting systems to record, summarize, and report business transactions. These categories satisfy legal requirements and are meaningful to management.

Accrual accounting The reporting of revenues in the period in which they are sold and the reporting of expenses in the period of purchase, regardless of when the cash was received or paid.

Accruals The recognition of an expense that has been incurred but not yet paid or revenue that has been earned but not yet received.

Accumulated depreciation Total past depreciation of a capital or fixed asset. It is reflected as a deduction of fixed assets on the balance sheet.

Action plans Plans describing the specific actions that the organization will take in the short term to achieve its long-term strategies.

Activity A description of the work that gets done in an organization. It is a combination of people, technology, materials, processes, and environment that produces a given product or service.

Activity analysis   A process that examines the major activities of the organization and categorizes them in a meaningful manner.

Activity-based costing (ABC)   A cost management approach that identifies the processes involved in supplying a product or service and the resources that these processes consume. It uses this information to assign costs, eliminate waste, and improve processes.

Activity-based management (ABM)   A discipline that focuses on the management of activities to improve continuously the value received by customers.

Activity cost   The total cost of all resources assigned to perform an activity.

Activity dictionary   A document that defines all the significant activities that the organization performs.

Activity level   A measure of volume or usage that varies according to the cost object.

Activity measure   A measure that quantifies the frequency and intensity of use of an activity or operation by a product or service, such as machine hours, labor hours, or units produced.

Actual cost   A cost that shows what has already happened and is based on historical data.

Actual yield   The actual output obtained from the manufacturing process.

Administrative costs   The support costs of running the organization—for example, human resources, accounting, tax, treasury, information systems, legal, and corporate.

Allocation base   A measure that determines how costs are assigned to the cost object.

Allocation rate   See *cost allocation rate.*

Assets   The organization's economic resources—anything of value that is owned or legally due to the business.

Average cost   Establishes a relationship between costs and activity levels or volume. It is calculated by dividing some total cost (the numerator) by some total measure of activity (the denominator). The activity level is expressed in a unit of measure that is meaningful to the users.

Balanced scorecard   A four-quadrant model that allows managers to view the business from four different perspectives: customer, internal, innovation and learning, and financial.

Balance sheet   A financial statement that shows the financial position of the business as of a specific date (e.g., as of December 31, XXXX). It presents all of the organization's economic resources and all claims (either external such as creditors or internal such as stockholders) against these resources.

Batch-level activities   Activities that consume resources each time a batch or work order is produced. Activity measures should relate the resource consumption to the number of batches produced.

Bill of materials (BOM)   A document that shows the components needed and the quantity required to manufacture a product or batch.

Book-to-physical-inventory adjustment   The difference between the inventory dollars as recorded in the financial records compared to the dollar value of what is physically in the warehouse.

Breakeven point (BE)   Represents the volume level where the total revenues and the total expenses are equal. At this level, there is no profit or loss. The breakeven point can be expressed in units or dollars.

Budget   A financial document that quantifies in monetary terms the action plans of the company over a short period of time, typically a year.

Capacity   The amount of output that can be obtained from a process during a given time period. It is generally measured in units of output per unit of time. Capacity can be constrained by people, facilities, or equipment.

Capacity utilization   The extent to which a company uses its production capacity; expressed as a percentage of the expected output. It is calculated using the following formula: (Actual output ÷ expected output) × 100.

Capital   See *net worth.*

Capital asset   An economic resource that provides benefits to a company over one or more years beyond the period of acquisition. Also known as *fixed asset.*

Capital budget   Shows the expenditures required for major investments and the purchases of property, plant, and equipment by area.

Capital costs   Expenditures incurred in the acquisition of capital assets. Also known as *capital expenditures.*

Capital expenditure   See *capital costs.*

Capitalize   A term used to describe an accounting process whereby a capital expenditure is recorded in the general ledger as an asset. A capitalized item is reported in the balance sheet.

Cash basis accounting   A basis of accounting in which revenues and expenses are recognized on the basis of cash received or cash paid.

Cash budget   Presents the expected cash receipts and cash disbursements for the budget period.

Cash flow   Cash that enters or leaves the business.

Cash inflow   Cash that enters the business or, conversely, cash that does not leave the business.

Cash outflow   All the cash that leaves the business.

Chart of accounts   A listing of all the categories within an organization that may be used to classify financial information.

Commercial risks   Those factors such as changing social values, competitive actions, and trade barriers that can affect the amount of revenues or cost savings realized from a project.

Committed costs   Costs that result from contractual obligations (e.g., a maintenance contract or purchase agreement) or are a consequence of past decisions (e.g., depreciation). Generally these costs cannot be altered in the short term and represent fixed amounts that can be calculated very precisely.

Committed funds   Capital appropriation funds for which a purchase order has been issued to a vendor.

Continuous budget   A budget preparation method that adds a new budget period as the period just ended is dropped. Also known as a *rolling budget.*

Contribution margin (CM)   The excess of sales over the variable costs of the product or service. It is the amount of money left over after recovering the variable costs to cover fixed costs and generate a profit. The CM can be calculated in total, per unit, or as a percentage of sales.

Contribution margin income statement   An internal financial statement that shows the contribution to income by an organizational unit such as a sales office, a product line, a department, or an activity.

Contribution margin ratio A ratio that shows on a percentage basis how much money a product contributed to recover the company's fixed costs. It is calculated as follows: (contribution margin in dollars ÷ sales) × 100.

Controllable cost A cost that can be significantly influenced by a particular individual for an area or department over a period of time.

Conversion costs The sum of direct labor and overhead costs used to manufacture a product.

Corporate mission statement Establishes the identity of the organization and provides a framework to establish the long-term direction of the organization.

Cost Estimated measure of the resources consumed to provide a product or service.

Cost allocation rate A rate used to assign the indirect costs to services. It is analogous to the manufacturing overhead rate.

Cost center Organizational unit whose managers are accountable only for costs. A cost center manager typically controls the inputs to the process (e.g., manpower and supplier relationships) but has no control over sales or the generation of revenue.

Cost drivers Factors that affect the resources required by an activity and therefore cause costs to be incurred by the organization. Cost drivers are structural causes of the cost of an activity and differ in the extent to which they can be controlled by the company. Examples are product or process design, customer specifications, corporate requirements, and government regulations.

Costed bill of materials A document that shows the quantity and cost of each component of a product and adds these together to obtain the materials cost per unit or batch.

Cost object An item for which a separate cost measurement is desired.

Cost of capital See *required rate of return*.

Cost pools Costs that are grouped together by department, production process, or work area for the purpose of assigning them to products, services, or processes.

Cost rollup An accounting process that sums the significant cost components of a product and calculates a total unit cost.

Critical success factors (CSF)   Key dimensions of performance that determine the long-term success of the organization.

Current assets   Cash or other assets that can reasonably be expected to be realized in cash, sold, or consumed during the next year or during the normal operating cycle of the business (if longer than a year).

Current liabilities   Obligations that are due within one year or the normal operating cycle of the business, whichever is longer. These liabilities are generally paid with current assets or other short-term liabilities. Examples are accounts payable, notes payable, and wages payable.

Customer contact and customization   A dimension used to classify service organizations that describes the level of customer interaction and the degree of customization involved in providing a service.

Depreciation expense   A portion of the total cost of capital assets to be charged as expenses in a particular period.

Depreciation tax shield   Tax savings that result from taking a depreciation deduction on the income statement.

Design capacity   See *practical capacity*.

Detailed flowcharting   A method used to set labor standards that shows a precise diagram of the job and examines this diagram for improvement.

Differential costs   See *incremental costs*.

Direct cost   A cost that can be directly traced to the item being measured.

Direct labor cost   The labor cost related to the time spent manufacturing a product.

Direct materials cost   The costs of all raw materials used to manufacture the finished product.

Direct method   An allocation method that assigns the cost of support departments directly to the operating departments and ignores intermediary users.

Discounted cash flow (DCF) methods   Capital-budgeting methods that measure the cash inflows and outflows as if they occurred at a single point in time. These methods recognize that money has a cost—the interest forgone. The commonly used DCF methods are net present value (NPV) and internal rate of return (IRR).

Discounted payback period A variation of the payback method that considers the time value of money. It is the time required for the discounted cash flows to equal the original investment.

Discount rate See *required rate of return*.

Discrete manufacturers Manufacturing companies that make different products as either a single unit or a distinct, identifiable batch or job.

Discretionary costs Costs incurred at the option of a manager. These costs are neither fixed nor variable. Training, travel, and supplies are considered discretionary expenses.

Economic risks The external nontechnological risks that are a cost of doing business, such as a change in government regulations, the rate of economic growth, or a rise in interest rates.

Engineering change order (ECO) A document used in manufacturing organizations to incorporate changes in the manufacturing process or the product design.

Expected cost Total actual or estimated cost of a batch or lot divided by the standard yield.

Expensed A term used to describe an accounting process whereby an expenditure is recorded as consumed in the general ledger. An expensed item is reported in the income statement.

Expenses The cost of goods and services consumed in the course of earning revenues.

Facility-sustaining activities Activities that sustain the organization's general business process.

Factory overhead costs All other manufacturing costs that are not included as direct labor or direct materials.

Financial accounting Accounting information that is designed primarily to meet the needs of external decision makers such as banks, stockholders, or regulatory agencies, and is governed by generally accepted accounting principles.

Financial budget Consists of the capital budget, the cash budget, the budgeted balance sheet, and the budgeted statement of cash flows.

Financial forecast Projects the financial results of an organizational plan for a specific time period. In contrast to a budget, a forecast may or may not be used to measure management performance.

Fixed asset See *capital asset* and *property, plant, and equipment.*

Fixed cost A cost that does not change in total with changes in volume or activity levels.

Flexible budget A budget preparation method that adjusts the budgeted costs to reflect actual activity levels. It compares actual costs for a given volume level with the budgeted costs for the same volume level.

Flowcharting See *detailed flowcharting.*

Forecast A planning tool that projects the financial results of organizational action plans for a specific time period.

Four-way variance analysis An overhead variance analysis that calculates separate variances for fixed and variable overhead.

Frontline labor Those employees who are directly involved in providing service to a customer, for example, a bank teller, an insurance agent, or a customer service representative.

Full cost See *total cost.*

General ledger The file, book, or database that contains all the company's accounts.

Generally accepted accounting principles (GAAP) The standard accounting concepts, rules, and procedures that govern accepted accounting practices at a particular time.

Gross margin The difference between sales and cost of sales. Gross margin as a percentage of sales is an important performance indicator. It is commonly used to evaluate cost control and overall product or service profitability.

Head-count plan Details the staffing requirements for the upcoming year or planning period.

Hurdle rate See *required rate of return.*

Hybrid systems Costing systems that combine elements of both job order and process costing.

Implementation risk The failure to meet project plans due to human behavior or organizational factors. Some factors that may contribute to implementation risk are reorganizations, employee compensation systems, employee morale, and training.

Income statement A financial statement that shows a summary of the revenues and expenses incurred by the business over a period of time.

Incremental budget   A budget preparation method in which managers justify only those expenses beyond a specified amount.

Incremental costs   Expected future costs that differ with each alternative. Also known as *relevant costs* or *differential costs*.

Indirect cost   A cost that is common to more than one cost objective.

Indirect labor costs   The labor costs of employees who support the manufacturing or service delivery process, but do not work directly on the product or service. See also *support labor*.

Intangible assets   Assets that have no physical substance but have a value based on rights or privileges that belong to the owners. Examples are patents, copyrights, and goodwill.

Internal rate of return (IRR)   The interest or discount rate at which the present value of the estimated net cash inflows, including the initial investment, is equal to zero.

Investment center   Organizational unit whose managers are evaluated based on profitability and return on capital invested.

Investments   Assets that are generally long term in nature, are not used in the normal operation of business, and are not expected to be converted to cash within the next year. Examples are securities held for long-term investment and land held for future use.

Item master   A file in the inventory control system that contains detailed information about all parts used and produced by an organization.

Job category method   A method of assigning labor costs to activities that uses total salaries by job classification or an average salary per position to assign labor costs to activities.

Job order costing   Costing system that accumulates the costs of an individual job, contract, or customer order. It is appropriate for companies that manufacture products in identifiable batches or provide customized products or services, such as law firms, aircraft manufacturers, shipbuilders, and auto repair shops.

Key performance indicators (KPIs)   Quantifiable measures that the organization uses to evaluate and communicate performance against expected results.

Labor efficiency variance   A variance that measures the savings or the additional cost incurred because the hours worked were different than the standard allowed.

Labor intensity   A dimension used to classify service organizations that describes the quantity of labor and the skill level of the workforce required to perform the service.

Labor price variance   A variance caused by paying more or less than the standard labor rate. Also known as a *labor rate variance.*

Labor rate variance   See *labor price variance.*

Labor standard   The time required to complete an operation when working under standard conditions. Labor standards are used for planning and measurement.

Labor variances   The differences between the actual labor cost incurred and the expected labor costs for the output achieved.

Liabilities   Obligations of the organization. They are divided into two categories: current liabilities and long-term or noncurrent liabilities.

Long-term direction statement   Defines the long-range goals of the organization and must support the corporate mission.

Management accounting   Accounting information that is primarily designed for internal use and is not governed by generally accepted accounting principles.

Management control   The process by which managers influence other members of the organization to implement the organizational strategies.

Manufacturing costs   The costs required to produce a product for resale. It is the sum of labor, materials, and overhead.

Margin of safety   The difference between the actual or projected sales and the breakeven point. The margin of safety answers the question of how far sales can drop before the company will stop generating a profit.

Marketing and selling costs   Costs that are used to market and sell a product or service. These costs may include new business development, product marketing, sales, service, and support.

Mass service organizations   Service organizations that have a high degree of labor intensity and a low level of interaction with the customer. There is little customization for the consumer.

Materials and supplies cost   The cost of consumable items used in providing a service.

Materials efficiency variance   The difference between the actual quantity of materials used and the standard quantity that should have been used for the output achieved, multiplied by the standard unit price. Also known as a *materials quantity variance* or a *materials usage variance.*

Materials price variance The difference between the actual and the standard unit price of materials multiplied by the actual quantity of materials purchased or used.

Materials quantity standard Predetermined amount of materials required to manufacture a product as described in the design specifications.

Materials quantity variance See *materials efficiency variance.*

Materials usage factor See *scrap factor.*

Materials usage variance See *materials efficiency variance.*

Materials variance The difference between the actual material cost and the standard material cost for the actual volume of units purchased, sold, or produced.

Maximum capacity See *theoretical capacity.*

Merchandising costs The costs of acquiring merchandise for resale. It includes not only the purchase price of the item but also freight, tax, insurance, and any other costs required to prepare the merchandise for sale.

Modified accrual approach Under this method, the organization maintains its books on a cash basis throughout the year and makes the appropriate accounting entries at year-end to convert the financial records from cash to accrual accounting.

Motion studies A method used to set labor standards that breaks down the actions of workers into identifiable parts to determine where improvements can be made.

Net book value (NBV) The original purchase price of the equipment less the depreciation amount that has been systematically recognized as an expense during its useful life.

Net income Represents the net increase in stockholders' or owners' equity resulting from the operations of the business. It is the difference between revenues and expenses.

Net present value (NPV) Discounted cash flow method that calculates the expected monetary gain or loss on a project by discounting all the projected cash flows to the present, using the required rate of return.

Net worth Represents the stockholders' or owners' claims against the company assets once all liabilities have been paid.

Noncurrent or **long-term liabilities**   Debts of the business that are due beyond one year or the normal operating cycle of the company. Examples are bonds payable, long-term debt, and mortgages payable.

Nonrecurring expenses   Expenses that are incurred infrequently, often due to a special circumstance such as a government fine, the implementation of a new computer system, or a new product introduction. Because of their infrequent and unpredictable nature, these expenses are often difficult to budget.

Nonvalue-added activities   Activities that do not contribute to customer value or satisfy an organizational need.

Occupancy costs   All costs incurred to maintain the facilities and its surrounding areas.

Operating budget   A financial representation of the short-term plans of the organization across all functions. It consists of an income statement and all supporting budgets.

Operating department   A department where the production occurs or the service is provided.

Operating income   The difference between gross margin and operating expenses. It is the income generated from the main business operations.

Opportunity cost   The profit forgone from the best available alternative as a result of choosing a particular course of action. This cost is not reflected in the accounting books and is often implicit in the decision-making process.

Other assets   Miscellaneous assets owned by a company.

Other service overhead costs   Consist of all other service costs that are not included as service labor, materials and supplies, technology costs, or occupancy costs.

Overhead allocation   A method of assigning overhead costs in some meaningful and systematic way to individual products.

Overhead costs   See *factory overhead costs* or *other service overhead costs*.

Overhead rate   Rate used to assign overhead costs to products or services. It is calculated by dividing the total overhead costs for the facility, department, or work area by an appropriate activity measure.

Overhead variance   The difference between the actual overhead costs incurred and the total overhead costs charged to the products or services for the period.

Owner's equity See *net worth.*

Parent part Manufacturing term that refers to a finished product.

Payback method A capital-budgeting method that measures the time that it will take to recover the total funds invested in a project.

Period costs Costs that are recognized in the period in which they are incurred. Some examples are sales and marketing expenses, research and development costs, and general and administrative costs.

Planned capacity The level of activity projected for a particular time period. It can be above, below, or at a practical capacity.

Planning A business process that involves the identification of long-range goals and the strategies and action plans required to achieve them.

Postimplementation evaluation A tool some organizations use to evaluate their investment decisions. The purpose of this evaluation is to determine how well the company has executed the project in light of the original analysis.

Practical capacity The output that a company would like to produce under normal operating conditions and for which the production system was designed.

Practical or currently attainable standards Standard costs that are achievable within a specific set of performance parameters.

Prime costs The sum of direct materials and direct labor costs used to manufacture a product.

Pro forma balance statement Financial statement that shows the projected assets, liabilities, and net worth of the organization for the planning period.

Pro forma income statement Financial statement that summarizes projected revenues and expenses by major functional category.

Pro forma statement of cash flows Financial statement that shows the expected cash inflows and outflows of the organization from operating, financing, and investing activities for the planning period.

Process costing Cost accumulation system in which the costs of all units produced within a given time period are calculated using broad averages. Process-costing systems are generally used by industries that provide like products or services in a continuous manner, such as food processing, plastics, chemicals, data processing, and transportation services. These systems accumulate costs by departments or processes.

Process manufacturers Manufacturing companies that build like products in a continuous manner following a uniform sequence of production operations. Process industries include steel, plastics, chemicals, distilled spirits, and petroleum.

Product costs All costs that are assigned to the items produced. These costs are reported as inventory until sold as required by generally accepted accounting principles.

Product hierarchy Manufacturing term that refers to the different levels of a bill of materials. The product hierarchy shows all components and subassemblies used in the finished product or parent part.

Production order See *workorder.*

Production plan Details the quantities of each major product that will be manufactured during the year and is expressed in physical terms (e.g., units, pounds, gallons). It is based on the sales budget or the sales forecast and the desired ending inventory levels.

Product structure See *bill of materials.*

Product-sustaining activities Activities that are necessary to meet the production of each type of product or product line.

Professional service organization A highly specialized service organization that requires high labor intensity and a high degree of customer contact. Customization is a key element of the service delivery process.

Profit center Organizational unit whose managers are evaluated based on the operating income or net income of the organization. A profit center manager should control pricing, sales and marketing strategies, and sources of supply—in other words, all major factors affecting revenues and costs.

Projected cost A future cost based on historical data, industry forecasts, supplier quotes, management estimates, and other sources of information.

Property, plant, and equipment Resources that are used in the continuing operation of the business and are not intended for resale. Also known as *fixed asset.*

Quantitative reasonableness tests Statistical analyses that can be done on an absolute or relative basis.

Quasi-manufacturing service See *service factory organizations.*

Reasonableness tests Tests that are used to assess the validity of the cost model and can be done on a subjective or quantitative basis.

Reciprocal method An allocation method that takes into account mutual services rendered among support departments. It allows the incorporation of interdepartmental services into the cost allocation model. The reciprocal method requires the use of simultaneous algebraic equations and can be quite complex.

Recurring expenses Expenses that are incurred on a regular basis and can be estimated based on historical data.

Relative reasonableness test Reasonableness test that compares the calculated cost of an item with historical, standard, or estimated costs of similar items.

Relevant costs See *incremental costs.*

Relevant range Range of activity level that defines the cost/volume relationship.

Required rate of return The minimum acceptable rate of return on an investment. Also known as the *hurdle rate,* the *cost of capital,* or the *discount rate.*

Research and development (R&D) costs Costs incurred for research and development of new products, processes, or technologies. A manufacturing facility may perform R&D functions if it is involved in the development or test of a new process or product.

Resource allocation The process used to assign the economic means available to a company, including labor, materials, equipment, and facilities, to a specific department, work area, or activity.

Responsibility accounting The system that measures the plans and actions of each responsibility center in monetary terms.

Responsibility center An organization, group, division, department, or work area for which a manager is held accountable.

Retained earnings Accumulated earnings that have been reinvested in the business.

Return on assets A financial ratio that measures the amount of profit received for every $1.00 invested in assets. It is calculated by dividing net income by total assets.

Return on capital A financial ratio that measures the amount of profit generated for every dollar of the owner's investment. Also known as *return on equity (ROE)*.

Return on investment method A capital-budgeting method that measures the incremental operating income that will be generated per dollar of investment. It is calculated by dividing the incremental operating income by the required initial investment and presenting this figure as a percentage of the initial investment. Also called the *accounting rate of return*.

Revenue All income flowing into the business as a result of services rendered or goods sold by the company. Examples of revenue are the sale of products, services rendered, fees earned, ticket sales, and interest income.

Revenue center Organizational unit whose managers are evaluated solely on the basis of sales. Managers of these units should exert significant influence over pricing decisions, sales and marketing strategies, and any other factors that may affect their ability to generate sales.

Rolling budget See *continuous budget*.

Routing file A database that identifies the sequence of processes or operations used to manufacture a product and shows the labor machine hours, or both, required by each operation.

Sales budget A projection of the expected sales volume and dollars for the budget year.

Sales mix The relative combination of quantities or dollars of products that compose total sales.

Scheduled capacity See *planned capacity*.

Scrap Raw materials or products that are damaged during the production process and cannot be reused. It can also include finished products that are returned by the customer but cannot be reworked or sold.

Scrap factor A provision for material losses that normally occur during the production process. Also known as the *materials usage factor*.

Semivariable cost A cost that has a fixed and a variable component.

Sensitivity analysis A "what-if" technique that shows how the financial outcome of a project will change as a result of a change in an underlying assumption.

Service costs The costs incurred to provide or deliver a service.

Service factory organizations Service organizations that are characterized by low labor intensity and a low degree of customer contact and customization. Also called *quasi-manufacturing service*.

Service labor cost The cost of those employees who provide services to the customer. It can also be defined as the total labor costs related to the time spent providing a service.

Service shop organizations Service organizations that provide a more customized service. They resemble a discrete manufacturer or job shop operation.

Short-run capacity The maximum output that can be attained without making an additional investment in plant or equipment or straining company resources.

Short-run time period Brief period of time in which the quantities of the available resources are fixed.

Specific employee method A method of assigning labor costs to activities that details the time spent by each employee in each activity.

Spending variance A type of overhead variance that isolates how much of the difference between actual and standard overhead costs was due to spending more or less money than what was called for in the budget.

Standard costs Predetermined costs that are usually expressed on a per unit basis.

Standard cost variance The difference between the actual cost and the standard cost of a product or service.

Standard yield The expected level of output from a manufacturing process.

Statement of cash flows Financial statement that shows the cash produced by operating, financing, and investing activities during the period. It compensates for a major deficiency in the income statement: the inability to account for changes in cash.

Statement of stockholders' equity A financial statement that shows the changes in the capital invested and retained in the company over a period of time.

Static budget   A detailed plan based on a single level of activity.

Step-down method   An allocation method that considers the services performed by one support department for another. This method requires a hierarchy of allocation levels; once a support department's costs have been allocated, it cannot receive any additional charges from other support departments.

Stockholders' equity   The sum of the capital invested plus the cumulative net income earned over the life of the company. See also *net worth*.

Strategic analysis   A thorough examination of the external and internal factors affecting the organization for the purpose of developing strategic plans.

Strategic gap   The difference between the current position and the desired position of the organization based on a strategic analysis of the internal and external environment.

Strategic planning   The part of the planning process that involves the determination of the goals of the organization and the strategies required to achieve these objectives.

Strategies   Long-term objectives that are defined for a specific period of time.

Strategy review   A review process that typically occurs at the start of the annual budgeting cycle in which management develops short-term plans that support the company's long-term objectives and establish the company priorities.

Subassembly   Manufacturing term that refers to an intermediate product used to manufacture another product.

Subjective reasonableness tests   Reasonableness tests that rely on the individual judgment of experts.

Sunk costs   Costs that have already been incurred and therefore are not relevant to the decision-making process. Sunk costs are the result of past decisions that cannot be changed. Classic examples are inventory and property, plant, and equipment.

Support department   A department that provides services to operating departments.

Support labor   A labor classification that includes those employees who provide essential support services to the frontline but do not have direct customer contact. Some examples are maintenance, supervisory, and administrative personnel.

Tactical plan   A short-term planning document that identifies the specific actions or projects required to achieve the stated objectives for the budget year.

Target income   A desired level of income beyond the breakeven point.

Technological risks   Risk factors that involve the failure to meet technological goals. Examples are vendor support, equipment performance, technological obsolescence, compatibility with existing technologies, and new technologies.

Technology costs   All costs relating to the acquisition and use of equipment and information technology.

Theoretical capacity   The maximum output that can be attained when the resources are used to their maximum potential. Also known as *maximum capacity*.

Theoretical standards   Standard costs that can be achieved under the best possible conditions.

Time studies   A method used to set labor standards that uses stopwatches and videotaping to time elements of a job.

Total cost   Represents the aggregate resources consumed by the organization or a part of the organization such as a department, a work area, a product, or a service. Also known as *full costs*.

Total labor hours available   The estimated number of hours that an employee has available to work after deducting legally mandated breaks, vacation, sick leave, training, and other nonproductive time.

Total labor method   A method of assigning labor costs to activities based on the total time spent on each activity by its employees.

Unit cost   The cost of one unit of measure (UM) of a good or service. The UM should identify the output of the goods or services of the organization in a meaningful manner.

Unit-level activities   Activities that are performed each time a unit is produced. The cost of these activities is directly proportional to volume.

Value-added activities   Activities that customers perceive add value to the products or services they purchase or that satisfy an organizational need.

Variable cost   A cost that changes proportionately with increases or decreases in activity levels.

Variance analysis   The process that examines the differences between actual and standard costs to determine their underlying causes and identify opportunities for cost improvement.

Vision   See *long-term direction statement.*

Volume variance   A type of overhead variance that shows how much of the difference between the actual and the standard overhead cost resulted from a failure to operate at the budgeted activity level.

Work activity analysis   A method used to set labor standards that lists in chronological order the work performed, the time spent on it, and the number of items completed.

Work order   A document that contains information on the product, the operations required, the quantity ordered, the quantity completed by operation, and other important tracking information. Also known as a *production order.*

Zero-based budgeting   A budget preparation method that breaks the cycle of continuous overhead growth by assuming zero resources; all resources must be justified.

Bibliography

"The Accounting Classification of Workpoint Costs." In *Statements on Management Accounting*. Statement No. 4BB. Montvale, N.J.: Institute of Management Accountants, 1997.

Akers, Michael D., and Grover L. Porter. "Strategic Planning at Five World-Class Companies." *Management Accounting* (July 1995): 25–31.

Anderson, James C., and James A. Narus. "Capturing the Value of Supplementary Services." *Harvard Business Review* (January–February 1995): 75–83.

Anthony, Robert N., and James S. Reece. *Accounting Text and Cases*. Homewood, Ill.: Richard D. Irwin, 1989.

Berlant, Debbie, Reese Browning, and George Foster. "How Hewlett-Packard Gets Numbers It Can Trust." *Harvard Business Review* (January–February 1990): 178–183.

Berliner, Callie, and James A. Brimson, eds. *Cost Management for Today's Advanced Manufacturing: The CAM-I Conceptual Design*. Boston: Harvard Business School Press, 1988.

Bierman, Harold, Jr., Thomas R. Dyckman, and Ronald W. Hilton. *Cost Accounting: Concepts and Managerial Applications*. Boston: PWS-Kent Publishing Company, 1990.

Brimson, James. *Activity Accounting: An Activity-Based Costing Approach*. New York: Wiley, 1991.

Brinker, Barry J., ed. *Emerging Practices in Cost Management*. Boston: Warren, Gorham & Lamont, 1990.

Chase, Richard B., and Nicholas J. Aquilano. *Production and Operations Management: A Life Cycle Approach*. Homewood, Ill.: Richard D. Irwin, 1989.

Cokins, Gary, Alan Stratton, and Jack Helbling. *An ABC Manager's Primer: Straight Talk on Activity-Based Costing.* Montvale, N.J.: Institute of Management Accountants, 1993.

Cooper, Robin. "Cost Classification in Unit-Based and Activity-Based Manufacturing Cost Systems." *Journal of Cost Management* (Fall 1990): 4–13.

———. "You Need a New Cost System When . . ." *Harvard Business Review* (January–February 1989): 77–82.

———. "The Two-Stage Procedure in Cost Accounting: Part One." *Journal of Cost Management* (Summer 1987): 43–51.

———. "The Two-Stage Procedure in Cost Accounting: Part Two." *Journal of Cost Management* (Fall 1987): 39–45.

Cooper, Robin, and Robert S. Kaplan. "Measure Costs Right: Make the Right Decisions." *Harvard Business Review* (September–October 1988): 96–103.

———. "Profit Priorities from Activity-Based Costing." *Harvard Business Review* (May–June 1989): 130–135.

Cooper, Robin, Robert S. Kaplan, Lawrence S. Maisel, Eileen Morrissey, and Ronald M. Oehm. *Implementing Activity-Based Cost Management: Moving from Analysis to Action.* Montvale, N.J.: Institute of Management Accountants, 1992.

Crosby, Philip B. *Quality Is Free.* New York, N.Y.: Penguin Books USA, Inc., 1980.

"Developing Comprehensive Performance Indicators." In *Statements on Management Accounting.* Statement No. 4U. Montvale, N.J.: Institute of Management Accountants, 1995.

Dickey, Terry. *The Basics of Budgeting.* Los Altos, Calif.: Crisp Publications, 1992.

Drtina, Ralph, Steve Hoeger, and John Schaub. "Continuous Budgeting at the HON Company." *Management Accounting* (January 1996): 20–24.

Ferrara, William L. "The New Cost/Management Accounting—More Questions Than Answers." *Management Accounting* (October 1990): 48–52.

Finkler, Steven A. *Essentials of Cost Accounting for Healthcare.* Gaithersburg, Md.: Aspen Publishers, 1994.

Finney, Robert G. *Essentials of Business Budgeting.* New York: AMACOM, 1995.

Gerstner, Louis V., Jr. "Can Strategic Planning Pay Off?" *Business Horizons,* December 15, 1972, pp. 5–16.

Gibson, Charles H. *Financial Statement Analysis Using Financial Accounting Information.* Cincinnati, Ohio: South-Western Publishing Company, 1992.

Gill, James O. *Understanding Financial Statements.* Los Altos, Calif.: Crisp Publications, 1990.

Gleim, Irvin N., and Dale L. Flesher. *CMA Review.* Vol. 1. 6th ed. Gainesville, Fla.: Gleim Publications, 1994.

Granger Morgan, M., and Max Henrion. *Uncertainty: A Guide to Dealing With Uncertainty in Quantitative Risk and Policy Analysis.* New York: Cambridge University Press, 1992.

Green, F. B., Felix Amenkhienan, and George Johnson. "Performance Measures and JIT." *Management Accounting* (February 1991): 50–53.

Hammer, Michael, and James Champy. *Reengineering the Corporation.* New York: HarperCollins, 1993.

Heskett, J. L., Thomas O. Jones, Gary W. Loveman, W. Earl Sasser, Jr., and Leonard A. Schlesinger. "Putting the Service-Profit Chain to Work." *Harvard Business Review* (March–April 1994): 164–174.

Hobdy, Terrence, Jeff Thomson, and Paul Sharman. "Activity-Based Management at AT&T." *Management Accounting* (April 1994): 35–39.

Horngren, Charles T., and George Foster. *Cost Accounting: A Managerial Emphasis.* Englewood Cliffs, N.J.: Prentice Hall, 1991.

Horngren, Charles T., George Foster, and Srikant M. Datar. *Cost Accounting: A Managerial Emphasis.* Englewood Cliffs, N.J.: Prentice Hall, 1997.

Horsch, James C. "Redesigning the Resource Allocation Process." *Management Accounting* (July 1995): 55–59.

"Implementing Activity-Based Management: Avoiding the Pitfalls." In *Statements on Management Accounting.* Statement No. 4CC. Montvale, N.J.: Institute of Management Accountants, 1998.

Jaroslovsky, Rich. "Called to Account." *Stanford* (June 1991): 18–29.

Johnson, H. Thomas. "It's Time to Stop Overselling Activity-Based Costing." *Management Accounting* (September 1992): 26–35.

Johnson, H. Thomas, and Robert S. Kaplan. *Relevance Lost: The Rise and Fall of Management Accounting.* Boston: Harvard Business School Press, 1987.

———. *Relevance Regained: From Top-Down Control to Bottom-Up Empowerment.* New York: Free Press, 1992.

Kaplan, Robert S. "The Four-Stage Model of Cost Systems Design." *Management Accounting* (February 1990): 22–27.

———. "One Cost System Isn't Enough." *Harvard Business Review* (January–February 1988): 61–66.

———, ed. *Measures for Manufacturing Excellence.* Boston: Harvard Business School Press, 1990.

Kaplan, Robert S., and David P. Norton. "The Balanced Scorecard—Measures That Drive Performance." *Harvard Business Review* (January–February 1992): 71–79.

———. "Putting the Balanced Scorecard to Work." *Harvard Business Review* (September–October 1993): 134–142.

Kaplan, Robert S., and Robin Cooper. *Cost and Effect: Using Integrated Costs Systems to Drive Profitability and Performance.* Boston: Harvard Business School Press, 1998.

———. "The Promise—and Peril—of Integrated Cost Systems." *Harvard Business Review* (July–August 1998): 109–119.

Keegan, Daniel P., Robert G. Eiler, and Charles R. Jones. "Are Your Performance Measures Obsolete." *Management Accounting* (June 1989): 45–50.

Klammer, Thomas. *Managing Strategic and Capital Investments: Going Beyond the Numbers to Improve Decision Making.* Burr Ridge, Ill.: Irwin Professional Publishing, 1994.

———, ed. *Capacity Measurement and Improvement: A Manager's Guide to Evaluating and Optimizing Capacity Productivity.* Burr Ridge, Ill.: Irwin Professional Publishing, 1996.

Kohnler, Eric L. *A Dictionary for Accountants.* Englewood Cliffs, N.J.: Prentice Hall, 1975.

McFadden, David W. "The Legacy of the $7 Aspirin." *Management Accounting* (July 1995): 38–41.

Needles, Belverd E., Jr., Henry R. Anderson, and James C. Caldwell. *Principles of Accounting.* Boston: Houghton Mifflin, 1990.

Newton, Grant W. *Certified Management Accountant Review.* Part 3: *Management Reporting, Analysis, and Behavioral Issues.* Westlake Village, Calif.: Malibu Publishing Company, 1994.

Porter, Michael E. *Competitive Advantage: Creating and Sustaining Superior Performance.* New York: Free Press, 1985.

"Practices and Techniques: Implementing Activity-Based Management: Avoiding the Pitfalls." In *Statements on Management Accounting.* Statement No. 4CC. Montvale, N.J.: Institute of Management Accountants, 1998.

Pryor, Tom, Julie Braunschweig-Sahm, and Guy Diedrich, eds. *Activity Dictionary.* Arlington, Tex.: ICMS, Inc., 1992.

Quinn, James Brian, Thomas L. Doorley, and Penny C. Paquette. "Beyond Products: Services-Based Strategy." *Harvard Business Review* (March–April 1990): 58–67.

Raffish, Norm, and Peter B.B. Turney, eds. "Glossary of Activity-Based Management." *Journal of Cost Management* (Fall 1991): 53–63.

Rehnberg, Stephen M. "Keep Your Head Out of the Cockpit." *Management Accounting* (July 1995): 34–37.

Roach, Stephen S. "Service Under Siege—The Restructuring Imperative." *Harvard Business Review* (September–October 1991): 82–91.

Schemann, William A., and John Lingle. "Seven Greatest Myths of Measurement." *Management Review* (May 1997): 29–32.

Schlesinger, Leonard A., and James L. Heskett. "The Service-Driven Service Company." *Harvard Business Review* (September–October 1991): 71–81.

Schmenner, Roger W. *Service Operations Management.* Englewood Cliffs, N.J.: Prentice Hall, 1995.

Shim, Jae K., and Joel G. Siegel. *Modern Cost Management and Analysis.* Hauppauge, N.Y.: Barron's Educational Series, 1991.

Simmons, Sylvia. *How to Be the Life of the Podium: Openers, Closers and Everything in Between to Keep Them Listening.* New York: AMACOM, 1991.

Standard Costs and Variance Analysis. Montvale, N.J.: Institute of Management Accountants, 1974.

Stevenson, William J. *Production/Operations Management.* Homewood, Ill.: Richard D. Irwin, 1990.

Stewart, Thomas A. "Why Budgets Are Bad for Business." *Fortune,* June 90, 1994, pp. 179–187.

Strupeck, C. David, Ken Milani, and James E. Murphy. "Financial

Management at Georgia Tech." *Management Accounting* (February 1993): 58–63.

"Tools and Techniques for Implementing Integrated Performance Systems." In *Statements on Management Accounting.* Statement No. 4DD. Montvale, N.J.: Institute of Management Accountants, 1998.

Turney, Peter B. B. *Common Cents.* Hillsboro, Ore.: Cost Technology, 1991.

Weber, Joseph. "Did Pfizer Doctor Its Numbers?" *Business Week,* February 14, 1994, p. 34.

Weisman, Dennis L. "How Cost Allocation Systems Can Lead Managers Astray." *Journal of Cost Management* (Spring 1991): 4–10.

West, Timothy D., and David A. West. "Apply ABC to Healthcare." *Management Accounting* (February 1997): 22–33.

White, Timothy S. *The 60 Minute ABC Book.* Bedford, Tex.: Consortium for Advanced Manufacturing International, 1997.

Index

ability-to-bear criterion for cost allocation, 207
absolute reasonableness tests, 159
accounting
  accrual, 7–8
  ensuring data integrity, 6–8
  as information system, 4–5
  system obsolescence, 8–11
accounting analyst
  and budget review, 56
  management reliance on, ix–x
accounting cycle, 4–5
accounting period, 8
accounting rate of return, 111–112
accounts, 5
accrual accounting, 7–8, 296
accruals, 7
accumulated depreciation, 293
action plans, 39, 218
activity
  tracing labor costs to, 314–316
  what it is, 239
activity analysis, 241, 242–248
  activities classification, 247–248
  activities definition, 244
  data gathering, 244–246
  data organization, 246–247
  finalizing and documenting, 248
  identifying areas for, 244
  scope determination, 242, 244

activity-based costing, 180, 235–261
  cost assignment using, 255–257
  evolution of systems, 257–258
  implementation approach, 239–242
  uses for, 236–238
activity-based information, 236–237
  advantages of, 238–239
activity-based management, 236
activity cost calculation, 248–251
  activity measure, 250
  activity performance measurement, 251
  calculation, 251
  cost basis selection, 249–250
  resources traced to activities, 250
  secondary activities assigned, 251
activity dictionary, 245
activity levels, 16
activity measure, 82, 96–97, 169, 249, 250
  characteristics, 254–255
  considerations when choosing, 254
  and cost behavior patterns, 251–253
  and cost drivers, 253

actual costs, 157
actual yield, 173
administrative costs, 21
allocated costs, 24
allocation base, 201
  cost pools and, 208
  selecting, 206–207, 209
American Institute of Certified
  Public Accountants, 292
annual business plan, 52–55
assets in balance sheet, 293
assumptions in budgeting process,
  documenting, 98–99
average actual cost of materials,
  164
average cost, 15
  per unit, 150
average gross margin per unit, 150
averages, weighted vs. simple, x

balance sheet, 4, 291, 292–294
  budgeted, 54
balanced scorecard, 130–131
bargaining power of customer, 43
barriers to entry in industry, 43
batch-level activities, 252
benefits
  of capital project, 107
  and cost allocation, 206–207
big bucket approach to capital budget, 108
bill of activities, 256
bill of materials, 77, 162–166
  costed, 165
book-to-physical-inventory adjustment, 87
breakeven analysis, 266–267, 270
  assumptions of, 270–272
  as management decision-making
    tool, 272
budget, 34
  choosing preparation method,
    65–67
  continuous, 64–65
  flexible, 61–63

incremental, 60
preparation methods, 59–67
standard costs and, 219
static, 60
zero-based, 64
budgetary slack, 59
budgeted balance sheet, 54
budgeted income statement, 88–89
budgeting process
  behavioral considerations,
    58–59
  for capital investments, 104–107
  documentation of assumptions,
    risks and opportunities, 98–99
  example, 304–309
  fixed percentage adjustments, 56
  guidelines, 67–68
  planning of, 47
  purpose, 49–52
  review process, 55–58

capacity, 77
  and product costs, 173–177
  service organizations and,
    196–197
  see also excess capacity
capacity utilization, 175–176
  contribution margin to evaluate,
    274–276
  by service organizations, 183
capital assets, 95, 103–104
  in balance sheet, 294
capital budget, 54, 98
  elements, 106–107
  justification example, 310–312
capital budgeting process, 104–107
  managing, 107–109
capital costs, 103
  classifications, 105
capital investment
  administration, 122
  cost classifications, 103–104
  nature of, 101
  net book value, 124
  postimplementation evaluation,
    123

capital investment cycle, 102–103
capital investment evaluation,
    109–122
  cash flow identification,
    109–111
  financial analysis, 111–119
  qualitative factors evaluation,
    122
  risk assessment, 120
  sensitivity analysis, 120–121
capitalized costs, 103
cash basis accounting, 7–8, 296
cash budget, 54
cash flow
  in capital investment evaluation,
    109–111
  discounted methods, 114–119
cash outflow, 110
cause-and-effect relationship, and
    allocation base, 206
Champy, James, 126
chart of accounts, 5, 6
commercial risks, 120
committed costs, 94
committed funds, 122
communication
  in budgeting process, 59, 67–68
  planning and, 35
comparative data, for expense esti-
    mates, 97
compensation, performance indi-
    cators integration with, 133
competitiveness of industry, 43
computer technology
  and direct cost classifications,
    214
  and labor expenses calculation,
    94–95
consensus building, in standard
    setting, 225
continuous budget, 64–65
contract
  contribution margin and bids,
    279–281
  cost allocations and negotia-
    tions, 202

contribution margin, 263–265
  applying, 273–281
  contract bids and, 279–281
  to evaluate capacity utilization,
    274–276
  gross margin vs., 276
contribution margin income state-
    ment, 265–266
contribution margin ratio, 264–265
control, planning and, 35
controllable costs, 128
conversion costs, 22
Cooper, Robin, 259
coordination, planning and, 35
core processes, measurement sys-
    tem focus on, 132
corporate mission statement, 38
cost allocation rate, 190, 209
  calculating, 204–205
cost allocations, 200–214
  example, 207–211
  practical considerations,
    213–214
  process, 203–205
  reasons for, 201–202
  trends, 214–215
cost behavior patterns, activity
    measure and, 251–253
cost centers, 127
cost classifications, 16, 17
  for capital investments, 103–104
  cost behavior pattern, 16–19
  decision analysis, 28–30
  by functional area, 21–22
  manufacturing costs, 22–25
  relationship to item measured,
    19–21
  service costs, 25–27
  timing of recognition, 28
cost drivers, 236, 239
  activity measure and, 253
cost estimates, 9
cost information, preparation, 299
cost object, 16
  in cost allocation process, 203
  defining, 156
  identifying, 184, 187

cost of capital, 115
cost of goods sold, 83–86
cost pools, 169, 201
 and allocation bases, 208
cost reports, 4
cost rollup, 171–172
cost systems, reexamining, 288
cost variances, 220
cost-volume-profit analysis,
  266–267
costed bill of materials, 165
costing approach, 155–159
 cost basis determination, 157
 cost calculation, 158
 cost component identification,
  157–158
 cost object definition, 156
 documentation of assumptions,
  158–159
 information gathering, 157
 purpose of costing exercise,
  156–157
 reasonableness tests, 159
costs, 149
 factors affecting, 166
 information about, 13–14
 term defined, 14–15
 see also activity-based costing;
  standard costs
credibility, of performance indicators, 135
critical success factors, 38, 132
current assets in balance sheet, 293
current liabilities in balance sheet,
  294
currently attainable standards,
  224–225
customer, 42
 bargaining power, 43
 contact and customization in
  service organization, 152

deadlines in budgeting process, 68
death spiral, 177
decision analysis, and cost classification, 28–30

demographics in strategic analysis,
  44
department
 activity view of, 240
 expenses, 81–83
 functional view of, 240
departmental budget preparation,
  91
 departmental spending, 93–98
 depreciation, 95–96
 estimates of other expenses,
  96–97
 organizational structure, 92–93
 short-term strategies and plans,
  92
departmental spending, 93–98
 on labor, 94–95
departmental-spending reports, 4
 accounting systems, 10
depreciation, 24, 103, 111
 accumulated, 293
 in departmental budget, 95–96
 and overhead, 171
 straight-line, 112, 124
design capacity, 175
detailed flowcharting, 234
detailed item approach to capital
  budget, 108
differential costs, 28
direct costs, 19
 for activities, 248–249
 determining for services, 185–
  186, 189
 identification, 21
direct labor costs, 23–24, 167
 in budget preparation, 78–81
 in service costs, 25
direct materials costs, 22–23
 in budget preparation, 77–78
 in service costs, 25
direct method for support department cost allocation, 211–212
direction statement, long-term, 38
discontinuous thinking, 126
discount rate, 115

discounted cash flow methods, 114–119
discounted payback period, 116–117
discrete manufacturers, 151
discretionary costs, 18–19, 94
documentation
 for activity analysis, 248
 in budgeting process, 98–99
 of costing assumptions, 158–159
downsizing, 93

economic risks, 120
economy, in strategic analysis, 45
efficiency variance
 for labor, 227–228
 for materials, 226–227
80/20 rule, 74, 84
employee, labor expense estimate by, 94
engineering change order, 164
engineering studies, for materials quantity standards, 222
equipment
 book value, 111
 disposal and cash flow, 110
 estimated market value, 111
estimates
 in capital budget proposal, 106
 of costs, 9
evaluation of performance, overuse of budget in, 58–59
excess capacity, 86
 and overhead costs, 176–177
 in service organization, 197
 and special orders, 277
expected cost per unit, 172
expensed costs, 103
expenses, 296
expert, 159
external demands, planning and, 35–36
external environment, 42–46

facilities in strategic analysis, 45
facility-sustaining activities, 252

feedback, planning and, 35
financial accounting, 9
Financial Accounting Standards Board, 292
financial analysis
 discounted cash flow methods, 114–119
 payback method, 113–114
 return on investment method, 111–112
financial budget, 71
financial condition, in strategic analysis, 46
financial information, preparation of, x
financial review of budget, 56
financial schedules in business plan, 54
financial statements, 291–297
 balance sheet, 4, 54, 291, 292–294
 format, 142–143
 income statement, 3–4, 292, 294–297
 and performance reports, 140–143
 questions, 8
 statement of cash flows, 4, 292
 statement of stockholders' equity, 4, 292
 types, 3–4
fixed assets, 95
 in balance sheet, 293
fixed costs, 15, 16–17
 in flexible budget, 61–63
fixed percentage budget adjustments, 56
flexible budget, 61–63
 obstacle to use, 63
flowcharting, 234
Food and Drug Administration, 151
forecasts, and budget changes, 65
four-way variance analysis, 228
franchising fees, 27

frontline labor, 26
full costs, 19, 263
functional area, cost classification
    by, 21–22

GAAP *see* generally accepted ac-
    counting principles
general ledger, 5–6
generally accepted accounting
    principles, 7, 201–202, 292
    and standard costs, 219
government, in strategic analysis,
    44
gross margin, 89, 160
    vs. contribution margin, 276

Hammer, Michael, 126
head-count plan, 54, 92–93
high-contact service activities, 182
historical data
    for activity analysis, 244–245
    for expense estimates, 96
    in sales budget, 71, 73
hurdle rate, 115
hybrid costing systems, 154–155

implementation risk, 120
income statement, 3–4, 292,
    294–297
    contribution margin, 265–266
incremental budget, 60
incremental costs, 28
incremental expenses, for capital
    investments, 106
incremental revenue, from special
    orders, 277–278
indirect costs
    for activities, 248–249
    assignment in cost allocation
        process, 209–211
    in cost allocation process, 204,
        205
    identification, 21
    for services, 186, 190
indirect labor, 24
    costs, 167

indirect materials, 24
industry structure, analysis of, 43
information
    activity-based, 236–237
    for costing approach, 157
    gathering for activity analysis,
        244–246
information systems, in strategic
    analysis, 46
informational meeting, in budget-
    ing process, 68
initial investment, and cash flow
    from capital investment, 110
input-output relationship
    for activities, 241
    service vs. manufacturing,
        181–182
Institute of Management Accoun-
    tants, 131
intangible assets, 293
integrated performance measure-
    ment system, 131
intermediate-range plans, 41
internal controls, 6–7
internal environment, in strategic
    analysis, 45–48
internal rate of return, 114
    net present value vs., 118–119
internal use, financial information
    for, 9
interviews, for activity analysis,
    245
inventory
    adjustments, 86–87
    and cash flow, 110
    control system, 165
    and production plan, 76
    standard costs to value, 219
    valuation methods, 233
investment centers, 128
investments, in balance sheet, 293
item master, 165

job category method for tracing
    labor costs, 314

job order costing, 153–154
job order environment, service
    costs in, 194–196

Kaplan, Robert, 239, 259
key performance indicators, 39,
    125, 129
    categories related to, 135–136
    credibility of, 135
    defining, 133–136

labor
    departmental spending on,
        94–95
    in product costs, 167–168
    in service organization, 182
    total hours available, 79–80,
        300–302
    tracing costs to activities,
        314–316
    variance analysis, 227–228
labor intensity, in service organiza-
    tion, 152
labor standards, 167, 223–224
last cost of materials, 165
liabilities, in balance sheet,
    293–294
licensing fees, 27
long-range plans, 41
long-term direction statement, 38
long-term liabilities, in balance
    sheet, 294

macrolevel activities, 246
maintenance, 24
management
    activity-based, 236
    attitudes about accounting, 9–11
    expectations for budget, 67
    performance measurement as
        feedback for, 137–138
    and responsibility center organi-
        zation, 128
management accounting, 9
management control system, 219
    standard costs as, 217–218

management narrative, in business
    plan, 52–54
manufacturing costs, 21
    budgeted, 77–83
    and cost classification, 22–25
    variances, 87
manufacturing organizations
    vs. service organizations,
        180–183
    types, 151
margin of safety, 268
market, in strategic analysis, 42
marketing and selling costs, 21
mass service, 153
materials and supplies, in service
    costs, 26
materials costs, 162–166
    estimates, 164–165
materials quantity standards,
    222–223
materials usage factor, 163
materials variances, 225–227
maximum capacity, 174–175
merchandising costs, 21–22
microactivities, 246–247
mission statement, example,
    298–299
modified accrual accounting, 7
motion studies, 234
motivation, standard costs and,
    219

net book value of capital asset, 124
net income, 296
net present value, 114, 117–118
    vs. internal rate of return,
        118–119
net worth, 294
new products, 50–51
nonfinancial performance indica-
    tors, 128–129
    financial impact of, 138–139
nonrecurring expenses, 94
nonvalue-added activities, 248,
    260

objectives, in strategic planning, 37
observation, for activity analysis, 246
occupancy costs, 27
operating budget, 51, 52, 70–88
  budgeted manufacturing costs, 77–83
  cost of goods sold, 83–86
  other costs, 86–88
  production plan, 75–77
  sales budget, 71–75
operating department, 211
operating expenses, 88
  and capital projects cash flow, 110
operating income, 89
operating managers, costing systems for, 238
operational schedules, in business plan, 55
opportunities
  in budgeting process, documenting, 98–99
  in business plan, 54
opportunity cost, 30
organizational structure, and departmental budget preparation, 92–93
organizational unit, contribution margin for, 266
overhead, 22, 24–25, 81–83
  and activity-based costing, 237
  in product costs, 168–171
  in service costs, 25
  standards, 224
  variances for, 228–229
overhead rate, 82, 169–171
  fixed and variable components, 83
overtime, 23
owner's equity, 294

paperwork, standard costs and, 219–220
parent part, 162

payback method, 113–114
  discounted, 116–117
performance evaluation, overuse of budget in, 58–59
performance goals, activity-based information and, 238–239
performance indicators, nonfinancial, 128–129
performance measurement
  in activity-based costing, 242
  limitations of traditional approach, 129
  new approaches, 130–133
  summary example, 313
  system review, 136–138
  traditional approaches, 126–129
performance reports, 138–140
  financial reports and, 140–143
performance standards, 217–218
period costs, 28, 177
periodic inventory method, 199
Pfizer, 36
planned capacity, 175
planning
  of budgeting process, 47
  and capital investment, 108
  reasons for, 34–36
  what it is, 34
planning cycle, 33, 36, 37
policies, in strategic planning, 37
position, labor expense estimate by, 94
practical capacity, 175
practical standards, 224–225
price variance
  for labor, 227–228
  for materials, 226–227
pricing behavior, and sales budget, 73
primary activities, 247
prime costs, 22
pro forma balance sheet, 54–55
pro forma income statement, 54
procedures, in strategic analysis, 46

process costing, 154
process manufacturers, 151
product costs, 28, 161–178
  capacity and, 173–177
  labor costs, 167–168
  manufacturing yield and,
    172–173
  materials costs, 162–166
  overhead, 168–171
product family, evaluating
    profitability, 266, 273–274
product hierarchy, 162
product structure, 162
product-sustaining activities, 252
production orders, 151
production plan, 51, 75–77
production volume, and activity-
    based costing, 237–238
products, service vs. manufactur-
    ing, 181
professional service, 153
profit centers, 128
profitability
  evaluating for product family,
    266, 273–274
  product contributions to, 150
  standard costs and, 219
projected costs, 157
  of materials, 165
purpose, of cost allocation, 204

quantitative reasonableness tests,
  159
quasi-manufacturing service,
  152–153
questionnaires, for activity analysis, 246

raw materials, estimated purchase
  prices for, 77–78
reasonableness tests, 159
reciprocal method, for support department cost allocation,
  212–213
recurring expenses, in department,
  93–94

relative reasonableness tests, 159
relevant costs, 28
relevant range of activity, for costs,
  18
rent, 24
required rate of return, 115
research and development costs,
  21
resource allocation
  in budgeting process, 51
  planning and, 34
  in strategic planning, 37
responsibility accounting,
  126–128
retained earnings, 294
return on assets, 144
return on capital, 144
return on investment, 111–112
revenue, 296
revenue centers, 127
review, of financial reports, 7
reward system, performance indicators integration with, 133
rework, 88
risk
  assessment for capital invest-
    ment, 107, 120
  in budgeting process, document-
    ing, 98–99
  in business plan, 54
  and discount rate, 115–116
  sensitivity analysis and, 121
rivalry, 43
rolling budget, 64
routing file, 78, 167
royalties, 27, 86

salary increases, in budget, 95
sales budget, 51, 71–75
sales mix, 73
  effect of, 270
scheduled capacity, 175
scrap, 87
scrap factor, 163
secondary activities, 247

Securities and Exchange Commission, 292
semivariable costs, 18
sensitivity analysis, 120–121
service costs, 21, 25–27, 179
   and cost classification, 25–27
   example, 187–194
   in job order environment,
      194–196
service costs development,
      183–187
   costs classification, 184–185,
      187
   cost object identification, 184,
      187
   direct costs determination, 185–
      186, 189
   indirect cost assignment, 186,
      190
   indirect cost identification, 186,
      189–190
   total service costs calculation,
      187, 190–194
service factory, 152–153
service labor, 26
service organizations
   capacity and, 183, 196–197
   estimate of resource require-
      ments, 51
   manufacturing organizations vs.,
      180–183
   operating expenses breakdown,
      85
   standard costs in, 230–231
   types, 151–153
service shop, 153
setup time, 178
shift work, cost comparison, 192
short run, and fixed costs, 16
short-run capacity, 18
short-term plans, 41, 49
short-term strategies and plans,
      and departmental budget
      preparation, 92
simplicity, in cost information sys-
      tem design, 289

simulations, planning and, 36
special orders, 277–279
specific employee method for trac-
      ing labor costs, 314
spending variance, 228
staffing
   head-count plan, 54, 92–93
   see also labor
standard cost variance, 218
   analysis, 4
standard costs
   advantages and disadvantages,
      218–221
   future of systems, 231–232
   level of, 224–225
   as management control system,
      217–218
   of materials, 164–165
   process for setting, 221, 222
   in service organizations,
      230–231
   what they are, 217
standard yield, 172
Stanford University, 202
statement of cash flows, 4, 292
statement of stockholders' equity,
      4, 292
static budget, 60
   vs. flexible budget, 61–62
step-down method, for support de-
      partment cost allocation, 212,
      213
stockholders' equity, 294
straight-line depreciation, 112, 124
strategic analysis, 40–41
strategic gap, 41
strategic planning, 36–40, 287–288
   and capital investment priorit-
      ies, 108
strategies, 38–39
   and budgeting process, 67
strategy review, 50
subassembly, 162
subjective reasonableness tests,
      159

substitutes, threat of, 43
sunk costs, 29, 273
suppliers' bargaining power, 43
support departments, cost allocations, 211–213
support labor, 26

target income volume, 269–270
tax rate, breakeven formula to consider, 283
technological changes, in strategic analysis, 44
technological risks, 120
technology costs, 26–27
theoretical capacity, 174–175
theoretical standards, 224
time studies, 234
timing of cost recognition, and cost classification, 28
total costs, 15
total labor hours available, 79–80
  calculating, 300–302
total labor method for tracing labor costs, 314–315
total unit cost, 172
training, in budgeting process, 68
transactions, coding, 6

unit cost, 15
unit-level activities, 252

unit of measure (UM), in sales budget, 73
"upside" sales, 75
users, and report format, 143
utilities, 24

value-added activities, 248, 260
variable costs, 15, 16, 17–18
  in flexible budget, 61–63
variance analysis, 218, 220, 225–230
  of standard costs, 4
variances, 10
  sources of, 229–230
vendor quotes, for expense estimates, 96
vision, 38
volume variance, 228

warning signals, performance indicators potential as, 132–133
work activity analysis, 234
work orders, 151
work sampling, 234
workorder, 252

zero-based budgets, 64